ACCIDENTAL COURAGE

"Whoever tries to keep his life safe will lose it, and the man who is prepared to lose his life will preserve it."

Luke 17:33

Happy Birthday, David

Jn Kuto

1/03

RODALE

ACCIDENTAL
COURAGE
FINDING OUT I'M A BIT **BRAVE** AFTER ALL

JOE KITA

Printed in the United States of America
Rodale Inc. makes every effort to use acid-free ∞, recycled paper ♻.

"I Will Survive" by Frederick J. Perren and Dino Fekaris © 1978 Universal-Polygram
International Publishing, Inc. on behalf of itself and Perren Vibes Music, Inc.
All rights reserved. Used by permission.

Title-Page Photograph by Mitch Mandel/Rodale Images
Text Design by Susan P. Eugster
Cover Design by Massand Peploe Ltd.
Cover Photograph by Robert Daly/Getty Images

Library of Congress Cataloging-in-Publication Data

Kita, Joe.
    Accidental courage : finding out I'm a bit brave after all / by Joe Kita.
       p.   cm.
    ISBN 1–57954–494–0   hardcover
    1. Courage—Case studies.   2. Fear—Case studies.   I. Title.
    BF575.C8.K58   2002
    179'.6—dc21   2002009234

Distributed to the book trade by St. Martin's Press

2   4   6   8   10   9   7   5   3   1 hardcover

Visit us on the Web at www.menshealthbooks.com,
or call us toll-free at (800) 848-4735.

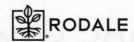

WE **INSPIRE** AND **ENABLE** PEOPLE TO IMPROVE
THEIR LIVES AND THE WORLD AROUND THEM

Contents

CONTENTS

Acknowledgments

So many people helped with this project that I'm afraid I'm going to miss someone. Anyway, here's an honest go at it: to Neil Wertheimer for his belief in my writing; to Dave Zinczenko and Ed Fones for their financial support; to Steve Perrine for the germ of this idea; to the entire staff of *Men's Health* magazine for their verve and creativity (it's infectious); to Cindy Ratzlaff, Mary Lengle, Tom Mulderick, and Dana Bacher for their near-manic enthusiasm (for everything); to Stephanie Tade and Steve Salerno for their interim guidance; to Jeremy Katz for his expert editing; to Greg Stebben for his help wrangling the celebs; to Patrick Taylor for his entrepreneurial spirit; to Steve Kandianis for his help designing my Web site; to the Rodales for their company and a chance; to Maria for her love, tolerance, and good humor; to Paul and Claire for continuing to scare the hell out of me regularly; to my mother for reminding me I'm not too old to be put over her knee; to my dad for never questioning my dreams; and, finally, to the bogeyman: You, sir, no longer scare me.

Before

I guess it's fitting

that a book about fear

should begin with an apology.

Apologizing is what frightened people do. That's our way out. That's how we cope. I tell myself, and anyone who catches me in my cowardice, that I'm sorry. My behavior and all my phobic worries embarrass me deeply, but I just can't help myself. To save my self-esteem, to remain a respectable human being, I subsequently do the next best thing: I try to avoid what induces my fears. But by not facing them, I'm avoiding facing myself. And that, I'm realizing, is unforgivable.

The level of fear in this country has never been higher. But it isn't run-through-the-streets-screaming fear. It's not terror. In some ways, I'd almost welcome that. It would be cathartic, because when my legs stopped sprinting and my heart stopped drumming, I'd be safe. At least for a little while, I'd have escaped.

But this new fear is relentless, surreptitious—and it's everywhere. It's 3:00-A.M. fear—a strange sound from who knows where, a shadow, a feeling, a darkness that has you pinned to the bed, waiting, praying, wondering what's out there and whether you're next. It's as pervasive as night itself. It's the futile struggle against the unidentifiable that causes helplessness. And since we can't run, since it's easier to be numb, we close our eyes to it. Indeed, the majority of those with fear will never try to confront or conquer it. Instead, they'll make excuses and apologies and, like me, just learn to live with it.

Let me tell you a few secrets. I checked under my bed until I was 13 years old. I cower in thunderstorms. I'm a nervous flyer. I'm obsessed with death. I sometimes have panic attacks before large crowds. I can't pee in public. I'm scared of being alone. I dread getting old and fat. I'm paralyzed by heights. I worry about being in a car accident. I believe in ghosts. I'm afraid of pain and change and letting go and so much else. . . .

Yet I'm totally functional, successful, normal. You'd never know I'm so scared, because I rarely show it. But that's what fear is all about. It's a deception, both of others and of ourselves. And that's why it's so dangerous. Like termites, it eats at the framework of society, multiplies exponentially, and then one day reduces us to dust.

Because I was curious, because I was hopeful, because I could feel myself crumbling, I asked some famous tough guys if they were ever frightened. These are men I admire. These are some of my fearless heroes. I didn't know if they'd be honest, if they'd reveal their weak spot, or if I even wanted to hear about it. But to my surprise, few had trouble being truthful:

Norman Schwarzkopf

I was a battalion commander in Vietnam in May 1970. I was in a helicopter when I got the report that a soldier had stepped on a mine and was hurt. We flew there, and I studied the scene from overhead. The area was filled with old foxholes, trenches and, most likely, more mines. I had the pilot hover, drop me on the ground, then lift off with the wounded soldier. BAM! Another mine went off. The soldier who tripped this one was screaming, his leg horribly twisted. Meanwhile, other men started panicking, screaming that they were in the middle of a minefield and were going to die.

"You're not all going to die!" I shouted, but I knew I had to do something to stop them from running and tripping more mines. So I told the company commander to gain control of his men, and I started walking very, very slowly through the minefield toward the wounded man. It felt like it took me a thousand years to reach him. I was staring at the ground every second, looking for any little bump in the dirt that might indicate a mine. And my knees were shaking so hard I had to grab each leg and steady it before I could take the next step. Obviously, I'm here to say I made it.

Stephen King

I grew up in a tiny, tiny town, and when I was a little kid—probably 10 or 11—I had an insatiable appetite for horror movies, especially the Edgar Allan Poe ones, which all starred Vincent Price. One day I was at the supermarket picking up something for my mother, and I took a close look at the man standing in line in front of me. "Holy shit!" I said to myself. "I think that's Vincent Price!" The man turned around, very tall and very handsome. He looked down at me and I looked up at him, and I knew it was Vincent Price and he knew that I knew he was Vincent Price. . . . And he waited for me to say something, but I didn't dare. He just gave me this sort of sweet smile that said, "I understand how intimidating I am for a young fellow like you." And that was it—not a word passed between us.

Rick Mears

While I was making a pit stop during the 1981 Indianapolis 500, one of the crew pulled the gas nozzle out of the car, and the valve stuck open. The car and I were covered with fuel, and the heat of the engine ignited it. But methanol burns clear, so no one saw the flames. My skin wasn't burning because my suit was flame resistant, but it was getting real hot, and the flames were coming up inside my helmet. I had to keep closing my eyes so they wouldn't burn. I scrambled out of the car, ran to a fireman, and ended up setting him on fire because he couldn't see the flames. The scariest part, though, was not being able to breathe. When I tried, I could feel the heat start down my throat. The only one who realized I was on fire was my dad, because he knows I don't move that fast for anything. So he grabbed the extinguisher the fireman had dropped and put me out.

Mike Ditka

It was when I had my heart attack. Normally, I don't fear things I can't control. Sure I'm scared when I'm in a situation on a plane or something—yeah, that happens once in a while. And I don't like snakes! But other than that, I never had any fear about the challenges of life or what was going to happen to me. But when you have a heart attack like I did and come to the realization that you're not nearly as tough or invincible as you think you are, when you realize you're vulnerable, that's scary.

Besides these well-known characters, I talked with lots of ordinary men and women. There was a cab driver in Chicago whose dashboard was crowded with little religious statues. Rosaries dangled from his rearview mirror. He told me 12 cabbies were murdered in the city last year, and that some people are so desperate they'll make fake 9-1-1 calls in order to rob drugs from ambulances. "You do what you have to do to make a living," he said with a shrug, "and pray."

There was a tow-truck driver in Maryland who spends eight hours every summer day on the ramp to the William Preston Lane Memorial Bridge over the Chesapeake Bay. He's there to assist anyone who becomes too scared to drive across the four-mile-long, 186-foot-tall suspension span. As many as 10 people per day can't make it. They pull off the road, trembling. The most memorable, he told me, was a flight attendant who said looking down made her dizzy.

There was a computer consultant from Boston who boarded a Delta shuttle to New York at 7:30 A.M. on September 11, flew directly over the World Trade Center, and then minutes after landing witnessed the horror that could have included him. What he can't get out of his head is that the terrorists and doomed passengers were in Logan Airport at the same time he was. The guy he brushed shoulders with in the men's room. . . . The businessman with the leather briefcase he admired. . . . When he looks around now, he wonders who to trust and who may be next.

There are many more stories like these, many more examples of people living with fear every day. It's like their coffee. It's there when they wake up, percolating, and they're compelled to drink a full cup. It makes them aware, nervous, ready—but for what? It seems like such a black, pointless stimulant.

Most people I asked seemed grateful for the opportunity to share their fears. It's as if they'd been carrying a rock on their back for years and, at last, somebody had offered to help. Only one person refused. Only one person insisted he was fearless. Maybe you've heard of him:

Chuck Yeager

I never had any fears in my life. You media guys write about that crap, and I'm sure people talk to you about it, but I don't think you quite understand what the hell fear is. Basically, if you have fear, it's going to interfere with doing an acceptable job and possibly get you into trouble. As a military guy, I learned to put fear out of my mind. It's mental discipline. And so, when I say I don't have any fear, that's exactly what I mean—I don't let it bother me. Some people will tell you some hairy stories, I'm sure. But I can only use an expression: The tougher you can make the opposition, the bigger hero you are for hacking it. See what I mean? When I was in the war or trying to break the sound barrier, I had the ability to put fear out of my mind—because if I didn't, it would interfere with my survival. I'm either black or white. You either do or you don't.

And I never did, and that's the way most military guys are; you're trained for that sort of thing, and you don't let it interfere.

With all due respect to Mr. Yeager and his many accomplishments, I don't believe him. I think he's afraid of being honest, of admitting what he construes as weakness. He sees fear in militaristic terms—as an enemy that will either surrender or defeat him. But there's a vast middle ground where things aren't so clear. This is the battlefield for the rest of us. Fear is a basic human instinct ingrained for our survival. In certain circumstances, it's beneficial. It is also a fundamental emotion—one that even Christ felt when His death became imminent. To ignore it, to insist it's unproductive, is to sacrifice a part of what it means to be human. But to dwell on it, to let it compromise our potential, is to lose an even bigger part of life itself. Such is our dilemma.

In her book *Feel the Fear and Do It Anyway,* Susan Jeffers, Ph.D., details an experiment that's worth duplicating. Stand up, make fists of both hands, and extend your arms out to either side. Then ask someone to face you and try to push your arms down. Resist with all your might. Little will they budge.

Next, lower your arms to your sides, close your eyes, and repeat 10 times: "I am a weak and unworthy person." Really try to feel the negativity of that statement. Then open your eyes, extend your arms as before, and have the same person attempt to push them down. No matter how hard you resist, it'll be futile.

Finally, close your eyes once more and repeat 10 times: "I am a strong and worthy person." Really try to feel the positivity of that statement. Then open your eyes, extend your arms, and have the same person do as before. This time, your arms won't fall.

This isn't magic; it's the power of your mind at work, the result of a subtle yet significant perspective shift. And belief is what flicks the switch.

I've reached a point in my life, and maybe you have too, where

I'm tired of living in fear. The older I get, the more fears I seem to collect, and it's wearing me down. Instead of an expanding future, I'm seeing a collapsing one. Before I get too narrow minded, before I run out of excuses, I need to reaffirm that I'm a strong and worthy person. I need to raise my arms out to either side, face my fears, and dare them to push me down. I need to believe in myself. I need to find out what courage is all about.

I have a crazy, stupid, potentially lethal but liberating idea. One by one, I'm going to confront each of the things that scare me most. You may think some of my fears are pansy stuff, but I don't. What a nervous little man like me feels in the grip of his fear is no different, I supect, than what heroes feel in the face of theirs. The situations may be different and more horrific, but the courage needed to act isn't.

What I'm really trying to get at here is the root of all my fear. By discovering its source, by determining the one thing that's frightening me most, maybe I can finally be free of it.

I'm going to do this without any help. Not from the safety of a psychiatrist's couch or through the haze of antianxiety pills, but out in Schwarzkopf's symbolic minefield. I'm going to take a tentative step and then another and another. . . . I'm going to see what happens.

Then, if I get to the other side, I want you to follow in my footsteps.

"To conquer fear
is the beginning of wisdom."

—Bertrand Russell

THE bOgeyman

SLEEPING UNDER MY CHILDHOOD BED

It's 2:15 A.M.,

and

I'm under my bed.

I'm at my mother's house in Bethlehem, Pennsylvania, in the same bed-room where I spent my childhood. I'm lying on my back, nose brushing the underside of the box spring, muscles already aching. I haven't slept in this room for decades, but in the dark, from this perspective, nothing has changed. There's the subtle lemon scent of mom's furniture polish, the plush feel of the wall-to-wall carpeting, and the distant gong of the family grand-father clock. But I can't let this familiarity lullaby me. I must stay alert. I am waiting for *him*. And this time I'm not a helpless kid. I'm a 42-year-old adult in search of the bogeyman.

Go ahead and laugh. I know it's absurd, but when you're out to ex-plore this thing called fear, to tunnel into the place where it exists, you have to start somewhere. And what better place to begin than where it was born—in the black, subterranean lair of the bogeyman himself.

When I was growing up, I never saw him, never heard him wheeze, never felt his scaly fingers tugging at my sleeves, but I was certain he lived just two feet beneath me. While I slept, he slithered around beneath my bed and occasionally rose up to watch me. As long as my heart was beating, he was powerless. But if it ever stopped, I knew he'd be quick to pounce. He'd tear out my heart and eat my soul before any guardian angel could be roused. Then, just as swift, he'd move under a new kid's bed and resume his loathsome vigil.

Sometimes, deep in the night, I'd wake, imagining that my heart had fluttered and his rancid, expectant breath was on my face. I pictured him as a long-limbed, dirty-green blend of the Grinch, a hobo, and a praying mantis. But by the time I had screamed and my father had come running and the light was blazing, there was absolutely nothing. My dad would touch my clammy forehead as if checking for a fever and diagnose a harmless nightmare.

But I knew it wasn't that, and after he had tucked me in, turned off the light, and shuffled back to his bedroom, I'd lie wide eyed in the dark, waiting for the bogeyman's return. And before long I'd feel him under the bed once more, chuckling and poking his bony finger into the mattress, reminding me that it was only a matter of time. Eventually, he'd get me.

It was my first fear. To a boy armored only in flannel, it was so very real. I don't know where it came from or why it terrified me, but it clung to my psyche like a cobweb, tangling me up for years. When I was six or seven and my courage had begun to blossom, I started peeking beneath my bed right after night prayers had been said—a quick glance into all corners, then an equally fast jump beneath the covers. My strategy was to get to sleep before the fear settled in too deep. Sometimes it worked. Sometimes it didn't.

Kevin is the five-year-old son of a friend of mine. He's the quintessential little tough guy. One day while I was visiting and his dad was in another room, he abruptly stopped playing with his Tonka trucks, hitched up his miniature Levi's, and asked with confidential sincerity:

"When you hear a scary sound at night, that's just the house settling, right?"

I nodded.

"I thought so."

And with that Kevin went back to playing with his trucks.

Just checking. Just getting a second opinion on what dad had diagnosed. Just reassuring himself.

Until now, I'd never told anyone about my bogeyman fear, or that I kept checking under my bed until I was a teenager. I suppose my dad suspected, but he let me save face on those nights when I quivered by offering a drink of water instead of a sympathetic shoulder. Perhaps it was this cover-up—his well-meaning but false reassurance that nothing was wrong, and my willingness to accept it and be calmed—that kept me from getting my fear out in the open where it belonged. Maybe I didn't fear the bogeyman as much as I feared admitting I believed in him.

Hang in there, Kevin.

3:45 A.M. The damn grandfather clock striking every quarter hour. A seam in the rug growing higher. The label you're never supposed to rip off under penalty of law tickling my nose. Mom's snoring rattling her Hummels. No wonder the bogeyman is so ornery and frightful. Trying to sleep under these conditions would make anyone demonic.

I drift in and out of consciousness, unsure of where rational thoughts end and dreams begin. I'm surprised, in the midst of this silly experiment, that I'm unable to look back on my first fear and deem it frivolous. It must be because I still remember being squeezed so hard by it, and having everything spill out until I felt empty, misshapen, and worthless. I remember the taste of that fear (like cotton candy without sugar), the feel of it (like a single drop of ice water slithering down my spine), and the smell of it (like burning confidence). And because it's all so vivid, I can't dismiss it.

The part of the brain that's responsible for fear is called the amygdala. Because fear is necessary for survival, the amygdala is fully

formed at one's birth. And although only about the size of a pea, it is powerful enough to control the entire body. In fact, it can elicit a response in
twelve-thousandths of a second. It is primitive at the same time it is perfect. The amygdala is programmed to recognize basic, life-threatening
situations. This is why fears of heights, open water, and snakes are so
common. Each of these perils has killed millions of our ancestors. But the
amygdala is also capable of learning new fears, through either trauma or
observation. And once imprinted, whether by genetics or recent events, it
never forgets. You can learn not to attach as much significance to a fear or
to dampen your reaction to it, but that fear will always be with you. And
those that form in early childhood before the logical, verbal parts of the
brain have developed are the most stubborn. These are the ones we feel in
our gut. These are the ones we struggle to put words to. These are the ones
that we least understand but that scare us the most.

The fear of the bogeyman is like that. It's so widespread among children because it's actually the fear of the unknown. Darkness and ignorance
are threats because they reduce our ability to react to what can hurt us.
And being small and relatively defenseless compounds this. It's that simple.
In order to handle this fear, kids use personification to make it less vast. A
bogeyman is terrifying, yes, but he's slightly less so when you know where
he lives. Better for him to be somewhere than everywhere.

There's nothing under my bed anymore except dust bunnies and
frayed carpeting. That much is obvious. But I can sense that the bogeyman
isn't dead. Part of me still feels him watching, waiting. Part of me knows
that my heart is 30 years older, 30 years weaker, and he's a patient bastard.
And part of me still feels the same shame.

I have my own house now, complete with a master bedroom that I'm
supposedly the master of. I no longer check under my bed before I go to
sleep, but that's because there are storage drawers there. I guess you could
say that's a smart use of typically wasted space, or maybe it's just a
convenient way to plug up his cave. (Come to think of it, installing
those drawers was my idea.)

I also have a home security system. It's been one of my best invest-ments. Once I activate it with my secret code, no one can pierce the perimeter of my abode. If someone tries, lights flash, an alarm sounds, and a threatening machine-voice repeats, "Intruder! Intruder!" until I either de-program it or the cops come. This is the moat around my castle, the barbed wire I've furtively uncoiled. When I wake at night disoriented from a dream or alerted by something out of the ordinary, my first fuzzy reassur-ance is there's no need for worry: The security system is working. Or at least I hope it is. Usually I'll prod my wife and double-check. "Did you set the alarm?" I'll ask. Only when she mumbles yes do I rest peacefully again.

But in case someone forgets to set it, or there's a power outage, or my phone line gets severed, or my secret code is hacked, I have a second line of defense. She's a 13-pound Jack Russell terrier with the heart of a Rott-weiler and more bark than a Yosemite redwood. She may be too squat to reach a trespasser's jugular, but she knows where the Achilles is located. When I'm lying in bed listening, waiting, I know it's safe if I hear her gentle snoring.

But in case the intruder has a steak or is someone she doesn't suspect (80 percent of homicides are committed by acquaintances), I keep a base-ball bat close at hand, a Daisy BB gun in the closet, and a blackjack in my sock drawer. A pathetic arsenal, I know, but better alternatives than my soft fists and brittle elbows. I'll use them if I have to.

And in case that's not enough, I kneel by my bed every night and pray to God to keep all I own and love safe. I rely most on sincerity, but some-times I offer a trade—continued protection for more benediction. Six Hail Marys, three Our Fathers, and an Act of Contrition is the current exchange rate.

But why do I need all these layers of vigilance? What do I think is lurking out there in my well-lit, neatly trimmed suburban bushes? Some-times after everything is set and I'm tucked into bed, I don't feel safe, I feel ridiculous. After all these years could I still be afraid of the bogeyman?

6:15 A.M. Dawn brings the smell of brewing coffee and warming pecan twirls. I could just as easily be 10 years old, getting up for school, throwing my pajamas in a pile, looking expectantly out the window for snow (even in April). But this morning I'm feeling old and sore. I push aside the dust ruffle, shimmy out from under the bed, and slowly try to stand. It takes a few agonizing minutes to straighten myself.

"So I guess the bogeyman didn't get you," my mother taunts, as I hobble downstairs, bleary eyed, uncertain whether the steps or my joints are creaking.

"I beat the crap out of him," I boast. "You're going to have a hell of a time cleaning up the mess. And while you're at it, rip the tag off that mattress."

But he hasn't been subdued. No longer can I be fooled. When I punch the buttons on my alarm system each night, double-check my arsenal, and ask my dog and my God to be watchful, it's not the fear of burglars that's at work. It's the knowledge that I still haven't come to grips with *him* yet. And by avoiding confrontation, by insisting all along that it's just my house settling, I've let him grow stronger. And now he's in so many corners. . . .

Besides control, I've lost something else, too. It's the option of crying out for help, of hitching up my Levi's and asking for reassurance. If I have a bad dream and awake screaming, no one is going to come running. No one is going to put his hand on my head, make a comforting diagnosis, and offer me a glass of water. No one can make it right again. No one except me. Or so I've come to believe.

Robert Maurer, Ph.D., is an associate clinical professor at UCLA School of Medicine who studies stress and fear. I once attended a lecture of his in which he explained how gorillas react to danger. When researchers surprise them with a fake leopard or other predator, they immediately huddle together. Then, from the safety of their pack, they assess the threat. Eventually, the alpha male emerges to either chase or fight it.

Maurer pointed out that this is the same instinctive reaction children have to night frights. They run to the safety of their pack, which is their parents' bed. But as they age, this is discouraged. They're chastised and maybe even punished for it. It's a process that happens to all of us. We grow up. But in doing so, we lose touch with how we're meant to deal with fear. We deny ourselves the option of sharing it, not just physically but also emotionally. Men especially. So with no way to diffuse it, we lie awake alone at night, overwhelmed by our worries and our inability to soothe them. Fear no longer just scares us; it humiliates us.

Maybe the reason I've become so paranoid is because I keep pushing fear under beds, into corners, and outside electronic perimeters. I keep my mouth shut about it, because I've been taught that any admission of fear is a diminishment of self. And the older I get, the more shame I feel for not having outgrown it. But how are we to ever muster the strength to face our fears when that first step is considered such a weakness? If I'm to get to the bottom of this, I need to forget about saving face and protecting myself. I need to risk crying out and telling the world what I saw in those shadows. I need to determine if what I fear is simply admitting that I fear.

As author Philip Roth once said: "It turns out that I am even more scared of confessing to being scared."

Humiliation

JUST TRYING TO PEE

Some fears

don't make you scream;

they make you whimper.

Some fears don't widen your eyes in terror; they lower them out of embarrassment. Some fears are so private you can barely admit them to yourself. Some fears make you sob every day you're alone with them and feeling helpless. Some fears can't be shared because of the sarcasm and shame they'll evoke. Some fears gradually wear you down, make you never want to leave home, and cause you to feel broken. Some fears make you stop living long before you actually do. Some fears no one can understand—not even you.

I want to believe that everyone has at least one fear like this, but it can't be true. If it were, then I wouldn't feel such humiliating solitude. If everyone has these fears, then no one has them. Such is the dilemma I'm caught in.

It's time to get something off my chest. It's my biggest, most embarrassing secret. I have never shared it with anyone because, if it were known, it would turn my ego upside down. Everyone fears the bogeyman at some point in his or her life, but only a few pathetic souls fear what I'm about to admit. Or at least that's what I tell myself. This thing is so stupid yet so shrewd, so inconsequential yet so huge that I don't know how to present it other than to just state it:

I can't pee in public.

There, I said it. I can't take a satisfying leak in a goddamn public restroom because I'm afraid someone might be watching, listening, or waiting. I tense up, and no matter how long I stand there, only a few drops dribble out. Some bathrooms are worse than others. Some have urinals without dividers. Some have open troughs. Some have stalls without doors. Some give me no choice but to sit down like a girl. All because I can't piss like a man. Go ahead and snicker. Call me a self-obsessed fool. It's crazy, I know, especially when I see my confession in black and white, printed on the page. It's only five words. All that buildup, then this. How curious. How *weird*.

Believe me, I share your skepticism, your urge to smirk. I'm aware that it's an entirely irrational fear, but that knowledge doesn't make it any easier to handle. In fact, it makes it worse. To have something so insignificant get ahold of you and control you is not just frustrating, it's demeaning. After a while, you inherit its insignificance.

I've had this problem since third grade, when an old nun we'd nicknamed Fang began supervising us in the bathroom. She said we couldn't be trusted, called us "bold, brazen, impudent fellows." She stood behind us with arms crossed as we took our obedient places at the urinals. She gave us 60 seconds. I could never pee with her standing there. I felt her black, rosary-bead eyes on the back of my head, and I couldn't relax.

Have you ever held your urine for an entire day? At first, the need is sharp and immediate, but if you resist long enough it eventually settles into a dull, simmering burn in your lower abdomen. Wait a while longer, and you start to feel sick. It becomes difficult to focus, move, sit. But all the time you're pretending everything is fine.

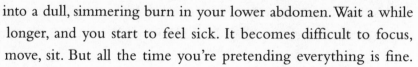

You're the tough guy who has taken a bullet and permits himself only a grimace. All because the pain of being found out is so much greater than the physical pain in your bladder.

I spent most days at school that way. Even after Fang left, I still couldn't go. My fear had somehow grown. To cope, I became devious. I'd raise a tentative hand midway through geography and ask to be excused. Or I'd volunteer to deliver a note to the office or fetch a book from the library if the teacher needed it. Or I'd watch the nuns during recess and manage to sneak inside when they weren't looking. Even now I can recall the sweet relief of striding into that bathroom when it was completely deserted, standing amidst the tiny tan-and-white tiles and the smell of urinal cakes, and emptying every last drop. *Ahhh.*

Although I hated living like this, I took pride in such victories. Just like the hit television show of the time, I was a miniature Fugitive. Every day I survived by my wits and avoided being caught. For a while, I imagined that my special brand of wait training was building me an impressively strong bladder. Although my biceps may have been puny, I had the kidneys of Arnold Schwarzenegger.

Fears can be such slippery, sedulous monsters. They slither out of deep dark holes in our childhood, leave a slime trail across our lives, then worm their way into the even deeper and darker crevices of our supposed maturity. And even though the fear of peeing in public may not evoke the same empathy as the fear of flying or public speaking or death, I'm here to tell you that it's no less intimidating if you have it. True fear doesn't have gradations. It is one emotion. And the same is true of the courage needed to confront it.

Because of my pesky fear, there's a sizable portion of life that I've ringed with caution tape and declared off limits. Forget about flying 24 hours to visit my brother-in-law in Australia, taking a train or bus cross-country, or celebrating New Year's Eve in Times Square. Big sporting events, deep-sea fishing charters, and rock concerts are all out of the question, as is going to nightclubs and even some bars and restaurants.

Before I agree to anything, I have to consider the possibilities for peeing. Does the chance for having fun outweigh the risk of discomfort and embarrassment? More times than not, it doesn't. However, when the offer is too good to refuse (like box seats at Yankee Stadium), I'll cope by dehydrating myself. For 12 hours beforehand, I won't drink anything. I'll even refuse the beers my buddies are buying, lying that I don't mind being their designated driver.

Sometimes, though, all this plotting doesn't work, and I get trapped. I'm back in third grade, at the end of the day, almost doubled over. Once, on an overnight train from Nairobi to Mombasa, I couldn't urinate into the open hole they called a bathroom, despite having drunk four liters of Tusker beer. My agony lasted for 20 hours, fed by the fear that I'd end up in an East African hospital. I was never so happy to check into a hotel room. And another time, on an Outward Bound sailing trip with co-workers on the Chesapeake Bay, I found myself confined to a ship with no options other than pissing off the bow. It was a character-building experience, just like the brochure promised. A new record: 22½ hours.

The clinical name for this condition is paruresis, which is Greek for "difficulty voiding." It's more commonly known as bashful bladder, shy kidneys, or being pee-phobic. I first saw mention of it in a men's magazine, and I was stunned that it was medically credible. There's even an organization, called the International Paruresis Association (IPA), dedicated to helping people overcome it.

According to the IPA, 20 million North Americans have occasional difficulty urinating in public. That's equivalent to the population of Texas. Of these, approximately two million lead lives significantly compromised by it. Nine out of 10 sufferers are male, and they generally consider it more shameful than even impotence or incontinence. To reach out to them, the IPA holds three-day workshops in major cities throughout the United States and Canada.

And that's how I've come to be sitting in a conference room at the Philadelphia Hilton on a Friday night with 17 other nervous guys. I've paid $300 and sacrificed an entire weekend, but that's not what's making me cringe. It's waiting for this to begin. As I look around the room, my subconscious is smugly trying to convince itself that I'm not as broken as these other idiots, that my paruresis isn't so bad, that a full refund is still possible. One guy looks like Pee-wee Herman and another like dumb Joey from *Friends*. Somebody from Detroit is gushing that he's been at two of these workshops, and "they're fantastic, really great." I want to ask him why, if they're so helpful, is he back again? Meanwhile, a burly guy with a shaved head boldly sips a pint of beer—staring straight ahead, no doubt trying to intimidate us with his choice of diuretic. Everywhere, there are pitchers and pitchers of untouched ice water, sweating nearly as much as we are.

Finally, IPA cofounder Steven Soifer shuffles in carrying a box of books and assorted pamphlets. He's wearing a bushy beard, a brown felt fedora, and nondescript clothes that are badly rumpled. Despite his welcoming smile and apparent calm, it's as if he's trying to hide as well. The first thing he mentions is the bathroom situation. There's a public facility across the hall with two urinals separated by a partition and four stalls. He also points out that the key to his adjacent suite is on the back table. It has two private bathrooms with locks.

On this news, more than a few of us fill our water glasses and tilt them to dry lips. We can relax. He's one of us.

For the next two hours we tentatively tell our stories, just like at an AA meeting: "Hi, my name is ____, and I'm a paruretic." Attendees range from a teenager, who drove from North Carolina with his parents, to a 60-year-old retired psychologist, who gave up trying to treat himself. Everyone's tales are remarkably similar. No one is certain exactly how his paruresis began, but everyone ballparks it as sometime during early adolescence. Most recall some vaguely traumatic experience, such as being taunted by someone in a bathroom or failing to go in a pressure-packed situation. The incident sparked a long fuse of worry, frustration, and embarrassment that exploded into this.

13

Where we're different, though, is the degree to which this condition handicaps us. It's obvious we're all serious paruretics, or we wouldn't be seeking help. But some of these men are far worse than I. One actually dropped out of medical school because of it. Another quit his job in order to work from home. A third lost his girlfriend because he rarely took her anywhere. And a fourth has taken to catheterizing himself. This involves inserting a long thin tube into the tip of the penis, then sliding it up the urethra and into the bladder.

"I just decided that no matter what I have to do," he says, with voice quivering, "I'm not going to stay home and give in to this fucking thing. I'm going to fight it every day."

"It's true," adds a fellow named Patrick. "Avoiding the problem only makes it worse. Mine got so bad, I could hardly go with *me* in the room."

We all smile at this, but grimly. We know the feeling.

Soifer says some people have been hospitalized with paruresis, others have committed suicide because they just couldn't deal with it, and a few have even been imprisoned. "There's a parolee who is serving a five-year sentence because he was ordered to take a drug test he could not fulfill."

Unfortunately, there is no pill or surgical procedure to remedy the problem. Many urologists and therapists are even unaware of it. According to Soifer, a professor of social work at the University of Maryland, the best treatment is "behavioral cognitive therapy." This is a fancy $100-an-hour psychological term for what's reducible to a nickel's worth of common sense, namely: "Face the damn fear." The key, however, is not confronting it all at once. Instead, Soifer explains, you need to take small steps. It's like climbing a ladder. At the bottom is the safest rung—your home toilet, for instance, with *Waterfall Sonata* playing on the stereo. At the top is the worst place imaginable—say, halftime at a New York Jets game. To make steady progress, you must gradually expose yourself to increasingly higher rungs of discomfort. It's sound logic that's been successfully used to treat many different phobias.

To help us make our climb, Soifer says, he'll be assigning "pee buddies." These will be guys from the group who share a similar level of anxiety. Starting tomorrow, we'll drink lots of liquid, then practice peeing with them.

To me, this sounds ridiculous, humiliating, and gay. Judging from the pained expressions on the other guys' faces, I can see they feel the same way. What's the goal here—to eventually piss with one of my buddies holding my dick? I don't know if I want any part of this.

But Soifer senses our unease and remains encouraging.

"You're all extremely brave," he says in lieu of good night. "The big stride was showing up here. The rest is just little steps."

The following morning, I'm a whirl of conflicting emotion. I'm ecstatic because I'm finally doing something about this. I'm hopeful because Soifer says "the process" helps four out of five people. I'm committed because my dream is to piss a vociferous stream with the whole world watching. But at the same time, I'm nervous because these practice sessions promise to be painfully awkward. I'm worried because maybe I'll fail, and the fresh defeat will make things worse. I'm embarrassed because I'm paying hundreds of dollars for what amounts to toilet training. I'm suspicious because these buddies of mine could turn out to be perverts. And I'm disappointed for letting myself think like that.

Soifer outlines the day's schedule. "The first practice begins at 10:30," he explains. "You should have a strong-to-moderate urgency by then, so start fluid loading now."

Coffee, tea, juice, soda, water . . . there are enough beverages in the room to fill a kidney-shaped pool. While we swig, Soifer explains that although paruresis may seem entirely psychological, it has a strong physical component. Two things must happen in order to pee. First, the bladder must signal the brain that it's full, and second, the brain must relax the muscles involved. But in paruretics, adrenaline interferes with this last process. Adrenaline is the hormone that readies the body against a perceived threat. It's what makes your heart beat faster and your

15

muscles tense. It's the fuel for the fight-or-flight response. Our job today is to begin reprogramming the neural pathway that controls this, so that restroom/urinal/stranger no longer registers in the brain as jungle/gaping mouth/tiger.

"In an ironic sort of way, all of you have learned the process of controlling your bladder too well," Soifer explains. "Now it's time to start unlearning."

My pee buddies are Tony and John. Tony looks like a dockworker—a squat, dark-haired Italian with a thick mustache. He's a recovering alcoholic, but "this thing," he says with a shake of his head, "had me in bondage." That is, until a few months ago, when he started attending IPA support group meetings in New Jersey. Just the other day, he was able to pee at Home Depot. "Three urinals with dividers," he says, smiling proudly.

John is the other side of Tony's dime. He's balding, bespectacled, and extremely anxious. He almost missed his flight to Philadelphia from Minnesota because he was running from bathroom to bathroom in the airport, searching for an empty stall. "I was in a full-blown panic," he says, pacing nervously and massaging his brow. "I've never been to a workshop or a support group meeting. My worst fear is being found out."

By 10:45 we're making uncomfortable small talk in John's hotel room. Despite drinking so much earlier that we're practically dancing with need, no one wants to go first. Part of this problem, it seems, stems from being almost *too* considerate. Finally, Tony volunteers. He'll try with the bathroom door open, and with John and I halfway across the room talking by the television. It's like we're actors on a set, and Tony is the director. He positions us just so, then dodges behind the camera for a go. We try not to think about him in the bathroom, but it's impossible. After about 10 seconds, we hear a shy tinkle that is just beginning to intensify when it stops. That's what Soifer wants. Get started, continue for three seconds, then halt. This way, we can practice multiple times per session.

John tries next. He wants us standing by the TV, volume up, bathroom door closed. He takes a deep breath, pauses, then ventures in. He's only gone a few minutes, but when he reemerges he's wringing his hands less. Things must have worked.

Now it's my turn. I begin far down my ladder by turning up the volume on the television, locking the bathroom door, and running the water full blast. In fact, I'm disappointed there isn't a fan. But despite all this insulation, I still feel pressured. Part of me senses them listening. I try to shut them out. I close my eyes. I tell myself this is bullshit. And after a while I'm able to start a stream.

We alternate like this for almost an hour. I gradually advance from total muffled seclusion to having the TV and the faucet off, and the door shut but unlocked. I know this sounds like paltry progress, but to be able to piss in total silence with strangers in the room is an honest breakthrough. My confidence is brimming along with my bladder. John enjoys similar success, and Tony is actually able to squirt out a hesitant stream with us standing behind him in a simulated line. I start to celebrate his achievement with a high five, until I remember where his hand has been.

One thing fear won't tolerate, though, is cockiness. It feeds off conceit, grows stronger, then returns with a crushing dominance. Buoyed by my success, I foolishly decide to open the door wide and pee with Tony and John just outside. I stand over the bowl and wait. But when nothing immediately happens, the old doubt rushes back in, and I tense up. Looks like I won't be graduating just yet.

I must remember: little steps.

It's noon at the Reading Terminal Market, just down from our hotel. The aisles are packed with people shuffling past pyramids of vegetables, spits of barbecuing chicken, tangles of king crab claws, slabs of thick steaks, and just about every other edible imaginable. Everyone's eyes are wide with wonder and hunger. You don't come to a place like this with a full stomach or, for that matter, a full bladder.

The men's room here is to paruretics what the Press Club podium is to stutterers. The six urinals are so tightly arranged that elbows must be kept pressed to ribs while you're going. A half-dozen stalls offer more privacy, but the line for them is longer than the line for Philly cheese steaks.

My pee buddies and I are here to witness an experiment. IPA co-founder Carl Robbins has been standing at one of these urinals for the past 15 minutes. To make matters worse, in his coat pocket is an electronic device that makes loud and convincing fart noises. He's trying to prove to us self-conscious souls that nobody gives a damn what we do in the bathroom. In fact, from time to time, he shakes his head and bellows: "I can't go! I can't go!" Not one person asks him to hurry up or even seems bothered.

"I once stood at a urinal in Camden Yard [the home of baseball's Baltimore Orioles] for 25 minutes," says Robbins, when I sidle up beside him. "Nobody said anything, not even the security guard."

He rips a long fart. A couple of kids at the sink giggle, but that's it.

Our assignment is to not only observe Robbins's antics but also perfect the art of not peeing. We're supposed to dally at a urinal just like he's doing, in order to desensitize ourselves to our fear of public restrooms. He wants us to become aware of our anxiety, wait it out, and realize it's just another feeling—nothing else. "Fight it, and it gets worse," he says. "Accept it, and it releases."

To underscore his point, Robbins distributes Chinese handcuffs when we reconvene in the conference room after lunch. He encourages us to slip our pinkies into the flimsy sleeve and notice that the more we struggle to escape, the tighter it gets. But when we relax, it's as if nothing had ever been there.

Indeed, while it's a frightful situation that jump-starts a phobia, it's our own anxiety that keeps it running and gradually depresses the accelerator.

There are lots of examples of this, including stuttering, blushing, and even impotence to some extent. "Your primary paruresis is the inability to pee," explains Robbins, a counselor at an anxiety-and-stress-disorders clinic. "It has no meaning; it's just a dysfunction. Your secondary paruresis is the shame, humiliation, and avoidance you attach to it. The fear your mind creates makes the problem worse."

Robbins says there's a crucial difference between being the object of life and the subject of it. In fact, this subtle distinction is the key to acquiring courage and overcoming many phobias. "Where is your attention when you walk into a bathroom?" he asks. "It's probably on people's perception of you. This is the same thinking that fuels many other fears. Take public speaking, for example. Someone with that fear is wondering: 'Do they like me? Do they think I'm smart? Have they noticed my lisp?' Just like you in the bathroom, they're making themselves the object of the experience. To overcome fear, you need to take back your own eyes, to see yourself through them. This is what it means to be the subject of life. It's a fundamental claiming of yourself. It's standing before that audience, whether real or imagined, and saying, 'I don't care what you think. I have a message to deliver, or something I need to do, and I value it.'"

He draws two circles on a flip chart—a small one in the center that he labels *self*, and a much larger, encompassing one that he calls *ego*. "The ego is the self's marketing department," he explains. "It's the image that we surround ourselves with. The ego has only one thing it values, and that's how others perceive you. The self, though, has countless values, including freedom, integrity, honesty, courage. . . . Make your own list. This is the important stuff. This is what defines who you really are. When you're in an anxious situation, ask yourself what else besides image you care about. Then insist that the world accept you for who you are."

Inspired by this advice, I make good progress in the afternoon practice session. John and I are assigned a new pee buddy. (Chris replaces Tony.) This is designed to raise our anxiety, but eventually I'm able to piss with the bathroom door fully open, both of them in the room, and the TV on low volume. I'm beginning to feel confident, to see that the word *pee* consists of just three tiny, inconsequential letters. But at the same time, after observing veterans like Chris who had attended multiple workshops, I'm also realizing this is only the beginning. No one will leave here cured. At best, we'll depart improved.

Chris is perhaps the most dogged and determined member of the group. He's the burly guy with the shaved head who was drinking beer at the outset. He's also the one who had to quit his job because of paruresis. He realizes he may never beat this thing entirely, but he refuses to stop trying. He knows that the moment he stops, he goes all the way back to where he was.

I admire Chris's dedication. I want to tackle this as hard as he has. But when I go out alone for dinner and consider visiting the restroom afterward, all the old excuses return. I rationalize that my urgency isn't very high, that I'm not far from the hotel, that I can easily hold it another 20 minutes. So I pay the bill and leave. But as I'm walking along the sidewalk, I notice the streetlights are casting a yellow glow on me. It's the color of cowardice.

"You know, there's a wonderful treatment for paruresis—more effective than any of this," I hear Robbins saying. "It's called avoidance. The only thing is, it has some side effects—namely, you don't have a life."

I'd like to say that I was pissing all over Philadelphia on the workshop's final day, that I was hanging my willy off the Betsy Ross Bridge and making giant ripples in the Schuylkill River. But the reality is I only stepped tentatively into a few public restrooms, and there were no further breakthroughs. In fact, the more I hung out with all my new pee buddies, the more I started worrying about becoming completely neurotic. These guys had far more problems than just paruresis; that became obvious. Quite a few were on antidepressants. One had a bizarre stumbling problem that caused him to trip on carpet ripples and sidewalk cracks. And another broke down before the group, confessing that his alcoholism had resurfaced this weekend and he'd spent the previous night at a strip club. He termed it just the latest chapter in his "extraordinary life of problems."

I felt sorry for him, and I don't mean to belittle anyone's demons. It's just that I have enough to worry about myself. I believe it's not specific phobias or conditions that we inherit, but rather a propensity to them in general. Dwell on the possibilities too long, and you risk making them your own. A fearful person's mind is exquisitely fertile.

I was evasive when Chris and Tony asked me to join their support group. It's one thing to have a pee buddy at a seminar, but it's another thing entirely to have one in the real world. That's too weird.

Soifer and Robbins conclude the workshop with a story about the Scotland Yard bomb squad. When researchers examined the men who did this nerve-wracking job, they found them unexceptional in every way but one: They were absolutely fearless when defusing bombs. They exhibited none of the common physiological reactions to being in such a stressful situation. No elevated heart rate, no tensing muscles, no release of adrenaline.

How did ordinary men attain such an extraordinary state? Not through training alone, the experts concluded. In fact, no matter how many manuals these men read or how many sophisticated simulations they did, it wasn't until they defused an actual explosive in a life-or-death situation that the fear left them.

That's our parting lesson. No matter how much progress we think we've made this weekend, the fear is still ticking inside us. Although it's been muffled, it's just as powerful. Our next job is to circle it warily in our everyday world, appraise it using our newfound tools, stand next to it despite sweaty palms, and methodically deactivate it forever.

"I recommend urinating in one public restroom daily for at least a month," says Soifer. "Remember: If you're not scaring yourself on a regular basis, you're not working hard enough."

I write this last statement in my notebook. It's the final line there—sage advice not just for paruretics but for tentative people everywhere.

I have one more thing I need to do as part of the recovery process. In 17 years of marriage, I've never told my wife, Maria, about this. My excuse for being away this weekend was that I was covering a urology conference for *Men's Health* magazine. But I can tell by the tone in her voice when she asks how it went that she suspects something else. So I tell her about shy-bladder syndrome, show her the books and pamphlets. I confess to having it. She shakes her head. As a registered nurse with more than 20 years' experience, she's used to pain and suffering. She reserves most of her sympathy for her patients, of which I am not one.

"If this is all that's wrong with you," she says, "consider yourself lucky."

And that's it. No hugs. No reaffirmation of her love. No offer of a warm sponge bath. Instead, she asks me to fetch the olive oil from the pantry and muster the kids for dinner.

I'm disappointed and angered by her callousness. How dare she minimize what has caused me such grief and required so much courage to confront. I stew on it, like I have stewed on this condition for so long.

But eventually, I realize she's right. How dare I *maximize* this? How dare I attach so much significance to it that I lose sight of all the other ways I'm blessed? How did I let this happen? How did a silly thing like not being able to pee in front of a half-blind, 80-year-old nun more than 30 years ago result in this belittling, life-altering handicap?

I'll tell you how.

It's because I've been holding it in for so long.

Emasculation

DRIVING IN A DEMOLITION DERBY

My wife has a friend
named Sue,
to whom she tells everything.

And Sue, in turn, tells everything to her husband, Bob, who is the megaphone in our crowd. This is how word of my bashful bladder leaks out. Maria mentions to Sue that I was at a "learn-to-pee" workshop, Sue mentions it to Bob, and Bob thinks this is hilarious. Don't get me wrong; I love the guy. We've been friends since college, and if I learned something equally embarrassing about him, I'd consider buying airtime on a local radio station. One Christmas, I gave him an ice-cube tray filled with frozen semen because he couldn't get his wife pregnant. So I guess I had it coming.

"Guess why Joey missed the party last week?" he asks friends, coworkers, and even my children. "He was learning how to pee!

"Hey Joe, I got tickets to the Mets on Saturday night at Shea. Great seats. Right between the beer stand and the bathroom. You in?"

And so it goes whenever I'm with him. I smile and try to act like it doesn't bother me, but it does, especially when Maria and our teenage kids are around. I can see them wincing and shaking their heads. I can sense their disappointment and embarrassment. Maybe it's my imagination, but I feel I've let them down in some way, if only as a role model of strength and invincibility.

A man's job is to stand up to fear. It's his responsibility to battle the monsters, to protect his family, and to make a twisted world appear a little straighter. If he can't do that, then he's not a man, at least according to tradition. Suddenly, this journey I'm on to find the source of my fear has become doubly dangerous. Not only am I risking my pride and my neck facing each one, but I'm also jeopardizing the respect of those I love.

"Courage is not the absence of fear," I once read, "but rather the judgement that something else is more important."

What's vital to me is preserving the regard of my family. If I lose their respect, what purpose, other than delivering a paycheck, do I serve? I'll remain a provider, but not of what counts. What I need to keep giving is example, inspiration, and guidance.

So I get the urge to do something brave, something ballsy, something that'll convince my family that I'm not a pussy. I want there to be a moment of drama, a scene filled with smoke, an interminable instant of doubt from which I'll emerge unscathed and victorious. For the first time in my life, I want to go into battle. I want to be a warrior.

I notice the advertisement in our local newspaper.

Demolition Derby
The Great Allentown Fair

I didn't even know they had such events anymore. And as I read the fine print, as I coddle the ember of an idea, I get a chill. I can remember every car accident I've ever been in. Even the near misses and the ones I witnessed are seared into my brain like a cattle brand. All I have to do is summon their memory, and they play like old movies:

▶ My father turning left off Route 378 into a place that sold garden statuary. He was taking my mother to buy a birdbath. I was alone in the backseat, all of four or five, when a car traveling too quickly in the opposite direction hit us broadside. This was before air bags and mandatory seat belts, plus we were riding in a Volkswagen Beetle. The collision spun us around and left a big dent in our right front quarter-panel. I'll never forget the stunned silence that ensued—all of us sitting there, shocked at what had happened, neat rows of driveway jockeys staring at us from the garden-shop lawn. Then my father's quaking voice: "Is everyone all right?" And my mother, clutching his arm: "Oh my God, Joe." When I heard their fear, I got scared. In fact, I couldn't speak for the next 24 hours. I wasn't injured in any way; my voice just left me. To my parents' credit, they didn't panic; they didn't rush me to the hospital. They bought a birdbath. I recovered.

▶ My dad and me, 10 years later, riding in his new Ford Thunderbird. He had moved up from Beetles; it was the biggest, shiniest car in the neighborhood. We were waiting to merge onto Freemansburg Avenue. For some reason, he started to go, hesitated, then stopped. Meanwhile, the driver behind us, assuming we'd gone, promptly rammed us. It wasn't much of an impact. Neither of us suffered a scratch. But his Thunderbird did—gouges all across the back. He shook his head and spit. I had never seen my father make a mistake as blatant as this.

▶ Chugging cans of Genesee Cream Ale in a tiny, blue Maverick with a sputtering engine. Four, five, maybe even six teenagers crammed inside—on our way to a wrestling match at a rival high school on Route 309. The driver, incensed by something his girlfriend said, beating the dashboard so hard with his fist that radio stations switched. Me thinking he's drunk; this is dangerous. Then a sudden, sharp curve, and we were off the road. No guardrail. Crashing through underbrush. Brakes straining. Coming to rest at the edge of a deep culvert. "Holy shit!" someone said. My buddy threw it in reverse. No one asked for any more beer.

▶ Driving to work along Hanover Avenue, alone in my gleaming Camaro Berlinetta—eight-track blasting, sunglasses on, my world. I was passing a van rigged for transporting large panes of glass. Suddenly, without signaling, it changed lanes and smashed into me. The metal rigging ripped through my front end like a knife through tough steak—sawing, shredding. The noise was a thousand fingernails dragged across black slate. We skidded to a stop, took deep breaths, then crept across the street to a gas station where I called the police. The other driver was apologetic, admitting it was his fault, that he never looked. I wanted to punch the idiot.

▶ Watching my daughter play soccer on a Saturday morning in Neffs, the town's landmark church steeple rising protectively to the west. Suddenly, the squeal of children was replaced by the squeal of tires. A Bronco swerving to avoid another car, then tipping and actually rolling over and over like a toy. It eventually came to rest on its roof with a final, sickening thud. Momentarily, we were all statues. Then people running, phoning, and the driver miraculously crawling out.

Car accidents are the leading cause of death in men under age 45. In fact, the risk of dying in one is significantly greater than perishing while skydiving or even bungee jumping. Driving is, by far, the most dangerous thing we do on a daily basis.

In order to survive, to continue to be able to drive, we put these statistics out of our minds. I know a middle-age woman who has had 22 separate accidents. Yet it doesn't stop her from commuting 80 miles round-trip each day. "None of them were my fault," she says with a shrug. It's her firewall against fear.

Car accidents remind us that *we're* vulnerable vehicles, too. We have sturdy shells, dependable welds, and all the necessary safety options, but the unforeseen can still happen. We can crumple in seconds, and no amount of insurance will be able to restore us. A car accident is the closest most people get to death. Perhaps that's why "heart stopping" is the usual description. In that adrenalized instant is a glimpse of the end, an inkling of life's futility, and a grudging realization that we should have paid more attention to the other guy.

"Are you thinking about entering one of *those*?" my son asks, looking over my shoulder at the newspaper ad for the demolition derby.

"Yeah, I am."

"That would be really *cool*," he says.

I call the number that afternoon.

The first thing I notice on the rule sheet I subsequently receive is this warning: ★★★No Alcohol or Drugs Allowed in the Pit Area. Anyone in Violation Will Be Removed and Possibly Arrested★★★

The second thing I notice is this restatement of the previous warning: ★★★Alcohol Will Be Confiscated and Not Returned★★★

The third thing that catches my eye is this restatement of the re-statement, with a bit more typographic emphasis: <u>NO ALCOHOL OR INTOXICATED PEOPLE IN THE PITS!!!</u>

Obviously, this is a major concern—bigger, it would seem, than the fact that "all drivers must wear an approved safety helmet" (rule #3), the car's "stock gas tank must be removed" (rule #8), and "a working hydraulic-operated brake system is mandatory" (rule #13). These are all listed, in much smaller type, *after* the previous warnings.

Before this story progresses any further, I should confess that I have a truly meager amount of automotive knowledge. The extent of my main-tenance skills is inserting the gas nozzle in the correct hole and periodi-cally changing the windshield-wiper fluid. This lack of mechanical expertise is going to prove challenging because, I'm realizing, a substan-tial amount of work must be put into a demo car before it can be de-molished. For instance, the exterior must be stripped of all chrome, plastic, glass, and anything else that could shatter or become a lethal pro-jectile. This includes lights, hubcaps, and even door handles. Like-wise, the interior must be pared of all carpet, headlining, upholstery, and other flammable material. This includes the rear seat and even the sun visors.

But it's not so much the dismantling that has me worried. With a couple of phone calls, my kids could have a gang of teenagers in my driveway with crowbars and liters of Mountain Dew ready to make quick work of it. Rather, I'm concerned that the rules contain allusions to major modifications I have no clue how to do. For example, as mentioned, "the stock gas tank must be removed." Okay, that's seven words of explanation for a process that deserves at least a chapter in Chilton's. Once jettisoned, it must then be replaced by "an approved five-gallon metal or plastic marine tank to be securely fastened with chains or metal strapping to the area vacated by the rear seat." No mention, however, of how to get the gas from there to the engine.

There are some more puzzling omissions. It's my understanding from some Internet research that the entire exhaust system must also be stripped, since a dislodged tailpipe could prove hazardous. And the battery must be moved from the engine compartment (where it's vulnerable to impact and explosion) to the floor below the passenger seat. But there's not a word about either of these things on my rule sheet.

Now I don't mean to sound egotistical or above my fellow drivers, but I'm a college graduate. I am well-read. Frankly, I'm stymied by the assumption that this sort of stuff is done by ordinary people every day all across America. Like opening a can of tuna, there's no need to detail that step among the instructions on the label. Only a knucklehead wouldn't know how to do it.

It's becoming clear that I need two things if I'm going to do this: 1) an expert advisor with firsthand experience, and 2) a Panzer of a car.

According to the International Demolition Derby Association (IDDA), the best demo car is a 1964-to-1968 Chrysler Imperial four-door, followed closely by the 1967-to-1973 two-door version. These models are prized because of their bombproof construction. In fact, they're so indestructible many derbies outlaw them. Next on the list is 1974-to-1976 Chevrolet station wagons. Since it's smarter to back into opponents (to protect your engine), the more steel you have in your aft end, the better. All SUVs, limousines, Hummers, trucks, buses, and hearses are banned. Compact cars are permitted, sometimes in separate classes, but anyone who roars out in a Geo Metro or Toyota Stanza deserves to be removed from the gene pool.

Prices vary according to a car's desirability. The fair-market value for rust-free Imperials, according to the IDDA, is approximately $1,000. But many drivers refuse to pay more than $100 for a car. They contend it violates the spirit of the derby, which is to find a piece of junk that nobody wants and further trash it. Although a durable vehicle and a smart driver can win back their investment many times over (purses range from $500 to $1,000 at this level), money isn't the reason most guys do this. Apparently, it's trophies—those priceless pieces of worthless faux wood and plastic that symbolize manhood. And the bigger, the better. No matter how much the wife nags, the boss yells, the kids disrespect, or the dog growls, a man can look at his trophies on the mantel, scratch himself, and know that for at least one moment, he was on top of the world.

In addition, there's the heady experience of having your name announced on the PA system, of making an entrance before thousands of cheering fans and, temporarily, being the entertainer. Who needs alcohol or drugs? This seems intoxicating enough.

Shopping for a demolition derby car is much more challenging than browsing for a new automobile. They're not all lined up on a dealership lot. You have to ferret them out, cruising rural routes, peeking into barns, scrutinizing the death notices of little old ladies whose estates are liquidating their church cars. In the process, you're bound to offend some people who take pride in their older vehicles. For instance, I notice a newspaper ad for a Cadillac. It's described as lovingly cared for, meticulously maintained, and generally garaged—a 1973 for $350, which sounds reasonable. But when I mention on the phone to the owner that I'm thinking of using it in a demolition derby, she turns surly.

"That car was my Walter's pride and joy. He would roll over in his grave if I sold it to anyone who would do that!"

I didn't argue with her, but in my opinion, to go out in a demolition derby is an honorable end for any vehicle. If I were a Lincoln Continental or even a Ford Pinto, that's the way I'd want to go—smashed and steaming on the field of battle amidst a 21-backfire salute. You've served us well, old soldier. Now it's time to meet your Crusher.

I pull into the preowned lot at Krause Dodge in Schnecksville, Pennsylvania. I've heard there's a fellow here named Denny who has more derby experience than anyone in the area.

"I'm looking for a demo car," I say, shaking his calloused hand.

He studies me, like all used-car salesmen. I take the opportunity to do the same. He's about 60, walks without a limp, and has no apparent scars, burns, or missing limbs. Despite his occupation, he has an honest look about him.

"Ever done one before?" he asks, squinting.

"No, this is my first, but I hear you're the king, that you can set me up."

He tries to shrug this compliment off, but I can tell he's eating it up.

"Yeah, I got a lot of trophies."

I scan the lot, encouraged. "Anything here that might work?"

"As a matter of fact, I have one I was going to fix up for myself, but it doesn't look like I'm going to get around to it. Follow me. I'll show it to you."

We walk to the last row of the lot, behind the garage, well out of sight of the road. The asphalt gives way to weedy gravel. It's the antithesis of a showroom. Old vans, rusting Jeeps, forgotten models from my father's generation. Behind them all is a gully. It's as if they're being given one final chance to attract a buyer before being pushed off the edge.

"This is it," says Denny, stopping in front of a gun-metal-gray car with a maroon interior. It's so nondescript, I would never have noticed it. I can only guess at the make, model, and year.

"It's a good one," says Denny, nodding his head.

I don't know how to reply. Unlike the first sight of a Porsche or a Ferrari, this doesn't take my breath away. And being that my experience with demo cars is minimal, I can't yet be awed by its potential.

"It's a '78 Chevrolet Caprice Classic with a 350 V-8. Runs good."

And that's his entire sales pitch. No discussion of mileage, options, or tread wear. No ushering me around the car, pointing out all the cup holders. Not even an offer of a test-drive. With a demo car, all that's meaningless. To survive a qualifying heat and be competitive in the feature, it needs to run strong for a total of only 20 to 30 minutes.

Still, being a shrewd salesman, Denny senses I need more reassurance. So he leans close and whispers, as if there are other demo drivers on the lot who might overhear: "You can win with this."

"You think so?"

"I *know* so. You can win with this."

"Will you help me fix it up? I mean, I don't know much about this."

"If I was going to do that, *I'd* drive it. But I can set you up. I have a buddy in Slatington named Barry. He might be able to give you a hand. With this car and his help, you could win."

Indeed, four-door Caprice Classics rank sixth on the IDDA's most-wanted list. He's not pulling my clutch. He bought it for himself.

"Stand back while I open her up and check for hornets," he says, turning the key in the door. "They like to make nests in the dashboards."

It takes a portable battery, a liberal dowsing of starter fluid, and a half-dozen cranks to awaken the beast, but once it's running I realize he's right: It sounds good. I sit behind the wheel, imagining . . . what? Certainly not driving to the dairy for ice cream on a summer Sunday with my kids in the backseat. Definitely not loading up the trunk with ham and kiffles after a holiday visit to Grandma's. But rather, smashing into helpless adversaries, hearing the groan of twisting steel, and screaming maniacally.

It feels good. It feels right.

"How much do you want for it?"

"I'll sell it for what it cost me: $150."

"You got a deal."

Without a doubt, it's the most unusual vehicular purchase of my life. To think that for $150, you can buy an entire, driveable automobile is amazing. Of course, there's no final delivery prep by the service department. There's a big, bold As Is, No WARRANTY sticker in the window. And when Denny makes the deal official, he hands me a "Certificate of Junk Transfer." But I'm actually proud. In fact, on the day I come back to claim it, I bring my family—just as if we were purchasing a new Lexus.

"Isn't she a beauty?" I say to them, with a ta-da flourish.

"Exactly how long is this going to be sitting in my driveway?" asks Maria, with her hands on her hips.

"Just a couple of months. Then it's gone. I promise."

My son, who just got his learner's permit, is anxious to drive it. And for once, I don't feel apprehensive about handing him the keys. We pile in and sputter off like the Beverly Hillbillies, with Denny waving and yelling to make sure we all come back now, y'hear? Once on the road, we command instant respect. A blue BMW starts to pull out in front of us and then thinks better of it. A black Suburban, which usually stops for no man, politely surrenders the right-of-way at an all-stop intersection. A bunch of cocky teens, edging defiantly into the road, promptly yield. It's obvious to everyone: This car has no conscience.

Before we lodge it in our driveway, we have some fun. We take it to the supermarket and run shopping carts into it. We visit one of my son's buddies and ask him what he thinks of Paul's new wheels. We pick up the dog and let her lick the insides of all the windows. We deliberately spill a Yoo-Hoo.

I must admit that the only time I've had more fun in a car was when I took Patty Pavlish to the drive-in and unhooked my first bra. But the real thrill is just beginning. After Paul parks it, I tell him to go borrow the neighbor's biggest crowbar. I order my daughter, Claire, to drag the sledgehammer out of the cellar. And I tell my old lady to wiggle into her finest cutoffs and halter top, and fetch me a beer. Her man is going to be working out here. (Two hours later, I'm still waiting.)

EMASCULATION

My crew descends upon the Caprice Classic like jackals on a carcass. At times, things get primitive. My youngest emits a feral grunt after she rears back and delivers a fender-bending whack. The boy makes an oh-yeah fist and does an end zone dance after shattering both headlights. The dog rips out a patch of carpet and shakes it. And all the while, a steady stream of neighbors comes to visit. They ask what we're doing, chuckle with appreciation, and then volunteer their tools and assistance. This could easily become a community project. It captures the imagination.

Six-year-old triplet boys live across the street. They're the most fascinated of anybody, no doubt because we're doing what they've forever been warned not to do. All afternoon, I see three sets of wide eyes peeking from windows and bushes. I make it clear to their father that I will not be held responsible for any inspired damage.

Before long, our driveway is littered with bolts, bits of upholstery, shards of steel, hubcaps, mats, mirrors, and the entire backseat. In addition, we've filled six large garbage cans with miscellaneous debris. Where it's all coming from I can't tell, because the car still appears relatively whole. They definitely don't make 'em like this anymore. Plastic must not have been invented yet.

As the car is transformed over the next few days, so am I. My hands become scratched and grease creased. My clothes develop impressive stains. And I am infused with the subtle odor of motor oil. Yet I am shiny bright inside. To come home each afternoon and work out the stress by hammering, wrenching, and ripping is bliss. To discover that my little girl was out here by herself prying off some part makes me strangely proud. And to stand with arms folded in my driveway, telling a neighbor about the project's next phase, is the essence of small-town community. Maybe we'll raise a barn together next year.

Overall, it's an effect I didn't anticipate. I'm used to measuring progress in a white-collar world by shuffling papers and schedules. This is so much more satisfying and definitive.

Hello, I'm Barry."

Like a stubborn cork, he slowly pops himself out of his truck, hitches up his jeans, takes a few deep breaths to steady himself and, finally, extends a meaty hand. The effort has exhausted him. He's a big man—about 360 pounds, in his early fifties, but with a boyish tousle of brown hair and a look of mischievous enthusiasm. It's as if he's come over to play, not work. While he's shaking my hand, he looks right through me to the car, his eyes revealing excitement and a tinge of pleasant memory.

"Denny was right," he says, running his fingers fondly across the hole where the door handle used to be. "It's a good one. I used to run these, you know. Won some trophies."

I nod my head, trying to look suitably impressed. He raises the hood and spends a few silent minutes surveying the guts, occasionally emitting deep harrumphs.

"I didn't touch anything in there," I insist, just in case he's noticing something amiss. "I didn't want to risk yanking out anything important."

But Barry doesn't share my trepidation. To my astonishment, he promptly reaches in, unscrews a few nuts, and removes the entire fan assembly.

"We won't be needing this," he says.

I'm speechless. The part is about the size of my chest. I assume its job is to cool the engine, which seems like an important process. But here I stand, holding it in my hands, as if it were an errant wing nut.

"We won't be needing these either," says Barry, handing me a spaghetti tangle of wires and hoses that he just ripped out from God-knows-where. "Get me a ½-inch socket, will ya?"

And so we find our working relationship: Barry under the hood, under the dashboard, or under the car, and me hustling to drag away a part or get him the tools he's asking for. At times, I feel like a kid helping his dad or like a gofer at the neighborhood garage. But this is what I hired him for: to take charge, to be my chief mechanic.

Barry beams whenever I call him that. It's obvious he considers it a position of great honor—second only to driving in the derby himself. A day at the races, an afternoon in the pits, is heaven to him. "The wife says it makes me frisky," he says with a wink. But it's been years since he's competed. He ruefully admits that besides not having the time, his wife doesn't want him (or perhaps herself) getting hurt.

"She made me promise I wouldn't get behind the wheel if you chicken out," he says. "Hand me the wire cutters."

"Did you ever get injured?" I ask, delivering them like a surgical instrument.

"Only once," he says, twisting a coat hanger around the radiator. "I was in one of them crazy derbies where you wear a paper bag over your head. My buddy was next to me in the front seat telling me where to go. But I never knew when I was going to get hit, so I couldn't brace myself. Man, was I sore the next day.

"There!" he says, straightening up and surveying his work. "Now if someone hits you head-on, the radiator won't get pushed into the engine and chewed up. The fan is out of the way, and these coat hangers will act as braces."

As if to celebrate a job well-done, Barry rips a high-pitched fart. My dog pricks up her ears and takes a wary sniff.

"Just checking to be sure everything's still working," he says, chuckling, making no attempt to blame it on the torque wrench. "Now hand me that jack."

Barry cranks the front of the car precariously off the ground, lies on his back, and begins shimmying underneath for a look around. By the time he has squeezed himself into position, I can't tell if it's the jack or his stomach doing the lifting. "Not too bad," he says, from the depths of the undercarriage. "We should be able to drop that tank pretty easily once we siphon the gas out of it. The exhaust system shouldn't be a problem either."

With great effort, he slides back out, leaving a sweat stain on the asphalt. He's breathing like a horse after six furlongs.

"You okay, Barry? Everything still working?"

"Yeah, yeah, I'm just getting tired is all. Time to go home and hit the sack."

Barry works nights at a vague job that involves driving a truck. He also apparently has a part-time day job. Thus, he's only available to help with the car Saturday and Monday mornings—and only then if it's not excessively hot.

"I can't stand the heat," he says, mopping his face with a greasy rag. "I'll see you next week."

But bit by bit, we make progress. The car undergoes a slow, but purposeful, evolution:

▶ We buy a new battery and bolt it to the floor of the passenger seat. Because cars stall often in competition, some drivers use two or even three batteries to ensure plenty of starting power. As protection from acid leaks and explosion, Barry covers it with a flimsy floor mat. "Don't worry," he says, noticing my concern, "it'll be fine."

▶ We spray the engine with degreaser, letting it melt through the nearly 25 years of accumulated crud. This helps dissipate heat and minimize the chance of fire. But just in case, we also cut two holes in the hood through which any flames can be quickly doused.

▶ We carefully slide the windows out of all four doors, and hire a glass-removal service to take out the rear window and windshield. It costs almost half as much as the car itself, but it saves us from having to saw around the perimeters with piano wire—a painstaking process.

▶ We pad the inside of the driver's door with eight inches of golden foam torn from the backseat. Although it's illegal to hit another competitor here, it's a necessary precaution against inevitable impacts. For extra protection, some guys fill their doors with cement.

▶ We get rid of the tailpipe, muffler, and manifold, in addition to clipping the fuel lines and removing the gas tank. A plastic, three-gallon marine container gets chained to the floor behind the driver's seat, and the fuel lines are reattached to it. The fact that the gas supply will now be less than three feet from the back of my head is not reassuring. "Don't worry," says Barry, noticing my concern, "it'll be fine."

▶ We reinforce the front bench seat by looping a safety belt through the armrest hole. This is to prevent it from breaking free and pivoting backward after a hard collision. If you can't sit, you can't hit.

▶ We punch holes in the hood, trunk, and doors with big chisels and mallets. Sweat flies and blisters form as each of Barry's mighty blows clank and echo. These holes will allow us to chain everything closed, another safety requirement.

We do a hundred other things, and we could do a hundred more—some not totally above board. Barry says some guys reinforce their frames in devious ways, by either welding the shock bumpers or stuffing rags in the springs to make the car ride higher. Others put cement blocks in the trunk for better traction and ramming power. And a few even twist and hone the corners of their fenders into tire-slicers. Evidently, some drivers feel that the cars *and* the rules are meant to be bent. Although race officials inspect every car beforehand, some examinations are more cursory than others (especially if the judge happens to be a brother-in-law). To his credit, though, Barry insists on playing by the rules.

Finally, it's time to fire this puppy up. I offer Barry the privilege since he's my chief mechanic. I can tell he's excited as he shoehorns himself into the cockpit, pumps the accelerator, turns the key, and coaxes the engine to life. It stutters, hesitates, then RRROARRR! Without a muffler, the Caprice Classic is deafening. It no longer just "runs good," it growls menacingly. Like a German shepherd warning an intruder, the rumble comes from deep in its throat. Barry guns the engine again and again. My dog bolts. The triplets cover their ears. Barry's smiling, I'm smiling . . . but when he shifts into reverse, then drive, then—wait a minute—reverse again, the car won't budge. Barry suddenly looks sick. Everything's *not* working.

"Son of a bitch!"

For an instant, my life with this car passes before my eyes. All the sweat, all the work—wasted. Barry looks puzzled and pissed. He gets out of the car, hitches his trousers, raises the hood. This time, I'm afraid, he's going to yank out something really big. But he reaches for the dipstick instead and squints at the level of transmission fluid. Sure enough, it's dry. The smile returns. We're going to be all right.

After the engine and structural work is complete, it's time for the most important step of all: painting. A demo derby is one part mechanical preparation, one part driving skill, and one part entertainment. Some derbies even reward crowd favorites by allowing the audience to vote on which of the remaining, steaming wrecks advances to the final. But settling on a motif for your beast is often the toughest job of all. Prepping a car is cold and logical. Decorating one, however, takes imagination and flair, which is something most grease monkeys are a quart low on. So I'm thinking I can gain an advantage here.

An automobile is a challenging canvas. It's mobile, it's three-dimensional and, at first, it's difficult to surmount the feeling that you're committing criminal mischief. There are only a few rules. The driver's-side door must be painted white in order to make it more noticeable. Any number you choose must be painted boldly on the roof and doors. And a big X or some other type of mark must be drawn across the tires to aid judges in determining movement. Beyond any lewd, lascivious, or offensive themes, everything else is fair game.

The possibilities are numerous. For names: Killer Kita and the Chevy from Hell . . . Sloppy Joe . . . Up Yours . . . Capt'n Krunch . . . Joe-Mama . . . Filthy Animal . . . Cruisin' for a Bruisin' . . . Smokin' Joe . . . My Life Is a Wreck . . . Crash Gordon . . . Let's Get Smashed . . . and (my favorite) Hit Me Hard in the Rear. For paint schemes: a white ambulance with big red crosses . . . a hungry shark with teeth across the front bumper . . . a black-and-white cruiser with gold sheriff's stars . . . the "Eat Me" birthday-cake car from *Animal House* . . . and (also attractive) the popemobile with "Bless you for not hitting me" on the quarter-panels.

But in the end, I buy $50 worth of assorted paint at Home Depot and turn the project over to the most creative artists I know—

my kids. My hope is that it'll give them a bigger stake in the project, while being a memorable bonding experience. (If I don't survive, at least they'll be able to say they gave me a stylish exit.) I encourage them to devise a plan, but like everything else they do they prefer to make it a spontaneous operation. So at 7:30 on a perfect morning, we stand in our oldest clothes with brushes in hand and wait for inspiration.

. . . And wait

. . . And wait.

"Aren't you going to let us eat breakfast?" asks Claire.

"No way," I say. "If you eat breakfast then all the blood will rush to your stomach, and you won't be able to think. The derby is *next week*. We have to get this done *today*."

Like cranky engines, it takes some priming to get them started. A brushstroke here, another there, and slowly ideas start to churn. The kids are partial to the can of Brilliant Yellow. It certainly contrasts nicely with the Charcoal Black and, say, don't crash-test dummies have a circular insignia on their heads colored like that? Paul looks it up on the Internet, makes a printout, and suddenly we have a theme that everyone is excited about. Big crash-test dummy insignias soon appear on the hood and trunk. They look good.

"What number should we put on it?" I ask.

"Gotta be 13," says Paul, and Claire instantly gets to work painting it in black on the doors and roof. We're rolling now.

But it needs more.

"How about if we paint the wheels the same way?" suggests the boy. "Make 'em look like four more dummy insignias."

Great idea.

"How about if we paint black-and-yellow stripes on the front and back?" volunteers the girl.

Do it.

"How about if we carry those stripes down both sides of the car?" says Paul.

"And write 'Caution' inside a few of them?" adds Claire.

We paint all day, stopping only for pizza that we eat while squatting in the driveway because we want to continue surveying our masterpiece. It looks fantastic, and I'm not just saying that. It's bright, it's colorful, it's funny, it's creative. With the stripes and caution labels, it looks like a cross between a tiger and a highway construction project. Like all proud artists, we sign it, adding our names and those of everyone who helped us to the remaining empty space. For good measure, the boy paints "Spank Me" on the trunk in huge, red letters.

And it is finished. We stand by proudly, spattered with the same yellow, black, and red, soaking up the compliments of our neighbors and the slowing traffic. The triplets are particularly impressed.

"Wow!"

"Cool!"

"Mom, can we paint our van? Please?"

All that's left now is to tune-up the engine and to chain down the hood, which Barry and I will do the morning of the derby. Now that the car is together, I can concentrate on putting my head in similar order.

The West End Fair is held annually in the town of Gilbert, about 25 miles north of where I live in the foothills of the Pocono Mountains. Although smaller and more rural than the Allentown Fair, it's supposed to have a pretty respectable demolition derby. I drag my family there on Monday night, buying their patience with snow cones, fried dough, turkey barbecue, and temporary henna tattoos. Since I've never seen a derby first-hand, I figure it's a crucial preparatory experience.

After paying $20 for tickets, we climb through the grandstand and emerge among hundreds of people. Most appear to be survivors of tractor accidents or alcoholic mothers. Everyone has the boiled, doughy complexion of pierogies and seems to possess a similar IQ. But man, are they friendly. As I nervously usher my family to our bleacher seats, they welcome us like Wal-Mart greeters. The men temporarily stop spitting tobacco juice into plastic cups to eye Maria and Claire and turn up the corners of scraggly mustaches. One woman with a black eye asks if I'd like some deer jerky. "Made it myself," she says, gnawing. "It's a whole lot easier than sausage." And after getting kicked in the back a few dozen times, I turn around and get to talking with a guy who's trying to control a rambunctious five-year-old named Talon. "I named him after my car," he tells me proudly. Dad is wearing a John Deere cap, and his two front teeth move while he's speaking.

"Welcome, ladies and gentlemen, to the West End Fair demolition derby!" blares the announcer from his crow's nest. The crowd thunders its approval with clapping hands and stomping boots. A cup of tobacco juice tips over on Maria's shoe.

Each driver tears into the dirt arena, slams on his brakes, and spins around as his name and hometown is announced. Occasionally, a raised fist appears from a window. I'm encouraged to see that none of the cars have very creative paint jobs, although each appears junkyard-mean and indestructible. They form two tight rows of 10 at opposite ends of the battlefield, with about 30 yards separating their rear ends.

"Are you ready?" booms the announcer.

"Five, four, three, two, one!" the crowd counts down.

And this theater of the bizarre explodes. Engines *vroom*, wheels spin, and transmissions grind as drivers stomp their accelerators and try to ram each other.

One guy in a small, nondescript car hurtles backward so fast that his helmet flies out of the window upon impact and his head pool-balls the dashboard. Officials immediately stop the action to check his condition. He crawls out of the car, waves to the crowd, and promptly falls over.

Lesson #1: Don't be overly aggressive.

Once he's taken care of and the mayhem resumes, a gray Lincoln that has been lurking in the corners gets bulldozed up onto one of the big metal pipes that surround the track. It teeters there like a seesaw, while the driver pounds his fist in frustration.

Lesson #2: Don't be too tentative.

As the action continues and the smoke builds, a couple of drivers team up on the only woman in the competition. She's driving a toenail-pink Volvo. They pummel her mercilessly, continuing even after her car stalls and she throws up her hands in surrender.

Lesson #3: Don't be a woman (or drive a pink automobile).

Finally, there are only two cars moving, and the judge waves the checkered flag as vehemently as if it were the last lap at Daytona. Both advance to the final. The driver of one immediately climbs onto his roof and begins jumping up and down like a gorilla.

Lesson #4: Don't be an asshole.

And so it continues, all night, through five heats and the eventual final. Hardly anyone in the grandstand leaves or even moves. The restrooms are deserted. It's redneck hypnosis. Three hours later, when the derby concludes, a haze hangs over the arena and the eyes of most spectators. I try not to think about what might happen in the parking lot.

Derby day dawns bright and sunny, glinting like showroom chrome. Barry arrives at the house early in his best pocket-T, ready to bring another trophy home.

"See how her back end rides nice and high?" he says, admiringly. "That's a good sign. When she gets hit, she'll crumple up, not down." After I determine he's talking about the car and not my wife, I agree.

Despite always knowing the car's destiny, now that the time has come I'm hesitating. I've become attached to #13 in the bizarre way men connect with all their cars, infusing them with a dignity that's partially our own. This is one of the few mechanical projects I've ever successfully completed. It's the soapbox racer I never built in Boy Scouts, the custom hot rod that's never taken shape in my garage. Like Barry, I'm damn proud of it. The ironic thing is, in less than seven hours I'm going to smash it to bits.

Yes: Today, I'm going to be in an accident—a multicar pileup, in fact. The certainty of it is strangely unsettling. Should I notify my insurance agent? A big part of the fear of accidents is the suddenness, the out-of-nowhereness. But I have had weeks to plot this collision course. Can it still even be called an accident if it's deliberate?

I don my helmet and goggles, and practice climbing out of all the windows. Paul times me, until I can escape from any window in less than 4.8 seconds. Meanwhile, Barry tightens the battery cables, tops off the gas tank, and yanks on all the door chains.

"Get in," he says. "We'll give it one final test run."

This time when I turn the key, the engine jumps to life—almost as if it's been crouching there, waiting. Maybe on some unknown quantum level the molecules of this motor grasp their fate and are fiercely ready. I back out of the driveway and practice driving in reverse around our cul-de-sac, drawing a horde of slack-jawed kids. After each run, Barry fiddles with the choke until the idle is high and loud and strong. The rumble is upon us.

I drive onto the flatbed that I've hired to take it to the fair, then jump in Barry's truck with my son. "Good luck!" Maria yells in chorus with all the other neighbors. "We'll see you there!" We all wave back. It feels like I'm going off to war.

They say it takes a lot of guts to enter a demolition derby, but I suspect that's just a polite way of saying it takes a lack of brains. Heat winners this evening will get $100 apiece plus a trophy, while $600 will go to the winner of the final and $250 to the runner-up. The rest of the 75 other competitors will get nothing, not even a T-shirt. In fact, it costs me $50 to register my car and two-man pit crew. When you consider that the event will draw 2,000 to 3,000 people at $11 apiece, it becomes painfully clear that the animals in this sideshow are being mistreated.

But nobody seems to care. The spirit in the pits is upbeat, hectic, and madcap. One guy is venting his hood with an acetylene torch. Another is whaling away at his bumper with a sledgehammer, while a third is trying to open a hole in his trunk with a pick ax. The cars are a lot more colorful than at West End. There's the Insaniac, Fender Bender, Flamin' Amish, Misfit, Mennonite Mafia, Krunchin' Kevin, Madcow,

43

Orange Krush, and Richie the Snakeman (complete with a stuffed boa constrictor on the roof).

They all look tough, especially the station wagons with their big-ass ends. To my surprise, many of the cars appear to be survivors from previous derbies. The guy parked next to us brags that his buckled baby won him a grand at Kutztown a month earlier. And a fellow across the lot admits that his charred chassis was in a sizable fire. "But she still runs good," he says. By comparison, the virgin appearance of my car is almost embarrassing.

Everyone seems friendly, and lots of guys come over to shake Barry's hand. One family team spans three generations, with separate cars for junior, dad, and gramps entered in different heats. Barry warns me to be wary, though. "They're all your friends until demo time," he whispers. "Then they're all your enemies." He zip-ties the key to the ignition and tells me not to lend any tools. Trust no one.

The most suspicious fellow in the bunch is someone my son dubs The Dirtiest Man in the World. He's not just greasy like everyone else, he's burnished a deep brown—as if he uses Quaker State for body lotion. His wild hair and beard are the color and texture of a black bear's, and his T-shirt wouldn't even be serviceable for wiping a dipstick. He struts purposefully around the pits, yet never seems to go anywhere. He is an adult Pig Pen, with a hostility problem.

Guys like him make me nervous—ones with a perpetual case of road rage, even when they're not driving. I can picture him madly laughing as he floors the accelerator and pulverizes me. Demo derbies allow the unstable to do what would otherwise get them jailed. I avoid his Manson-like stare.

Compared to many of the other crews, who are feverishly working on their cars, we're on a picnic. Indeed, after a very unofficial-looking official conducts a five-second inspection of our vehicle and writes "OK" on the hood in yellow crayon, Barry leaves to buy a sausage sandwich, a jumbo gyro, and some chili dogs. Shortly thereafter, he falls asleep on the grass in the shade of his truck.

Just before the 4:00 P.M. registration cutoff, a big pickup with a trailer squeezes in alongside us. The car it's towing looks virtually untouched. The backseat is still in, the doors are unchained, there are no numbers painted anywhere, and even the windshield remains. The driver, a quiet middle-age guy who meets no one's eye, has one hour to get it ready. He immediately starts working, and I watch him grow dirtier and sweatier as he makes steady and remarkable progress. Part of me is envious. If this is a strategy rather than just poor planning, then the guy is a genius.

I amend my opinion, however, when the unofficial-looking official flags the guy's fuel supply, which consists of a gas can that's pinned to the floor by a huge, three-foot-long bolt. As he correctly points out, if that thing gets bent or shears off, it'll be dangerous. The quiet guy says nothing. He just heads for the back of his truck, where he cranks the dials on a couple of tanks and fires up a torch. Is he about to do what I think he's about to do? I elbow Barry awake and call to Paul. Even though my grasp of garage-shop procedure is limited, if he's about to trim that bolt with a torch, then any fumes from that gas can could explode. Barry concurs, and I take cover—mostly behind him. The Dirtiest Man in the World ambles over and grins, as if approving of the ruinous possibilities. But the quiet guy pulls it off, spray-paints a runny #42 on each door, and the official writes "OK" on his hood.

With only 30 minutes remaining until the drivers' meeting, I'm getting anxious. At Barry's recommendation, I registered for the first heat. If by some incredible stroke of luck, I survive and make it to the final, then we'll have maximum time to unbend and Band-Aid our vehicle. To burn off some of my nervousness, I walk over to inspect the track. It's half the size of West End, and all the cars are to line up facing the grandstand. This reduces ramming speed and eliminates the mass crash at the beginning—both wise safety moves but significantly less exciting. The loose dirt-and-gravel surface is damp and pockmarked with piles of shit, left over from either the horse troupe that performed earlier this afternoon or last night's Blink 182 concert. It doesn't look like there are any plans to remove it.

Other drivers lean against the wall—spitting, smoking, trying to look calm.

"Two summers ago I lasted 30 seconds," drawls one guy in a Kiss T-shirt. "Then last year I was in for a minute. It's a sum-bitch."

"They say no rookie ever won," says the guy next to him. "I can believe that."

"The key is staying away from that stage," adds another. "See all those logs there? You don't want to get hung up on them. That happened to me before."

"Ever done one of these?" asks a stocky fellow with a haircut like Moe of the Three Stooges, who just stepped up beside me. He looks like he has a touch of Down's or something.

"No, this is my first," I reply.

"Well, let me give you some advice." He hesitates, as if about to hand me some kryptonite. "Don't get hit by any impacts."

"What's that?"

"Don't get hit by any impacts."

He nods his head in all seriousness.

"Attention, drivers! Attention, drivers!" It's the organizer, standing on the hood of a car, waving a bullhorn. He's tall, dark haired, and cocky, with sunglasses worn for effect. He makes us squint up at him as he preaches. Under no circumstances are we to hit a driver's-side door, he warns. If we do, we risk immediate disqualification. He says it over and over again, as if he's cautioning a roomful of two-year-olds about touching the oven.

When he's finished, he asks if there are any questions, but then he doesn't acknowledge any hands. Instead he waves the rule sheet, which "you all should have read already." It's obvious he loathes us. We are nothing but his gladiators.

"Okay, gentlemen, those in the first heat can follow me through the gate."

This is it. Barry puts his arm around my shoulder, tells me to protect my front end and not be overly aggressive. "Let the other

46

guys knock themselves out first," he says. Paul shakes my hand like a man and asks how much he'll inherit if I don't return. I cuff him in the head. But at the same time I notice, with concern, that other drivers are fitting themselves with neck collars and even fireproof suits. All I have are jeans, a long-sleeve flannel shirt, and my health-insurance card.

Unfortunately, hot dogging isn't allowed like at West End. We file obediently into the arena, like traffic through a tollbooth, and take our positions. I'm wedged in the middle of a 25-car lineup—a good place to begin. I turn off my engine and wait, noticing only two things. The first is that the grandstand is jammed and everyone is looking at *us*—pointing, murmuring, perhaps laying odds. I pick out a few coworkers, some neighbors, and Maria in a bright orange shirt. The second thing I spot is a group of firefighters in helmets and shiny black coats ringing the track. They're carrying extinguishers and looking serious.

I crawl out of the car and shake hands with the drivers alongside me, hoping that a good-luck wish might quell their animosity. They're both rookies, much younger than I, and their palms are equally sweaty. We stand together for the national anthem. It's one of the few times I've ever been at center stage when it was played, and I get goosebumps. Afterward the announcer introduces each of us, and we get to ham it up somewhat. But as he proceeds down the line, the grim reality of what I'm about to do settles in and the butterflies in my stomach become the size of bats.

I strap on my helmet, adjust my goggles, and fasten the seat belt. Barry has bullied his way to the wall about 50 feet in front of me. We exchange thumbs-up, and on the announcer's signal, all drivers start their engines. The roar is deafening. In fact, it's so loud, I'm not sure if my motor turned over. My dashboard lights are of no use since the sun is shining directly on them. I feel a worm of panic in my gut. The officials drop their flags, and everyone is immediately fighting for position. It's a mass shoving match, except it's steel that's rubbing, not shoulders.

But I can't move! I throw the transmission into reverse and press the accelerator, but nothing happens! I don't know if I've stalled or

47

if I'm pinned. I kill the ignition and try again. I can feel the eyes of everyone I know in the audience staring at me, willing me, wondering what's wrong. I turn the key again and again, worried now that I've flooded the engine. Helpless, I look for Barry. His face has the same pale, puzzled expression it did that day we were unwittingly out of transmission fluid. It seems like five minutes have gone by, even though it must be only seconds. I can't go down like this, not without delivering even one solid hit! I close my eyes and tell myself to relax. Then I turn the key and listen as closely as I can for the familiar rumble. And it's there! Just barely audible, but alive and ready! I shift into reverse, give it a little gas and, miraculously, start to move! By this time, the initial shoving has subsided, and there's more room to maneuver. I accelerate and plow into the unsuspecting front end of Richie the Snakeman. The crunch feels surprisingly good.

Already, quite a few cars have been eliminated. My strategy, although accidental, appears to have worked perfectly. By not moving, I let everyone else make the first mistake. I hit the Snakeman again and tear off. Despite the confusion and gathering smoke, there are discernible pathways through the wreckage. I hurl myself along them like a mouse through a maze, targeting whatever is in my way. Goddamn, this is great!

I can feel the adrenaline pumping, my heart pounding, my muscles tensing, my stomach tightening, my mind racing, my hands sweating, my senses sharpening . . . all the same symptoms I've felt dozens of times before when I was scared. But now, I'm *excited*. And suddenly, in the midst of this mayhem, I have a pseudorevelation. Fear and exhilaration are biologically identical. There's no difference in their rudimentary feel. It's the mind that evaluates the body's alert state and decides which way to take it.

It's like what happens on a roller coaster. All the riders are receiving the same stimulus. Everyone is feeling the same effects. But some are in the lead car with arms in the air and giant smiles on their faces, while others are cowering at the back with white knuckles and eyes stitched. Some want the ride to continue forever, while others want it to end *now*. The same experience, the same autonomic response, but far different interpretations of it. What's wrong? Or, more precisely, what's right?

BAM!

Without warning, the Insaniac comes out of nowhere and hits me head-on. But the Caprice Classic absorbs the blow and actually seems to push him off. I shift into drive and start after the prick, when I see what looks like a car on fire against the wall. Suddenly, officials are everywhere, waving us to stop. Firemen swarm the spot. I can't tell what happened or who's involved, but I can clearly see transparent-orange fingers of flame clawing at a white door. Just as I start to become concerned, they vanish in a blast of foam. The driver emerges unsinged to a standing ovation. I take advantage of the break to inventory the damage to my car. I'm definitely in good shape, rear end starting to buckle up, all four tires intact, and no apparent damage to the radiator. But what just happened is a vivid reminder that I mustn't get carried away. One of the most dangerous times is immediately after a fear appears to turn benign. It's during this fleeting period of false confidence that you're most vulnerable. I must remain alert and respectful.

God, it's hot in here. I can feel the padding inside my helmet growing squishy with sweat, and my goggles are starting to fog. The air smells acrid—a weird combination of fair food and burnt metal. Most of the remaining cars are losing their personalities, becoming unrecognizable wrecks with faceless captains. I wonder what mine looks like from the grandstand.

Flags wave again, and we're back at it. Somehow the little red indicator on my shifter has been knocked out of whack, and I can't immediately tell if I'm in drive, reverse, or neutral. This time the hesitation costs me, as I get crunched from in front and in back simultaneously. I feel the subtle rumble subside. A stall. And that's when I notice the Cadillac, gray and scuffed, and somehow I know what's going to happen next. Accidents are often like that. When it's no longer possible to escape, time crawls and you see how it'll all unfold.

The Caddy accelerates toward me—tires spitting gravel and shit, brake lights devoid of red. Then *impact*. I bounce off the driver's-side door, hands no longer on the steering wheel, head a pinball—and all the while, the cymbal clash of rending metal. I watch my hood actually buckle, and the Caddy's rear end come down on top of it—wheels smoking and spinning just inches from my head. The driver is trying to get away, but the entire back of his car is suspended, and mine is pinned underneath. There is so much smoke from my crushed engine and his frustrated transmission that I worry one of us will ignite. Then BAM! Another car hits my left side so hard the door is almost driven into my lap. Spears of metal from this vehicle poke menacingly through my open window. I try to wave down an official to disqualify this idiot, but there's no one in sight. I'm dripping sweat, or at least I hope that's what it is. Desperate, I crank the engine, willing it to turn over so I can escape. And, finally, it starts! But even in low gear I can't gain any traction. I'm not doing anything except overheating my engine.

In instances like this, when two otherwise driveable vehicles lock together, officials allow a few minutes for them to break free or get knocked apart. But neither happens to us, and we're eventually ordered to shut down. I've been eliminated.

The derby isn't over, however. I'm trapped in the middle of this craziness—at least for a while longer. I see The Dirtiest Man in the World careen by, wild eyed. What's left of Orange Krush sighs a thick plume of smoke and spits a few sparks. Somebody's entire fender goes flying through the air like a spear. But still no fear.

I look up through the smolder into the stands and see row upon row of awed, smiling faces. Such mass rapture I've never witnessed, even at professional sporting events. It's surreal how carnage provides the most riveting entertainment. I spot Maria in her orange shirt—hands over her mouth, eyes saucered, looking concerned but also (can it be?) proud. Like instead of yelling, "That's my husband down there!" she wants to scream, "That's my *man*!" Even though I'm out of the competition, I feel like a hero, if only because I did something all these people didn't. Maybe bravery, manhood, courage is just the willingness to step across that line every now and then.

I don't know who eventually won my heat, or who held the trophy high at the end of the night. I do know The Dirtiest Man in the World got upset after being disqualified and was escorted out. A front-end loader pushed my car off the track with me in it. I felt like a piece of dirt being swept out the door. When Barry and I had a chance to inspect the car, it was easy to see what had happened. The blow from the Caddy had crushed the right front wheel, and my efforts at escape had stripped the rubber from the rear. That's why I couldn't go anywhere. But if I'd used snow tires with more aggressive tread, or put inner tubes in the ones I had, or installed one of those big dashboard engine lights to tell me when I'd stalled, I would have done better. I know.

And that's what accidents are all about, aren't they?

You live (hopefully) and learn.

My God, Barry, let's get ourselves home. I do believe I'm feeling frisky.

LOSING
Control

DOGFIGHTING IN AN AIRPLANE

I got off

on fear.

I did.

It made me feel strong, masculine, important, sexual. It didn't just help me survive; it made me feel *alive.* It's a whole new dimension of apprehension—one I always suspected existed, but one I had never fully experienced. It's what results when you rise above fear. It is you as conqueror. And if that sounds too grand, then keep in mind that what's conquered doesn't matter. In my case, it was nothing more than a few steaming wrecks and my own sorry self. Just having the courage to put the key in the ignition and hang on to the wheel is enough.

And the feeling is addictive. It is a fear orgasm. After a surprisingly short refractory period, I want more. I need to do something else daunting, so I can strut before that grandstand again, whether real or imagined. This must be why extreme sports are so popular. The high you get from overcoming fear makes the satisfaction of hitting a fastball or a three-point jumper seem hollow by comparison. Skill in the midst of a good scare redefines competition.

Maybe courage is a muscle. Maybe by regularly training it, I'll build guts. Maybe the secret to getting off on fear rather than getting beaten by it is to simply continue to challenge it.

What really intrigues me, though, is not the flimsy curtain that separates fear from exhilaration, but rather how my brain chooses between them. What shifts perception from threat to thrill? How could those nights with the bogeyman have been so harrowing, yet my time alone behind the wheel so exciting? Given the same biological symptoms, why were the diagnoses so different?

Control.

It must have been the amount of control I thought I had in each situation.

In the demolition derby, I was well-prepared. I had a worthy car, a knowledgeable mechanic, and 25 years of accumulated driving experience. I had done my homework. But as a boy in my bedroom, I was a naïve inmate. I had my voice to call for help, and nothing else. It was like showing up for the final without cracking a textbook. So when the adrenaline started flowing and my heart began pounding, I had no confidence, no perception of control. I immediately doubted whether I could cope and, at that exact moment, my brain chose threat instead of thrill. It became focused on surviving rather than living. And, yes, there is a difference.

Maybe what I truly fear is not having control. Maybe what's gnawing at me and spawning all my nervous tics is sensing that as I grow older and life gets more complicated, I have less and less control. I'm fine when I'm in the driver's seat, but I'm a very restless passenger.

This is precisely the reason why so many people fear flying. Experts explain that it has less to do with being 30,000 feet in the air than it does with forfeiting control while we're there. When we're wedged into a middle seat in coach, we're entrusting our destiny to someone

54

else. And although it can be reassuring to surrender to authority and cultivate faith, there will always be a distrustful part of us that yearns to captain our own fate.

Half of all air travelers admit to being scared, and 20 percent rely on alcohol to handle it. The next time you're at an airport, think about that. One out of every five people you see is buzzed because he or she is so afraid. I wonder what the percentage is outside the airport.

Air Combat USA claims to provide the wildest aerial experience in the world. Barrel rolls, inversions, power dives, close-formation flying, even dogfighting are all performed in gutsy Marchetti attack planes with 260-horsepower engines and 27-foot wingspans. The truly amazing thing, though, is that *you* are at the controls. Except for takeoff and landing, you're flying the airplane (under the watchful eye of a copilot). No experience is necessary; your only training is an hour-long, preflight briefing. "It's kind of a slam-dunk, drink-through-a-fire-hose, get-thrown-off-a-cliff type thing," an instructor would later confide to me.

It seems like the perfect way to push my own envelope of daring, while at the same time testing the experts' control theory. When I'm in charge, when the flight stick is in my hand, does the fear level off and tip toward excitement? Is it breaking new ground that scares me so, or is it being a lemming?

I'm standing in the doorway to the briefing room at a small airport near Lancaster, Pennsylvania, momentarily distracted by something I just spotted inside on a chalkboard.

It's a stick drawing of a man parachuting from an airplane.

"Can I help you?" asks a young fellow with a bristle-brush haircut, aviator sunglasses, and a one-piece flightsuit, but I don't immediately hear him. I'm still staring at that drawing.

"Can I help you?" he repeats louder and more forcefully.

"Uh, yeah. Is this Air Combat?"

"Welcome, sir," he replies, snapping to attention. "My name is Rat. I'll be one of your flight instructors. This gentleman here is Ken. He's also in your class."

Ken smiles confidently when we shake hands, but his palm is noticeably damp.

I am afraid to fly. Nevertheless, I routinely board all types of commercial aircraft and travel just about anywhere. I manage to look convincingly bored and relaxed, but like many of my fellow passengers I am constantly on alert. Any change in engine pitch, any whiff of something acrid and, of course, any suspicious characters or turbulence instantly make me tense. Jet lag, I believe, is mostly an adrenaline hangover.

A friend of mine was once on a bumpy flight from Philadelphia to Los Angeles. Next to him was a woman, a stranger, who was growing increasingly nervous. Finally, somewhere over the Midwest, he smiled at her and offered his hand. She bit her lip and gratefully took it. And that's how they sat for the remainder of the trip. After landing, she gave him an embarrassed nod of thanks and they parted—still without ever saying a word.

I suspect there are a lot of air travelers like that woman—people who would accept a reassuring hand if someone offered it. But they'll never admit that. Although fear is instantly diffused once it's shared, most of us insist on clinging to ours and keeping it personal.

There have been two times when I've been really scared in the sky. The first was on a flight to Bermuda. The jet encountered some wind shear and dropped precipitously. One minute I was casually reading a magazine; the next it felt like the bottom had dropped out of the airplane. The captain immediately clicked on with a reassuring explanation, but I was momentarily terrified. And the suddenness with which it happened—in clear skies—has no doubt contributed to my lingering watchfulness.

My second scare occurred not in a plane but in the French Alps, where I let myself be pressured by some newfound acquaintances into parapenting. This sport is similar to hang gliding except that you're suspended beneath a rectangular parachute instead of a giant kite. By maneuvering the chute into updrafts of air called thermals, you can sometimes soar for hours.

Despite the obvious peril of this, no warning lights blinked on in my brain cabin until I was riding the ski lift to the top of a 10,000-foot mountain. That's when I realized how high up I was going, and that shortly I'd be throwing myself off the top. Even though I'd be harnessed to an instructor, I started leafing through my French phrasebook searching for how to say, "I've changed my mind."

But I never had the time. As soon as we got off the lift, the instructor spread our chute on the ground behind us, strapped himself securely to my back ("That better be the buckle poking me, Jacques!"), and then started yelling, "Go! Go! Go!" I had no choice but to run as fast as I could toward the precipice until I no longer felt the earth beneath my boots. I became a kid on a swing, legs dangling, hands death gripping, trying not to wet myself. And then the chute caught and we were floating, not falling, and the air suddenly became thick and supportive, not empty like I had imagined.

I hung on for the half-hour or so it took to reach the ground. We circled and swooped like a nylon hawk, and my emotions made similar wide turns—one minute concern, the next exultation, then back again with an unexpected shift in the wind. I was sliding down an invisible banister of air, knowing I should be whooping with excitement but unable to dismiss the danger. I landed on wobbly legs with a pale face, proud to say I did it but unwilling to repeat the experience.

Michael Blackstone, the president of Air Combat and a pilot with more than 24,000 hours of flight time, contends that the best way to conquer a flying phobia is to learn how to fly. Air currents, thermal dynamics, lift. . . . It's the control theory again. Accumulated knowledge clears you for takeoff.

"When you take flying lessons," he says, "you find that the plane is not being held up by a giant hand ready to slap you into the ground. Airplanes are quite stable, and I don't care whether you're talking about the Marchetti or a 767. They're all meant to be in the air and to recover from pilot screwups. I've lost entire engines on jetliners and was still able to fly them. Three or four things have to go wrong before you have a bad day at the office in an airplane."

Blackstone says matter-of-factly that I have a far greater chance of getting killed speeding on the freeway than I do in one of his airplanes. Air Combat flies approximately 3,000 missions in 15 U.S. cities each year, and since its inception in 1989 more than 22,000 people have paid $800 to $1,500 for a range of aerial experiences. Graduates include an eight-year-old schoolgirl and a great-grandmother named Helen.

None has crashed and burned.

Now it's my turn.

Rat is not the offspring of poor, prolific parents who named him such because he was one more burdensome child scuttling about the house. Rather, he acquired his nickname in the military after a drunken altercation with a rodent during a late-night foray across the Mexican border. "It was a big rodent," he says in his defense. "It stood up on its hind legs, I tried to put a move on it, and it bit me. I've been known as Rat ever since."

We all chuckle at this, but I can't help wondering whether a guy foolish enough to take on a rat can be trusted to convey the finer aspects of piloting an aircraft. Ken, a CPA from Delaware, compounds the situation by confessing that his nickname is Rear-End because it sounds like his last name, Riordan. This is the guy I'll be flying wingtip-to-wingtip with and eventually dogfighting. If there had been an ejection button on my folding chair, I would have considered aborting the mission.

I've registered for the half-day $895 Basic Air Combat Maneuvers course. This includes an hour-long briefing, a 50- to 60-minute flight, and a 30-minute critique of my videotaped performance. Rat hands me a white helmet and a faded-green flight suit. It has a set of wings sewn on the chest and an American flag on the sleeve. It instantly makes me look and feel like I know what I'm doing. (I should have paid more attention, though, to the fact that he had to rifle through a sizable pile before finding one that wasn't damp or soiled.)

Our briefing commences with a discussion of the planes we'll be piloting—nimble Italian-built fighters capable of 270 mph and worth nearly a quarter-million dollars apiece. He warns us that this is going to be a physically demanding experience. Not only will the temperature beneath the cockpit canopy exceed 100 degrees on this warm day, but the G-forces will make us strain like constipated Bulgarian powerlifters.

A "G" is the amount of force that gravity exerts upon the body. As you sit in your chair reading this, you're experiencing 1 G. Accelerating away in a dragster, you'd feel maybe 1½ Gs. But streaking upward in a Marchetti or banking hard left while maintaining the same altitude could convey as many as 6 Gs. This means a 200-pound pilot would instantly feel six times heavier—like he weighed 1,200 pounds. And such force, not surprisingly, produces some weird sensations.

"It impacts every molecule in your body," explains Rat. "But the most sensitive part is your eyeballs." First your vision fades from color to black and white, then your field of sight narrows until it seems you're looking through a toilet-paper tube. As the G-force increases and the blood pressure in your head drops, you eventually black out. This is called G-LOC or Gravity-Induced Loss of Consciousness. Military pilots, who can pull as many as 9 Gs in an F-16, train in a centrifuge to be able to withstand it. They consciously fight to trap blood in their heads by exhaling hard during acceleration and tightening their leg and stomach muscles.

Fortunately, G-LOC is a temporary, self-correcting condition. The pilot slumps in the cockpit as the plane continues on its set course. But since he's no longer pulling the throttle to accelerate, the G-force eases and he soon regains consciousness.

"You wake up a couple of seconds later and flop around a bit," says Rat. "You remember getting up in the morning, coming to the airport, and getting in the airplane. But you don't recall what just happened. There's no permanent brain damage—unless, of course, you're too close to the ground to save yourself."

The ground. That's another important concept. It must be afforded the same respect as the enemy because it can be as lethal as any missile. To help us avoid it, Rat explains the concept of a "hard deck." Although we'll be flying at approximately 8,500 feet, we'll actually have much less room in which to operate. That's because an imaginary surface will exist 2,500 feet above the earth. It's there for our safety, and it must be regarded as genuine terra firma. If either Ken or I break the hard deck, the mission is over. It's no different than if we hit the ground or got shot down. For similar safety reasons, there will also be an imaginary 500-foot bubble surrounding each aircraft. Unless we're flying in formation, we're not to get any closer to each other than that.

Although flying a Marchetti with essentially no training is intimidating, the idea of dogfighting pushes it beyond the boundaries of sanity. While there are other flight schools that put you in the cockpit of a Soviet MiG over Moscow, rocket you to 60,000 feet in an English jet, or even let you break the sound barrier over the Atlantic, none actually lets you take a shot at another aircraft.

Well, perhaps I should qualify that. While there's a gun sight, a trigger, unlimited ammunition, and lots of convincing bullet noise, you're not shooting real lead. It's up to the instructors to judge when you've locked on and then to activate a device under the plane that releases a plume of smoke. Nevertheless, it's convincingly realistic. And the strategy that's used to outwit an opponent and maneuver into kill position is the same as what's taught at Top Gun schools.

Rat grabs two miniature fighter jets mounted on wooden dowels to demonstrate what we'll be doing. "There will be no forward quarter attacks," he warns. "This means we're not going to shoot each other in the face. Directly ahead of you is 12 o'clock, to your right is 3 o'clock, to your left is 9 o'clock, and at your back is 6 o'clock. Anything in front of the three-nine line, we will not call a kill. It's just too dangerous

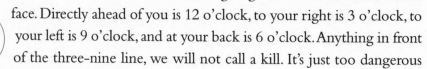

trying to put the gun sights on each other when you're closing from oppo-site directions." (He crashes the toy planes and mimics an explosion.)

Instead, he continues, we'll work behind the three-nine line. We'll chase rather than face. "The secret is keeping the horizontal line on your gun sight even with his wings at all times. And in the middle of the sight, you'll notice a dot. That's called the pipper. When it's on him, pull the trigger!"

It all sounds relatively straightforward, but Rat reminds us that rarely will we be tailing an opponent who's casually banking and rolling. Rather, he'll be using extreme diversionary tactics. This sparks a lecture on lift vec-tors, degrees of bank, level circles, lag pursuits, and something called "hi and lo yo-yos." Soon, my eyes resemble two glazed donuts. Even Rat's an-imated demonstrations with the model airplanes aren't helping me un-derstand it. Rear-End looks similarly blank. Does he really expect us to grasp all this? I mean, I've been driving a car for nearly three decades, and I still occasionally have trouble with K-turns.

Just when my brain is approaching warp speed, Rat scrubs off some of my anxiety by acknowledging that Air Force recruits spend 40 to 50 hours studying these concepts before trying them out. "Don't worry if you don't fully understand them," he says. "Your instructor will be there to help. The most important thing you need to know is this: 'Lose sight, lose fight.'"

That's our mantra. We need to twist around in our seats, look over our shoulders, and perform whatever Gumby maneuver is necessary to main-tain visual contact with the other aircraft. The minute I lose Rear-End, the second he disappears, my advantage disintegrates. I'm no longer the fox; I'm the rabbit. Or, perhaps a better analogy: I'm Snoopy on his Sopwith Camel.

Our briefing is temporarily interrupted by the return of the previous class from its dogfighting session. And as Rat had warned, our two counterparts look beat. They're brothers, both sixtyish. Their thin gray hair is matted to their heads, their complexions are pallid, and their flight suits sport dark gray circles beneath each armpit.

"Man, I need a cigarette," says one in a hoarse rasp. I can't immediately tell if he talks this way normally or whether it's because he's been screaming for the past hour. Neither of them acknowledges us. Their heads are still somewhere in the clouds.

With them are Worm and Spear. These are the other instructors, the ones who'll actually be sitting beside us in the cockpit. Fortunately, they look a lot less shell shocked. Worm appears to be in his late fifties, but he's lanky and fit. Spear is shorter, cockier, and younger by a few years. When they shake my hand, their grips are sure and firm. Although their nicknames are also strange (why doesn't anyone here use his real name?), they're less unsettling than some of the other Air Combat pilots that were listed on the roster—like Psycho, Skids, Mad-Dog, Gomer, and Nails.

"Let's take a look at your videotapes," says Spear to the brothers. "Ken and Joe, you can watch, too."

There are three cameras mounted in the cockpit. One looks through the gun sight, and the other two are trained on the pilot from different angles. It's the copilot's job to switch between them. Spear synchronizes the brothers' tapes on separate TVs, then fast-forwards to the start of their five dogfights.

The first thing that strikes me is that these guys are actually flying. The horizon is where it should be. The nose of the airplane is not pointing toward the ground. They appear in total control, hands casually gripping the stick, eyes expertly scanning the skies and console. It's inspiring. In fact, I feel my confidence rising. If these two old farts can do it, then I can, too.

But then the unexpected happens. One of the brothers reaches for something, digging around in a side compartment as if in a panic. Eventually, he pulls out a white plastic bag, puts it to his mouth, and starts vomiting. Not long afterward, on the other screen, the second brother repeats the maneuver. This appears to be a different type of kill—one that Rat failed to detail.

The Air Combat Web site states: ". . . fewer than 10 percent of our guest pilots suffer motion sickness." This is an encouraging statistic, and two reasons are given. First, being a pilot rather than a passenger provides more distraction. And second, focusing on the opponent instead of the horizon provides a more stable reference point. Still, the brothers' retching continues for a troubling length of time, with Spear eventually apologizing for not redirecting the camera.

Rat steps in to reassure us: "We're not going to fail you for getting air-sick," he says. "If you start feeling queasy, let the instructor know so he can ease off. He'll open the canopy to get some cool air, and give you a chance to relax."

Up until this point, I hadn't even considered getting sick, but now this vivid image is compounding my fear. I'm suddenly thankful I decided against ordering the huevos rancheros for breakfast.

"There's one more thing we need to talk about," says Rat, directing our attention away from the videotapes, "and that's egressing the airplane." At first, I think he's launched back into a discussion of combat maneuvers, but then I realize he's finally addressing that troubling sketch on the chalk-board—the one of the stickman parachuting.

"There are three reasons we leave the airplane," he says. "The first and best reason is because we've landed, and we're heading for the chicks and beer."

Chicks? Beer? (Did I miss that in the brochure?)

"The second reason is if there's a fire. And it needs to be a big fire; small ones we can deal with."

Fire?

"And the third reason is if a large piece of the plane is missing. If something small goes, we'll probably still be able to land safely. But if it's something big, like the wing, for instance, then that's going to make things unmanageable."

Like the wing, for instance?

"Should your instructor become incapacitated, it'll be up to you to get rid of the canopy. You'll notice a T-handle directly above you in the cockpit; give it a quarter-turn. There'll be another T-handle by your left knee. Pull that, and the canopy will release."

Instructor . . . incapacitated?

"After you've done that, release your lap belt and shoulder straps, detach the communications cord from your helmet, and dive over the side. Try to jump down off the wing, so you don't hit the tail section. That is, if it's still there."

If it's still there . . . ?

"Once you're clear of the aircraft, don't bother counting one potato, two potato . . . just pull hard on your parachute's D-ring. You'll feel a jolt when it opens. Put your hands on the risers and take one look at the ground. If you're heading toward a busy highway, pull in whatever direction you want to go. Then don't look down anymore. These are military chutes, and they won't set you down gently. It's more like jumping off a 12-story building. Just keep your feet and knees together and your legs relaxed. Collapse as you hit the ground, roll onto your back, and detach the chute. That's important. You don't want to get dragged down the road by it. We'll get our stories straight after that. Any questions?"

"Uh, yeah," I ask tentatively, "have you ever had to bail out?"

"No, this is all just theory to me. Now grab your helmets. Worm and Spear are almost ready."

What immediately strikes me about the Marchetti when I see it on the runway is how tiny it is. It looks like a die-cast toy. Although the plane weighs nearly 2,500 pounds, it seems so fragile that I'm hesitant to touch it. But it's a beautiful machine—subtle camouflage color, bright red nose, and stars on the wings and fuselage. It's a single-prop plane, meaning there's one propeller, and underneath are mounts for light bombs or missiles.

Spear (not God) will be my copilot. He's retired Air Force and supposedly has decades of experience flying F-16s, as well as commercial aircraft. He takes my picture standing proudly beside the plane because, he says, "everyone looks better beforehand." Instead of "Cheese," I say, "Here's looking at you, kid." He doesn't get it.

We climb into the cockpit, secure our safety harnesses, and hook up the communications equipment. I'll be able to converse with Spear, but I'll only be able to hear Worm and air-traffic control. Because he's the enemy, Rear-End will be incommunicado.

The console is a dazzling array of dials, buttons, switches, and potential warning lights. But the only two I have any flight experience with— the attendant call button and that little dial you turn for more stale air—are unfortunately missing. I do recognize the altitude gauge, but Spear tells me not to look at it. "Keep your eyes outside the cockpit," he says.

The only piece of equipment I need to operate is the flight stick. There's one between my legs (which is a reassuring placement) and a duplicate between Spear's. They move in tandem. Pull back to climb, push forward to descend, or angle it in either direction to turn. Thumb the button on top to open the communications line to talk, and depress the button in front when it's time to finish somebody off. That last one feels surprisingly at home beneath my trigger finger. Overall, the cockpit is more comfortable than I expected—more legroom than in coach, and an unrestricted view.

I take Rat's advice, though, and look for those T-handles—one overhead, another to my left, plus the chest buckle that secures my safety harness. That's my escape route. But how I'd ever retain the clarity of mind to do all that *and* muster the courage to leap over the wing remains unfathomable. I suddenly appreciate the blind genius of the push-button ejection system.

As I complete my cockpit inspection, I also notice the little white bag I saw in the video. It's tucked into a side pocket by my left leg. Just in case.

"All right, Joe, it's time to go," says Spear, flicking switches to start the engine. "We're gonna whoop on them, kick some butt, take names."

"I hope I don't whoop on myself," I reply, honestly.

"No way! We're gonna get mean! Kill or be killed! Okay, I'll taxi toward the runway, stop just short of it, then do some run-up checks. Duck your head—I need to close the canopy, or it'll get too loud in here."

With the propeller spinning, the entire plane starts vibrating. And it isn't a soothing jiggle, like you get sitting in the display chairs at Sharper Image. This is a full-body, grabbed-by-the-shoulders, wake-up shake. If I leave my teeth slightly parted, they chatter automatically.

Finally, the reality of what I'm about to do is settling in. Up until this moment, it was all theory, diagrams, and dare. But now I'm actually listening to ground control clear us for takeoff, and I'm scared. It isn't terror I'm feeling, though. I'm not about to scream, unbuckle my harness, and egress the airplane. Rather, it's grim resignation—the cold-sweat realization that I'm trapped, if only by my own stupidity, in a situation with too much momentum to prevent the inevitable from happening. I have control at the same time I do not. My brain is darting feverishly back and forth between threat and thrill.

We perch on the edge of runway 31. Spear locks the canopy, exchanges thumbs-up with Worm, and tells the tower that he's ready. I have one final, silly thought: I wish I had a nickname—some devil-may-care moniker that exemplified my bravery and brashness, some persona other than my own to hide behind. Suddenly "Joe" seems too personal, too vulnerable.

"Okay, this is it. My stick for takeoff. You ready, Joe?"

I nod my helmet, Spear guns the engine, and I'm once again racing toward that cliff in France, bracing myself for the step into nothingness. The gray tarmac and its white markings smear with our gathering speed. But this time, instead of falling off the end of the earth, I feel the ground gently lose its grip and we're climbing—powerfully so, almost as if the air itself is supplying traction. We've taken off in tandem, so a glance over my right shoulder provides a good view of the other Marchetti. It's like looking in a mirror. There I am, floating in the heavens.

 The weather is perfect for flying: light wind, no clouds, just a hint of haze building on the horizon. When I look down I see arteries of highway below us, with traffic inching along them like blood cells. The furrowed farm fields of Lancaster County are a patchwork, a fertile quilt covering the earth. It's all so magical, so beautiful, that my apprehension is replaced by security, privilege, and wonder. Maybe this isn't going to be so frightening after all.

Then . . . a jolt. We've hit some rough air, some turbulence. It feels like we're rolling over speed bumps at 150 mph. As I watch the wings bow, my sense of vulnerability instantly returns. We're being swatted by unseen hands to remind us that we're unwelcome here—like bothersome flies in the atmosphere.

"It's a little bumpy approaching 3,000 feet," Spear says reassuringly. "It'll smooth out shortly."

And sure enough, as we break that altitude, it does. The man knows what he's talking about.

"All right, Joe. You ready to fly?"

He says this as casually as if he's asking me the time. He really is going to surrender the controls of this quarter-million-dollar airplane.

"I'll try."

"Hold the stick nice and steady. Wings level with the horizon. Nose just slightly above it, because we're going to continue climbing for a while."

And just like that, with no more of an introduction, I'm in control. It reminds me of when I was 10, riding in my dad's VW, and he'd let me hold the steering wheel while he blew his nose or gathered money for a toll. It felt so wonderfully frightful that I simultaneously wanted it to continue and to end.

The Marchetti is incredibly responsive. The lightest movement of the stick instantly sends the plane in that direction. But it's not twitchy. It's more like an extension of my body, as if wings had sprouted from my shoulders and a tail section from my spinal column. I can see why pilots don't say, "I'm flying the plane," but rather "I'm flying."

"Ken is trying to fly formation on us," says Spear. "It'll take him a while to get the hang of it. Hold nice and steady what you got."

A glance off my right wing shows that Rear-End is in the same learning curve as I am. His plane is jimmying about as he tries to get

67

a feel for the stick and, at the same time, maneuver closer to my aircraft. This would seem like a lethal mix, but before long his flying smooths out, as does mine, and we're cruising along with less than 100 feet between us. As we each gain better control of our planes, I can feel the exhilaration, the strength, the self-importance, the thrill building.

"Good job," says Spear. "Now see that big white building out there? That's where we're going to be fighting. Head in that direction. Ken is sliding behind us to do some gun-sight tracking. Let's give him some left and right banks."

I tentatively push the stick to my left, but Spear puts his hand on mine and applies much stronger pressure. The Marchetti rolls in that direction. "There you go," he says. "Look over your left shoulder. See him? About 1,200 feet back, just getting into gun range? Now reverse the turn. Harder! Look over your right shoulder. Got him? He's at five o'clock, just slightly above the horizon."

I play mouse to Rear-End's cat for a few minutes, then we exchange positions. My focus is now through the gun-sight as I try to keep the horizontal line parallel to his wings. It's not easy at first, but I slowly get the hang of it. I learn I can also use the gun sight to gauge distance. When his wings fill half the inner ring, I'm a thousand feet back. When they fill it entirely, I'm at the 500-foot bubble.

"Go ahead, shoot him," says Spear. "Put the pipper on him and pull the trigger!"

I match his wings on a left roll and fire off a round.

"Hey, I think Joe has this figured out!" Spear radios Worm. "I think you guys are going to be in trouble."

Later, while watching the videotape of my flight, I'll notice that I was smiling at this point.

It would be the last time.

Once we reach the dogfighting zone, Rear-End and I review our combat tactics. I practice chasing him first, then turn over the aggressor's role and rehearse my evasive maneuvers. But unfortunately the geometry isn't any clearer up here, so I just follow Spear's orders. ("Roll inside in a low yo-yo, pull the nose out in front of him, more right bank, pull back, hard right. . . . ") I'm not enough of an expert to react swiftly and surely to all this, but I'm relieved to notice Spear's hand acting a split-second behind mine on his stick. There is a safety net.

The flying is getting more demanding now. No longer can I just sit back and enjoy the view. In fact, sometimes after a radical maneuver the ground isn't immediately where it should be. I have to constantly swivel my head to keep sight of my opponent, and when we pull 2 Gs during one hard roll, I feel the contents of my stomach compartment shift. Uh oh.

"Okay, Worm, we're complete coming off your right side," says Spear. "Joe, you ready to get it on? We're gonna be the fighter on number one."

The plan is to do six dogfights, alternating the aggressor's role. Each commences with our two planes streaking by each other from opposite directions. Even though we're pretty far apart, it's a heart-pounding way to start. Seeing the other guy blast by makes me realize just how fast I'm flying. Plus, it adds urgency. It's as if I'm cruising along on routine patrol and suddenly, off to the west, I spot a bogey.

"Here he comes," says Spear, pointing to a speeding black dot at two o'clock. "Fight's on! Bank right! Hard! Harder! Don't worry, you're not gonna break that stick. Now pull! Take it up in a vertical!"

My jaw drops, as much from the G-force as from the fact that we're climbing straight up. The horizon has vanished, the plane is now a rocket, and my skin feels like it's being pulled from my skeleton.

"Holy shit!" I yell.

"They're right in front of us," says Spear, unfazed. "Level . . . level . . . roll . . . pull. Look over your left shoulder! Got to keep 'em in sight, Joe. Lose sight, lose fight. Keep pulling! Pull harder! Right there, ease up a bit. Hold the nose down . . . more . . . more. See him? Okay, we're ac-celerating and closing. See the angles developing? Little closer. Get ready to shoot. . . . "

I pull the trigger and keep it depressed as Rear-End drifts in and out of my gun sight. I'm taking no chances. I'm unleashing a maelstrom. Finally, after about 10 seconds of continuous shooting, I score the hit, and a stream of smoke billows from his aircraft.

"Nice kill!" says Spear, slapping me five. "You definitely put enough bullet in him that time."

But I'm too overwhelmed to whoop. I'm still trying to grasp that for a brief time I was like an astronaut in a launch capsule. I feel like I've just stepped off the spinning tea cups at an amusement park—all giddy and disoriented. I can still see, hear, respond, but I do not fully comprehend.

"Okay, we're the bogey on this next one," says Spear. "Bank left. . . . Keep them in sight. . . . Hard left. . . . Fight's on!"

I'm moving sluggishly now. I hear muffled orders. My fingertips are thick on the stick. I've become slow and detached—body and mind disjointed. I have a disturbing thought: Am I one of those pathetic people who freeze in difficult situations—the pitiful, quivering mess who has to be slapped across the face and ordered to get hold of himself?

"As soon as the fight's on, you *have* to start doing something with the airplane," yells Spear, annoyed at my unresponsiveness. "He's in a low yo-yo. Look over your left shoulder. See him at seven o'clock? Keep him in sight, and let's take it into a hi yo-yo. . . . Uh oh, he's closing. . . . Might be too late. . . . Ow! I'm feeling those bullets! He got us!"

This last fight is embarrassingly brief, but even worse than my woeful piloting is the unavoidable fact that I'm feeling sick. It's an unmistakable clenching in my gut, as if a brute's fist is slowly tightening around my stomach. I swallow hard and lick my lips, which all of a sudden feel like Velcro strips.

"I felt my stomach on that one," I confess to Spear.

"No problem, I'll crack the canopy and get us some cool air."

I inhale deeply, swallow again, and try to settle myself by gazing at the horizon. I imagine my stomach to be a tiny bubble in a carpenter's level, slowly finding its equilibrium. Ironically, I realize I'm less afraid of flying now than I am of getting sick, of losing my self-respect. Vanity is more resilient than one expects.

"Feeling better, Joe?"

I nod, even though I'm not.

"All right, it's time for some full-up fighting," says Spear, relocking the canopy and making me wonder what it was we were doing before. "Take it uphill, Joe. Pull! Pull! Pull! Tighten those leg muscles. . . . Now give me some left bank. . . ."

Just like that, the sky swaps places with the ground, and I'm flying upside down. My brain can't grasp this distortion. It sputters for a few seconds, narrowly avoids a stall, and then begins questioning all rational thought. Maybe I'm not really in an airplane after all, maybe this throttle is a joystick, maybe Spear is an evil henchman and we're on a kamikaze mission. . . .

"Keep turning! Pull harder!" he yells, resorting to short, staccato commands to keep me focused.

"Man, I'm feeling that," I groan through gritted teeth.

"We're only pulling 2½ Gs. Tighten those muscles! Give me some left bank. . . . We got some angles on him. Uh oh, now he's starting to get some angles on us. We're losing our advantage! Keep pulling. . . . Harder! Take it uphill again!"

The duel seems unending. I can see why they call it a dogfight—engines snarling, bullets biting, fur flying. And all the while that brute's fist is tightening around my stomach—my face whitening along with its knuckles—until I say uncle.

"My stomach's feeling pretty queasy," I croak.

Spear nods and tells me to ease off the throttle, allowing Rear-End to swoop in behind and finish us off. But I feel no regret, no loss. Death, however staged, is a better alternative to how I'm feeling now.

"Pull the white bag out just in case," says Spear, cracking the canopy again. "Remember to push the mike out of the way if you have to use it. Worm, we're taking a breather."

The only thing worse than puking is trying to puke. Once you get rid of the bile, you feel better. That's what happened with those two brothers. "Blow and go" is what pilots call it. But all my anxiety must have combusted every last food particle in my stomach, because when I try to fill the white bag, nothing comes up. Dry convulsions wrack my body, and a cold sweat streams down my face and neck.

If you've been thinking up until now that Spear has a pretty cool job, consider that it's not yet two o'clock, and he has already witnessed two grown men throwing up. He's in the line of fire in more ways than one.

"Try to keep looking outside," he says, pressing himself against the far wall of the cockpit. "Focus on something in the distance. Soak up that fresh air."

But none of his advice helps. I'm past the point of no return. I want this to end. My hands are actually trembling. I doubt if even a slap across the face would revive me.

The rest of my Air Combat experience is a slow-motion blur. Each second feels like a minute, yet if not for the videotape I'd have only a fuzzy recollection of it. Rear-End and I fight three more times and end the afternoon with an equal number of victories. (I suspect, however, that they were being kind to me.) I reach for the white bag a second time, dry heaving and perspiring so badly that even Spear is impressed. ("I never saw anybody sweat like that," he says.) And at some point during the last few fights, we pull 3½ Gs and I black out. It only lasts a few seconds, and I can't tell whether it's from the G-force or just my barf-induced weakness. But I definitely go someplace else. One moment I have the pipper trained on Rear-End's tail, the next I awake to Spear yelling, "Pull the trigger! Guns! Guns! Guns!"

In the end, there is only confusion. It's just like I've heard veterans describe their time in combat. They were too mixed up to think or feel. They survived not on intelligence or cunning, but on luck and instinct. Had I been alone up there, I would have died. I couldn't react. I was completely useless. I no longer cared.

But I wasn't scared, not of losing control anyway. No, I willingly surrendered that. I wanted Spear to take that stick. Rather, there was something else. . . .

I did this partially to confront the fear of flying, the unease that I felt every time I buckled myself into an airline seat. And it will help with that. It has given me perspective. I'll no longer stand in wonder at a 747's thunder. I know now how air-worthy planes are—that despite their size they belong in the sky. I understand the concept of lift, and the support that's available from apparent nothingness. I can still feel the structural confidence of the Marchetti during even its most improbable antics.

I learned about turbulence, too. Those bumps that prompt commercial pilots to turn on the FASTEN SEAT BELT sign are nothing compared to being upside down or pulling 3½ Gs. It's a paper cut next to a stab wound. And as a result, my palms will be a lot less sweaty the next time I'm descending through storm clouds into O'Hare. And every time I catch a glimpse of the white bag in the seat back, I'll be thankful my stomach has a new baseline for queasiness.

But I'm no better prepared than I was to deal with genuine crisis. If something ever went seriously wrong on a flight—if hijackers stormed the cockpit or if I was ordered to put my head between my knees for a crash landing—I'd weaken and crumple just like I did in the Marchetti. I'd wait for somebody else to say, "Let's roll." And even then, I might not be able to follow.

I feel the soft, rubber bump of the wheels touching down. I am a 165-pound mound of blanched protoplasm. I'm unsure whether I can unhook my harness, stand up, and climb out. I feel that weak, that used up. As we taxi back to the hangar, I glimpse Rear-End celebrating with Worm in their cockpit. He obviously didn't get sick. He didn't just survive; he *lived.* Please, no beer, no chicks.

Spear cuts the engine, pops the canopy, and asks if I need a hand.

"No," I lie, my mouth so dry I almost choke.

My helmet drips when I take it off. My flight suit feels dishrag damp, and it smells. I wait beside my plane as Rear-End strides over, because I'm uncertain whether my legs can be trusted to take me that far.

"Man, that was great!" he says, pumping my arm. "What a rush! I never felt better!"

I try to smile back, to be equally enthusiastic.

"Yeah, that was something else," I mumble.

He grins at me broadly and slaps my back. But as he turns and walks away, I notice that balled up in his left hand, just like in mine, is a white plastic bag.

Every day is an act. We pretend, we deceive, we try so hard to make people believe. That takes courage, for sure. But what are we protecting? What are we so afraid of others detecting? No doubt weakness, inadequacy, and not having the right stuff. But there's something else.

I took the easy way out up there. That much is painfully clear. Because there was someone to whom I could pass the stick, someone who could save me, I took the opportunity. And although I felt awful, in retrospect I can't say I felt fear. I trusted Spear. Maybe what I have to do next is take away all safety nets and do something without a pit crew or a copilot. I have to be the one at the controls, the guy who has to measure up, the obvious culprit if things go awry. Yes, it's time to stand alone on the stage and either live or die.

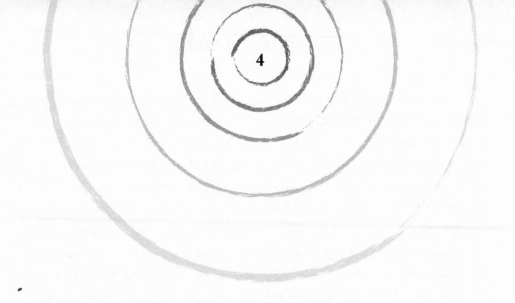

4

FIVE MINUTES AS A STAND-UP COMEDIAN

This next gentleman coming to the stage this evening is not a
professional comedian. He's here to overcome one of his biggest
fears, and that's getting up in front of a live audience. So I want
you to give a big Comedy Cabaret welcome to Mr. Joe Kita!

There's applause—or, more accurately, noise. That's what I hear as I
sidestep tables to get to the stage—a blur of thick sound neither welcoming nor troubling, just enveloping. And when I step up to the mike
and turn around, I see nothing. Even though I know there are about 60
people in the room, the spotlights in my eyes keep me from clearly seeing
anyone. They're just shadows, smudges, hints of men and women . . .

Settling in. Quieting down. Waiting for me to say something funny.

I grab the mike. It's sticky.

"Good evening. Did you hear the one about the two gay Irishmen?
Michael Fitzpatrick and Patrick Fitzmichael."

I pause for laughter. But there's nothing.

Rejection

There's an old Jerry Seinfeld bit in which he jokes that people at a funeral are less afraid of being in the coffin than they are of delivering the
eulogy. It's true. Public speaking is the most common fear in America. In
fact, it ranks significantly higher than dying, flying, going out alone at night,
or any other phobia you can name. It shows just how out of control fear
can get, if we let it. There is nothing threatening about speaking to a group
except what the mind fabricates. Neither the situation nor the behavior is
dangerous; it's only the significance we attach to it. It's everyone's paruresis.
For some reason, when people are watching, the words just won't flow.

I suppose there may be some ancient evolutionary force at work. I suppose that being social creatures, we need the acceptance of others to survive and thrive. So to risk being singled out, to take the chance of
appearing incompetent and being rejected, is to jeopardize our very existence. I suppose on some subconscious level, we can still sense this, although nowadays it's the ego we're trying to protect.

Notice that it's the fear of public speaking that's always ranked so highly
and not the fear of public nudity. With the latter there can be no deceit involved. But with the former, there's great effort in staying covered up.

My worst public-speaking experience occurred when I was a young
executive editor for a national magazine. I had been asked to explain the
creative process to a cross section of employees in our publishing company.
There were about 200 people in attendance, including several vice presi-
dents, and there was I—a mere boy—dressed in a suit and tie, standing behind the lectern, working through my introduction . . . when, without
warning, I almost shut down. My heart started hammering. My throat
closed up. I could barely get any words out. Everyone was looking at me,
and I wasn't sure I could proceed. I sipped some water. I inhaled. I dabbed
away invisible sweat. When I resumed speaking, I heard my voice quivering. Somehow, I fought my way to the end of it.

I'd had a panic attack—my first. In fact, I was under so much
stress during this time in my career that I also started experiencing

tunnel vision. People sitting just a few feet away from me in my office appeared as if they were at the far end of a tube. Then I began having panic attacks on the phone. When I had to make difficult calls or do radio interviews, all the same paralyzing symptoms returned. Although I never hung up, although I always toughed it out, it was an every-second struggle.

My fear eventually made me question what I was doing with my life. It helped me see that I was uncomfortable with the role of manager I was playing. It made me realize that I was pretending.

I quit my job and returned to writing. And sure enough, the fear receded. Yeah, I still get nervous making difficult phone calls or talking to large groups, but it's normal and manageable. I haven't had another panic attack. Instead of trying to fool people when I'm on stage, I tell them only what I'm sure of. I am no longer playing a role; I am merely being myself. I am not trying to impress; I am just attempting to clearly express. Sometimes fear can be a friend like that. It'll let you know, when no one else will, that you're not being true to yourself.

In order to face the fear of rejection, though, I'm going to have to put back on those imposter's clothes. To make this a worthy test, I can't speak about what I know best. I must be totally out of my element, in a realm where I have no experience or confidence. I must be on some stage where who I want to be is so far removed from who I am that there's a good chance the panic will return. I have to risk derision and failure and rejection and, ironically, getting laughed at. And what better place to do that than at a comedy club?

Before we get on with the show, I should admit that I was a bit of an entertainer in school. I did this killer Stevie Wonder impersonation when I was in eighth grade. Back then, I had glasses and thick, curly hair. If I picked up my chin, bobbed my head, and caught the right amount of backlighting, I could project a shadow on the classroom wall that looked just like the Motown man himself.

My best performance, though, came in Mrs. Young's typing class, sophomore year. She was a tiny, nearsighted old lady with eyes that looked like an umlaut had been typed above her nose. One day I brought in this huge screw. It was about 15 inches long and weighed a couple of pounds. There's no way it could have been a part of any typewriter. But midway through class, when everyone was tapping away, I dropped this screw on the floor. It made an incredible racket. Everyone stopped typing and looked up, while I screamed: "Mrs. Young! Mrs. Young! I hit the shift key and look what fell out!"

The poor woman was beside herself. She didn't know what to do. She told me to back away from the machine, as if it were a bomb. Then she hustled to the office to make an emergency call to IBM. Since everyone in class was in on my prank, we all had a great laugh while she was gone. For a while, I was Johnny Carson. But when she returned, it was with palpable rage and a pink detention slip.

But wisecracking in class (or in print, for that matter) is a lot different than trying to make an entire nightclub of paying customers laugh. That's public speaking squared. In business presentations, you can work from notes, use PowerPoint as a crutch, and expect the audience to at least be polite or asleep. On television and radio shows, you're sharing the spotlight with a professional who wants you to look good so that she does, too. But at a comedy club, you're alone. No notes, no slides, no TelePrompTers, no guarantee of any respect whatsoever. You're standing before Judge Judy, the Supreme Court, and God all rolled into one.

I suddenly realize that if I'm going to do this, I should understand the basics.

The lady at the Comedy Cabaret in Northeast Philadelphia recommends I look up Joey Callahan. He's a 35-year-old Irishman who's been doing stand-up for a dozen years in the area. Not only is he a regular performer at the Cabaret, but he also teaches comedy classes. He has written for Jay Leno and opened for Steven Wright, Joe Piscopo, and "Weird Al" Yankovic.

Callahan is funny on the phone, which I take as a promising sign. He's agreeable to coaching me and, most important, booking a slot at the Cabaret. But he offers no illusions about this being a glamorous business. He's worked more dives than the Cousteau family. He admits to having beer bottles thrown at him and knives flashed in his direction. But he also admits to drawing a buzz from this that is incomparable.

"It's like flying," he says. "Some nights you're fluttering, like a goose barely making it to Florida for the winter. But on other nights you're soaring, and it's the greatest experience of all. It's not the adulation of the crowd that makes you feel great, it's the energy and excitement that comes from making people laugh."

I'm not so naïve as to think I'll experience anything like that. I tell him my goal is to avoid smashing into a window like a blind sparrow. Actually, I'm of two minds on this. Part of me feels that to face this fear squarely, I need to do it on my own. The less polished and prepared I am, the greater the terror. But then, as Callahan notes, there are some basic principles of stand-up it can't hurt to know. He'll frame it out; I'll fill it in. Sounds like a deal.

The first thing I need is material, an act, something to do for the five minutes I'll be granted. That's right, five minutes. At first, I don't know whether to be relieved or disappointed. "Ever see the movie *Gandhi*?" asks Callahan. "It's about three hours long. That's what your five minutes are going to feel like."

I start writing down all sorts of observations. Like, for instance, why do real estate agents insist on putting their faces on For Sale signs? There has to be a joke in there somewhere. Or shouldn't stuttering be called something else? I mean, I have trouble pronouncing that, and I don't have a speech impediment. Likewise, aren't *morbidly obese* and *profoundly deaf* not only insulting but also redundant? And what the hell is an *ultra-thin super-maxi sanitary pad*? Who do women think they're fooling with these terms? "It's a heavy day, I have a splitting headache, and you better stay the fuck away from me."

"Profanity is cheap laughter," cautions Callahan. "I prefer not to use it. Not having that option will make you work harder to write clever stuff."

Okay, so I'll go highbrow, maybe even political. Like . . . I have a simple solution for the Middle East crisis. Just get rid of all those rocks lying around over there. Sweep the streets so when people get angry they won't have anything handy to throw at each other.

"That's a humorous observation, not a joke," Callahan points out. "There's a difference. Observations make people smile, jokes make them laugh. You want to tell jokes."

I spend an entire week one afternoon writing a bit I call The Guy Channel. Shows include: *This Old Spouse*, in which hosts Bob and Norm offer tips for renovating the old gal; *The Heavy-Equipment Hour*, which consists of a live feed from a construction site where cranes, graders, and dozers are at work; *The Bikini Weather Report*, featuring scantily clad meteorologists with high-pressure systems; and *Your Date for Tonight Is . . .* , a late-night, pseudo-reality show that enables lonely guys to go out with supermodels from the confines of their couch. Besides offering Dolby Surround Sound, The Guy Channel also synchronizes to the sound of a wife's voice. Whenever she starts speaking, it automatically increases in volume so she can't be heard. In addition, loud farts and belches occur periodically to camouflage the viewer's own. And every 90 minutes, programming is suspended, PISS BREAK appears on the screen, and men can go to the bathroom without fear of missing anything.

Hmmm.

Maybe what I need instead are props. I took accordion lessons for seven years when I was a kid, and I still own a Polka Master 2000. What if I punctuated each joke with an oom-pah-pah? What if I wore lederhosen?

"A lot of comics look down on prop acts," says Callahan. "They think you should elicit a response based on what you say, not what you do. Supposedly, it's a purer form of entertainment."

Okay, I'll admit, an accordion might not work. But how about a remote-control fart machine? I was so entertained by the one at the paruresis workshop that I bought one for myself. Suppose I slip it in my pocket and just stand on stage, totally deadpan, and pass gas for five minutes?

I must be looking desperate, because about a week before my scheduled appearance, I get an e-mail at work from my 13-year-old daughter. "Did you ever wonder . . . ," it begins:

> WHY glue doesn't stick to the inside of the bottle?
> WHY a boxing ring is square?
> WHY doctors call their business a practice?
> WHY lemon juice is made with artificial flavor, but
>   dishwashing liquid is made with real lemons?
> WHY the man who invests your money is called a broker?
> WHY there isn't mouse-flavored cat food?

"I found this on the Internet," she confesses in a P.S. "I thought you could use some help."

Wait! What about words that sound dirty, but aren't. Like *ganache*, *gnocchi*. . . .

Is that funny?

Or—hang on a minute—how about a riff on women and body lotion? My wife rubs so much stuff on herself before coming to bed that I have to wear a rubber for traction. . . .

The Comedy Cabaret is a white stucco bunker with bottle-glass windows and a weak ribbon of neon on the outside wall. It's attached to a Best Western Hotel. Callahan has warned me that a Friday night crowd is the toughest of all, because people are tired and impatient after a long workweek. I'm about an hour-and-a-half early, sitting in my truck in the parking lot watching the comings and goings. For some reason, there are a lot of foreign-looking people carrying in plastic bags. Maria, whom I've brought along for moral support, suggests that maybe the bags are filled with tomatoes and rotting fruit.

81

I continue to rehearse, as I've been doing all day. I've honed my routine to exactly five minutes. It's a Letterman-esque skit, the theme being The Seven Things Men Would Most Like to See. I've written the punchlines on cue-card-size placards, which will be unveiled in descending order. That'll be Maria's job. I've flattered her into serving as my beautiful assistant, hoping that a scantily clad woman might at least distract 'em.

"Should we go in and have a few drinks?" Maria asks, shivering in her low-cut, red satin blouse and miniskirt.

I feel like a pimp.

Hmmm. Alcohol. I hadn't thought of that. Would it be better to dull the edge of my anxiety with a couple of Bacardis, or would that just increase my chances of screwing up? I'm most terrified of forgetting my lines, of standing there speechless. In fact, I'm so troubled by this possibility that I considered writing my jokes on my fingers. But I decided that would be unprofessional—so I wrote them on Maria's.

The Cabaret is adjacent to the bar. I push open the door that separates the two and peek inside. The stage is a square, makeshift platform in front of a dirty red curtain. Stools and tables are scattered around it. It's one of those places that should never be fully illuminated. I see flaking chrome and ripped black leather. Not exactly Vegas, but hey, even Gallagher had to start somewhere.

I don't linger. There's no benefit to pressing my back against the cold brick until the firing squad is assembled. I head back to the bar and order a draft beer, plus a gin martini for my beautiful assistant.

It's an hour before the show begins, and I'm feeling a broiling in my gut. But it can't be heartburn. I haven't been able to eat anything. Callahan soon walks in, wearing an open-neck white shirt and a black sport coat. He looks the role.

"How are you feeling?" he asks, ordering a Yuengling.

"Ready," is all I can think of saying.

He introduces me to everyone—the waitresses, the barmaid, and the other comedians. There are three comics who'll be performing tonight, for guests who've paid a cover of $15 per person. The pros look so relaxed, so everyday. The female headliner is sorting coupons, for God's sake.

More people are starting to arrive. It looks like it'll be a good crowd. But, as Callahan recommended, I don't pay attention to any of them—especially not the guy with the beard and the scar who just rode in on that Harley, or the chick with the pancake makeup who can't permit herself to smile and risk cracking it. No, I'm all right. I'm not looking at anyone.

Maria orders another martini and Callahan one more Yuengling. We get to talking. He tells me about his family—his Italian wife and their two little girls, one of whom is having a birthday tomorrow. This job can be tough on them—nights in places like this and weekends on the road. He's driving out to State College next weekend, alone. I wonder if when I'm on stage I'll catch any hint of why he does this, what makes it so addictive.

The conversation helps. It keeps me in the present. That is, until I notice that my beautiful assistant is looking a bit flushed. In fact, she has just ordered her third martini.

"Don't worry, dear. I'm just having a good time," she slurs.

"Maria," I whisper, "you have to hold my cards! Your timing has to be perfect! Give me a break here!"

From the Cabaret comes a smattering of applause. The first act is going on.

"This guy will probably do about 15 minutes," says Callahan. "Then it'll be your turn. Remember, when we flash the lights at you, it's time to start wrapping it up. I'm gonna head inside. Good luck."

"Do I have time to use the bathroom?" asks Maria.

I start to pace. The fellow on stage is obviously doing great. There's much laughter and clapping. I suppose I can look at this two ways. Either the crowd will be more tolerant of me because he's warmed them up, or I'll be so flat by comparison that they'll boo me off. I know I should be taking advantage of these last few minutes to rehearse, but my mind is blank. I can't make it focus. I can't remember the order of

The Seven Things Men Would Most Like to See. In fact, I can't recall anything.

And where's Maria?

"Don't worry, you'll do fine," says the woman sorting coupons. "Look! Here's a good one: Buy three Chunky soups, get one free."

I wonder if I'm part of some comedy routine already, if the crowd in the Cabaret is watching me on a remote screen dealing with all this insanity. Maybe the joke's already on me.

"I'm back!" yells Maria, waving as if we're on opposite sides of a football field rather than in a tiny barroom.

"Are you going to be able to do this?" I ask.

"Of course I'm going to be able to do this. It's all part of my strategy, dear. If you have to worry about me, then you won't have time to worry about yourself. Now where are those cards?"

The guy on stage is winding down. It's almost time for me to go on. My five minutes, my 300 seconds, my personal *Gandhi*.

"I swore I put them right over here."

There's nothing I can do now. This is out of my control. If I make a fool of myself, at least I don't know any of these people. I purposely didn't invite any relatives or coworkers. Strangers are blinder (and kinder) than friends. Immediately after it's over, I can slip out the emergency exit and be on the turnpike home within 10 minutes. I never have to talk to Joey Callahan again. I can forget this ever happened. It was just a brief transgression.

Then . . . my introduction.

I hear it in slow motion from a hundred feet below the ocean.

This next gentleman coming to the stage this evening is not a professional comedian. He's here to overcome one of his biggest fears, and that's getting up in front of a live audience. So I want you to give a big Comedy Cabaret welcome to Mr. Joe Kita!

I feel absolutely nothing. No fear, no excitement, no apprehension, no confusion, no confidence, no courage. I make my way toward the stage as if I'm on autopilot. The routine is engraved in my brain. All I have to do now is press the button. The right button.

"Good evening. Did you hear the one about the two gay Irishmen? Michael Fitzpatrick and Patrick Fitzmichael."

The fact that there's no laughter doesn't matter. The lights are so bright it's like I'm back in my truck rehearsing by myself. I can hear my voice, but nothing else. There is no audience. This doesn't seem real.

"Okay, let me be honest with you. I'm not a stand-up comedian. I'm a writer for *Men's Health* magazine, and I'm doing a book on what it's like to face my greatest fears. Believe it or not, public speaking is the number one fear in America. Forget about the fear of terrorists, the fear of flying, the fear of heights, even the fear of seeing Martha Stewart naked—this is the big one right here. Standing in front of an audience and being judged."

I take a deep breath. I'm doing this.

"I honestly don't know what's going to happen up here. But I keep telling myself that if I bomb, it's no big deal. It's just part of the research for my book. Is anyone out there familiar with *Men's Health*? It's the biggest men's-magazine franchise in the world, with 25 million readers. We strive to teach men how to live long, prosperous, deeply meaningful lives. And the way to do that, we tell them, is really quite simple. Just build a great set of abs."

No boos yet. The mood is tolerant. Plow ahead.

"I asked the readers of *Men's Health* for some help with my act. I asked them what things they'd most like to see. Now remember, these are deep, thoughtful guys—guys with great abs. So, in descending order, here are The Seven Things Men Would Most Like to See. And to help me present them, I'd like to call up my beautiful assistant. I figure if my jokes aren't funny, at least she'll help distract you for the next three minutes."

Maria emerges from the audience with her cards, right on cue. Yet I'm only vaguely aware. The words keep coming, but I don't know from where.

"Women are always complaining about having to shave their legs and armpits. Well, let me tell you, they have no idea. They should try getting hair out of their nostrils and ears like us guys have to. The number seven thing men would most like to see? **Nair for the nose.**"

A few chuckles.

"I like watching women's figure skating. But it's not the athletic artistry I appreciate; it's when their little skirts flip up in the air. Evidently, lots of guys agree, and now they want to take it to the next level. The number six thing men would most like to see? **No-underwear women's figure skating.**"

Laughter. Whoa!

"It's tough being a guy nowadays. There are so many decisions, so much pressure. But unlike women, guys find it hard to ask for advice. They don't know where to turn. The number five thing men would most like to see? **Caddies not just for golf.** When you're facing a tough putt on life's rolling green, you deserve to be able to call someone over to help line it up—not to mention carry your clubs."

Must not be many golfers in the audience.

"Picture this: It's 2:30 in the afternoon at work. You're tired. You're not getting anything done. The number four thing men would most like to see? **Recess.** Ten or 15 minutes is all they need. A good chance to 'accidentally' pop the twerp from human resources in the nose during a game of Red Rover."

Keep going. Almost done.

"I think we're moving in the right direction with casual Fridays. But again, the men of America aren't satisfied. They want to take it a step further. The number three thing guys would most like to see? *Really* **casual Fridays.** We're talking robes and slippers here; hair combing and shaving optional."

Things have quieted down. Am I still reaching them?

"It's the middle of the night. You drank three beers before you went to bed. You stumble into the bathroom, unable to find the light. The number two thing men would most like to see? **Home**

urinals. No need to worry about putting up the seat to keep the missus dry. It's high time these were mainstream."

Big finish now.

"You've just closed the deal of the century. There are handshakes and back pats all around. It's time for a celebration. The number one thing men would most like to see? **Roving beermen.** They're not just at the ballpark anymore, they're *everywhere!*

"That's it, folks. Don't forget to pick up the next issue of *Men's Health*, in which we'll tell you how to add six inches to your penis! Thanks for helping me face my fear!"

More noise. What exactly it is, I can't be certain. I sidestep tables to get back to the bar, to escape, to be done with this. I want no part of an encore.

"You got a laugh!" says the coupon lady, using the singular and not the plural.

"Not bad," says Callahan.

"You were wonderful, dear!" says Maria, beaming.

"Hey, mister, when does that issue go on sale?" asks some desperate-looking guy who followed me out of the room. "Can you really add six inches to your penis?"

I am relieved, numb, in a world of my own. It's like I've just been pulled from the deep end of the pool and am slowly being revived. I pump Callahan's arm and thank him for saving me. I didn't feel like I was flying out there, but my time certainly flew. Overall, it wasn't as bad as I'd feared.

Somehow, I'm realizing, it never is.

Okay, so I only got one lousy laugh. So I've been waiting a week now, and I haven't been asked back (although Maria has). I was rejected—politely, but firmly. I experienced what I thought I most feared.

But it changed again—the slippery bastard.

In fact, when I was on stage, judgment and rejection weren't even on my radar screen. Rather, I was looking to do just one thing:

survive. And it became instantly clear that the audience couldn't help me with that. I alone was responsible for getting myself through this. Even if they had started to boo and throw beer bottles, it would have been up to *me* to dodge them. No, I was doing this for *my* benefit, not theirs, and what they thought or how they reacted didn't matter. Although I hadn't realized it at the time, I had prejudged myself. I had decided that in this venture, at least, I had inherent worth.

And because I didn't have a copilot, I couldn't fold. I had only myself. And once backed into that corner I found courage and confidence and the ability to do something difficult. But I also found fear. Only this time, it wasn't the fear that I'd be unable to act or that people would criticize me for it; it was the fear that I'd botch it.

What really unnerved me on that stage was the possibility I might fall down, knock something over, say something stupid or, worse, say nothing at all. I was scared of making a mistake, of being at fault, of having the finger of blame pointed at no one but me.

I should have guessed it. My biggest fear must be fucking up. After all, I'm a perfectionist.

5

Screwing Up

WORKING AS A HIGH-RISE WINDOW WASHER

Sophie Smith
is a hypnotist.

She bears no resemblance to any tarot card reader or carnival barker I ever met. In fact, she's a licensed psychologist and a grandmother, no less. We sit on couches in her living room of an office as a miniature water fountain gurgles and Enya plays in the background. It's very comforting. She takes notes as I talk. I like when people do that.

I tell her about yet another fear of mine: heights. How it stops me and shakes me and makes me cling, whether to the cliff I'm tight-roping or to the nearest human being. I tell her there are mountains I'd love to climb, observation decks I'd like to visit, even amusement park rides I want to do with my kids, but I can't. It's as if a giant hand were holding me back. I can feel it pressing against my chest whenever I'm near a precipice. Even though I want to step forward, I'm powerless.

I tell her that unlike most of my other fears, I can't pinpoint the origins of this one. There was even a time when I *enjoyed* heights, when I delighted in dangling my toes off bridges and sky rides. That was way back when I was a kid. Now, I don't even want to think about stuff like that.

I tell her that because I don't understand where this fear comes from; it seems more real and intimidating than the others—like it's there for good reason. I tell her I've been thinking a lot about this fear lately, and what it might represent. I suspect it's really the fear of making a mistake, of taking a misstep, of not being perfect.

But I tell her that's as far as I've gotten. Since I can't see its roots, I'm helpless to dig out this fear. And that's why I've come for professional help and, specifically, to explore hypnosis. I've read that it's a way to uncover repressed parts of the past—to make connections between experience and behavior.

Sophie says this is true. But she warns that hypnosis can also be dangerous. Some of what gets turned up can be disturbing, even life altering. Some patients have subsequently sued relatives and former teachers based on abuse they "remembered." She asks me to sign a legal release that says I understand the potential consequences of this therapy. As I'm doing so, I wonder if I should ask her for references. Is it wise, after just one consultation, to be letting this stranger into my head? I've been married for almost 20 years, and I still haven't let my wife go in all the way yet.

Sophie explains what hypnosis is not. There will be no looking deep into her eyes or staring at a swinging watch—no snapping of fingers, sleepwalking, or barking like a dog. Instead, she'll guide me to a "safe, comfortable, relaxing place of my choosing" and then sort of put me to sleep. I'll fade in and out of consciousness, sometimes aware but other times not. And while I'm in this state, she'll try to rewire me. The goal, she's careful to point out, is not to alleviate my fear of heights. (That's an instinctive alarm that protects my life.) Rather, it's to implant the notion that the next time I look down I won't freeze up. She'll attempt to put me in charge of this fear and, by association, everything else it represents. She'll try to make me courageous through the power of suggestion.

But first, she asks about my parents.

Uh oh.

Why do shrinks always have to know? I tell her my mother is an anxious person, that she probably has agoraphobia—the fear of leaving her house, of being social. For years after my father died, she traveled no farther than the hairdresser and ShopRite. Sophie nods knowingly and scribbles. "It looks like you came by this honestly," she says. "You inherited these tendencies."

But then there's my dad. He was an ex-marine. He never showed fear. So I'm a mixture. "He is helping you fight the fears that you inherited from your mother," she explains.

So that's why it feels like there's a war inside me. My mother was protecting me the only way she knew how. To her, the edge was just a lot closer, is all.

I tell Sophie I'll see her on Friday.

Now Joe, I want you to get comfortable and begin focusing on your breathing. Take a few deep breaths. In very slowly. Out very slowly. Good. Notice that it's automatic, it happens, just like your heart beating. Notice how effortlessly you're able to focus and let go of your concerns. And as you're focusing on your breathing, allow yourself to begin relaxing, such that with each inhalation you breathe in calm, peaceful warmth and with each exhalation you release any tension you notice in your body. Pretend there's a light above your head, a very soft white light, and it's going to check your body for you. It checks in your head to see if there's any tension. Allow yourself to exhale it as you find it. And let the light continue to check in your neck and shoulders. Good. Releasing any tension. And continue to check in your back and chest. And just release. Good. And in your arms and hands. You might begin to feel a little tingly or warm or cool. Whatever your experience, it's fine. It's just yours. Good. Continue to check throughout your torso, letting the light flow. Then let it go into your legs, letting them feel as they need to—very light, or a little heavy. Whatever you feel is fine. Then down into your shins and feet, and

91

finally exiting your toes and circling back around. The light will continue to flow through this whole experience, keeping you warm and relaxed.

"You said that home is your safest, most peaceful place. I want you to go there now. Notice all the colors and smells and sounds, how supportive the furniture feels because you know it's solid, giving you even more permission to relax, to let go. Take a moment to be there, as fully as you can, your body totally relaxed. Good. When you're fully there, I'm going to ask you to watch yourself go up the stairs to your bedroom. And with each step, you're going to get more and more relaxed, more and more calm, exhaling all the day's challenges, just relaxing in this place of peace and safety. This perfect place that is only yours. Good. And as you take the first step, allow yourself to experience this time as deeply as possible. Take the next step and notice how effortlessly you're climbing the stairs. It feels like you're floating up them. Third step. Good. Still noticing how effortless this is and how relaxed you can be. Fourth step. Your conscious mind beginning to let go, allowing your unconscious mind to do what it knows best. Five. Deeper and deeper relaxed. This amazing sense of wellness, wholeness. Six. Good. Continue up the stairs, the path that you know, and go to your favorite place there, carrying with you all the calmness, all the safety. Very relaxed. Good.

"Now while you're in this place of relaxation, peace, and safety, I want you to imagine that a video camera has taped you in one of those anxious situations you told me about earlier. Now you're watching this tape, still very relaxed, very peaceful. Notice how you feel looking at yourself on the screen, and that you have control over this. You can stop the tape, fast-forward it, or rewind it. Just notice. And since you have control, do what you need to do to make the situation as nonthreatening as possible. Freeze it, fast-forward, whatever is necessary—having complete control over the video at all times, allowing yourself to remain relaxed and calm in the safety of your home. Good. Now go to the end of the tape and turn the camera off. And take just a moment to relax even further, safe in your home, in complete control, allowing your breathing to be slow and deep. Good. Good.

"A short story. Once upon a time, there was a little boy who was very, very rich. He was so rich that he had a special room just for his toys and treasures, and he would go there every day to play. You would think he'd be a happy little boy with so many toys and treasures, but this was not the case. Actually, he was very, very sad because although he had many beautiful toys and treasures, there was one thing that spoiled it for him. Sitting in a corner of the room, barely visible, was a large green dragon. And this dragon never seemed to take its eyes off the little boy. Even though he knew it was a toy, it still spoiled his fun because he was very, very afraid of it. He had nightmares about the dragon rushing him, throwing him down, and trying to kill him. But he never told anyone about these dreams because he was afraid the green dragon would get even angrier. And so he was very, very unhappy. No matter how loudly he laughed, how hard he played, or how fast he danced and whirled in his special room, when he stopped, the green dragon would still be there looking menacingly at him. And this went on for some time. The little boy would begin each day playing with his toys, hoping to forget about the green dragon, but by evening he would be quiet and sad.

"One day another little boy came to visit. He looked around the room, his eyes growing wider and wider, and said, 'Oh, what wonderful treasures!' And he ran around picking up this one and that one, playing and clapping his hands. But the little rich boy was feeling very anxious. He kept stealing glances at the dragon. Suddenly, to his horror, his friend ran over to it. The boy cried, 'No! No! Don't touch that!' And his friend said, 'Why ever not?' The boy explained it was a fierce and ugly dragon that would surely harm him. 'I'm afraid of it,' he confessed. And with that, his friend turned the dragon around and showed him a long, shiny zipper running down its back. He didn't know what to make of that. And he watched with round eyes, still trembling with fear, as his friend began to unzip it. The dragon's green suit fell to the ground, and what do you think was in there?

"Another little boy, no different than himself.

"Now Joe, while continuing to stay relaxed, I want you to

93

imagine again, from the safety of your home, that you've turned that videotape back on. And you're watching yourself in the same situation that made you anxious earlier. There's quite a drop alongside you, and you're being respectful of it, but you're watching yourself handle it. You're only a little nervous. You're taking slow, deep breaths to remind yourself of how peaceful and calm and safe you are. You're proceeding without any resistance or concern. You're using the appropriate caution. You're noticing how beautiful it is up here, what a great view it is, and how strong and confident you feel, because you've mastered this just like you've mastered other things in your past that seemed insurmountable. Notice how very, very secure and confident you feel, and what a good feeling that is. Let yourself experience it fully. Your body feels confident. Your brain feels confident. Your heart feels confident. And I want you to enjoy this place and this feeling a little while longer. It's comfortable, peaceful, and you have this wonderful sense of well-being. Good. And when you're ready, I want you to turn off the video.

"And in just a bit, Joe, I'm going to re-alert you. But first, I want you to take a moment and let yourself be fully aware, as only your unconscious mind is capable of, that you can master this. Just like in the video, it will play out for you. It will become more and more effortless. Good. I'm going to count from five to one. By the time I get to one, you'll either be alert and fresh and ready to go, or you will drift into a peaceful sleep from which you'll emerge rested and with a sense of genuine well-being. You will know what you need to do, as I count from five, four, three—halfway there—two, one."

That's all there was to my hypnosis. Sophie spoke in a soft, slow, reassuring monotone, and it wasn't until later, when I listened to a tape of the session, that I became aware of all she had talked about. My awareness had indeed drifted. When I opened my eyes after her countdown, I felt relaxed and rejuvenated, but not cured. I had no immediate urge to take the elevator to the top floor. But Sophie laughed and said I

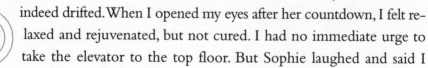

shouldn't expect that. Despite its reputation, hypnosis isn't magic. She told me to listen to the tape in a quiet place every day for at least a week—giving its lessons time to sink in. Only then should I consider confronting my fear.

Unfortunately, I had no startling revelations while I was hypnotized—or at least none I can plainly recall. Sophie said my brow furrowed twice during the trance, but I can't remember anything that made me wince—no memories of Mom holding me by the ankles out the attic window. Sophie warned that sometimes nightmares follow. Once the subconscious has been pricked, there's no telling how long it'll take things to surface.

When I get home, I fake-twitch, call my children by different names, and ask the same questions of my wife repeatedly. Because I don't feel dramatically different, I'm even a bit embarrassed by what I did. So far, I've spent $270 on this.

"Give me that kind of cash," says Maria, "and I'll sit with you on the roof until you get over it."

Maybe I was wrong to pick home as my safe, secure place.

For the next week I dutifully follow my prescription. I lie in bed, close my eyes, and listen to Sophie's voice on the tape once every day. And just like before, I float in and out of consciousness. And when I awake, I feel relaxed and rejuvenated, but never cured. As a midafternoon pick-me-up, this therapy is great. But it's impossible to tell if it's working at that deeper level I need it to.

Eventually, I'll need to test this. I'll have to walk out onto some ledge and risk a misstep. I'll have to face the fear in a black-and-white way in order to gauge the success of my lobotomy. It's both paralyzing and energizing to consider the possibilities.

▶ The Appalachian Trail isn't far from my home. In fact, from my upstairs window I can see the big blue mountain that it's on. I bet there are some places where the path is no wider than a balance beam.

▶ Dorney Park and Wildwater Kingdom in nearby Allentown has a roller coaster named Steel Force. It's one of the tallest on the East Coast. An open-step catwalk climbs 205 feet to its summit.

▶ There's a light bulb atop the antenna that crowns the Empire State Building. It's 1,454 feet, 6¾ inches high. The last time I was in New York City, I noticed it flickering.

But what catches my eye as I look toward the sky is a story on the Internet about a 38-year-old father of three who works for Valcourt Building Services in Elizabeth, New Jersey. His name is Rolando Simpson, and he has been washing windows on high-rise buildings for almost two decades. At a recent International Window Cleaning Association Convention in Reno, he was named Window Cleaner of the Year. Got the golden squeegee, the platinum pail, a nice plaque that he shines with Windex. He steps off the edge into what I fear every day. He makes a living from what my mind somehow interprets as dying. He doesn't need any psychologists or hypnotists to help him through it. In fact, when I explain on the phone what I'm doing, he laughs.

"I have no fear of heights," he says, with a thick Panamanian accent. "I don't even think about it. The only thing that ever scared me was divorce. But I survived that, too."

Rolando has no qualms about letting me spend the day with him. In fact, he's flattered by my interest. Now it's my turn to wonder if I can do it.

The day before I'm supposed to meet him, I listen to the tape again and again, filling my subconscious with premium suggestion, hoping it's not possible to overdose on hypnosis. At night I have trouble sleeping. I can't stop myself from worrying. It must be because I feel so unprepared. It's not like this training has given me bigger leg muscles that I can look down upon as proof of newfound ability to stand my ground. Rather, I can only hope that my subconscious has grown stronger, and that my fear response has indeed been rewired.

A hundred questions, none of which matter: How should I dress? What type of shoes do window washers wear? How much room is there on scaffolding? How high up will we be? Are there railings? Suppose I can't do this? Suppose I make a fool of myself in front of Rolando and his men? What if I make the mistake of looking down, get vertigo, and pitch over the side? Does the fear of heights immediately disappear at that point? Is it replaced by, say, the fear of hitting the ground? I don't want to find out. I taste the old poison: self-doubt.

It's 7:30 A.M., and I'm sitting in the Valcourt general manager's office staring in disbelief at a framed photograph. It's a shot of four guys washing windows on a skyscraper. Only they aren't using scaffolding. They aren't using cranes. These guys have rappelled off the roof and are working their way down on ropes.

"*This* is what Rolando does?" I ask.

"Yes, sir," the GM answers proudly, leaning back in his chair. "That was taken at 101 Hudson in Jersey City. It's the tallest building we do. Forty-three stories. Six hundred feet of rope. Takes one crew three days. Let me tell you, these guys are athletes."

These guys are *crazy*! No wonder Rolando doesn't have a fear of heights. Rolando must not have any brains! This is insane! How could I have been so stupid? How could I not have guessed this is how they do it?

"So does your publisher's liability insurance cover you on an assignment like this?" asks the GM. "I'm sorry but, you know, I have to check."

"Have there been accidents?"

"Nationwide, I'd say about 20 high-rise window cleaners get killed every year. So, yes, it's dangerous. But at Valcourt, safety is our goal. In fact, those very words are printed on the backs of our vans. . . . There was one incident, though. See that guy over there?"

He leans closer and lowers his voice, as if pointing out a prostitute in church. I follow his gaze to a young Hispanic man leaning nonchalantly against the wall. "He fell off a five-story building, landed on a bucket, and broke his ankle and back. It's unclear what happened exactly."

While I'm staring, Rolando pokes his head around the corner, extends his hand, and smiles. A gold tooth flashes.

"Joe! Sorry to keep you waiting. Are you ready to go?"

I have no choice but to follow.

Rolando leads me through the office and into the garage. He's a solid man—six-foot-two, 192 pounds, 33-inch waist. An athlete. He starts throwing huge bundles of rope, harnesses, and other equipment into the van. If I didn't know better, I'd say we were heading for the Tetons. He introduces me to José and Efrain. Neither speaks English, but they'll be part of our crew. I'm relieved that the fellow leaning against the wall hasn't moved.

"We're going to Princeton today," says Rolando, as he merges into rush-hour traffic juggling a muffin, an orange juice, two phones, and the steering wheel.

SAFETY IS OUR GOAL. I checked. It *is* printed on the back.

"When I interviewed for my first job back in '85, they asked if I knew how to clean windows," Rolando begins. "I told them, 'Of course, I know how to clean windows.' Then my supervisor took me up on the roof, I looked down and said, 'There's no way in hell I can clean *those* windows!' I was afraid, but I watched how he did it, and I stuck with it. Money is the best incentive. You make more cleaning outside.

"I only ever had one accident. I fell off a 60-foot ladder. Lucky for me, I landed on my partner. I broke my arm and chipped this tooth, but if he hadn't been there to break my fall I would have been hurt a lot worse.

"I don't look at what I do as hazardous, though," he continues. "There's absolutely no danger in it if you follow the rules and safety procedures. When there's an accident, it's never the equipment's fault, it's human error."

I glance back expectantly at José and Efrain, my crew—the guys I'll be depending on to tie the knots and set the ropes. Their heads are tilted back on the seats, mouths agape. They're asleep.

"So how tall is the building we'll be working today?"

"It's a three-story box in an industrial park. We'll be about 45 feet up." He makes it sound so incidental.

"Usually we do a building like that from the ground with extension poles, but for your benefit we're going to drop off the top."

Even though I'm clattering along in a van at 65 mph, amidst

snores and horns, I close my eyes and try to find my special, peaceful place—the one Sophie told me to go to whenever I'm feeling anxious. . . .

"I remember cleaning this building in D.C.," continues Rolando. "It turned out to be the Saudi embassy. No one had told the building manager we'd be cleaning that day, so here we come off the roof on ropes. In no time, the building is surrounded with cops. They had guns trained on us."

I try to envision that very soft white light checking my body for tension. . . .

"Bees are the worst. A lot of times in these parts, they make their nests under the eaves. So you have no way of knowing until you drop off that they're under there. I always carry bug repellant. I'll spray myself, then the nest, and just hang on."

Sure enough, I can detect some tension. It's in my head, neck, chest, back, arms, legs, you name it. I wonder if Rolando has any Enya tapes in the glove compartment. . . .

"It's real tough to work in the cold. It's not so much that your body gets chilled, it's your hands. It gets hard to control the ropes. Sometimes by the end of the day, I swear if I hit my hands on the dashboard they'd just shatter."

I try to play my videotape—the one where I'm only a little nervous, the one I'm supposed to be able to rewind whenever I want to. . . .

"There were some window cleaners in the World Trade Center when it got hit. All they had were squeegees, but they used them to chip a hole in the drywall and get out. I don't worry about terrorists, though. A more real risk is someone cutting your rope. Once you go off the top, you have no control of what happens on the roof."

I have this creeping feeling that hypnosis is bullshit. . . .

"Here we are," says Rolando, pulling into the industrial park. "Let's unload and get started."

But the windows, I want to argue, don't even look dirty. Perhaps they can wait another day.

99

José and Efrain wrestle the equipment from the van. Unlike Rolando, they're short and puny, and it staggers them. There's rope—bags full of white ½-inch work line and red ⅝-inch safety line. There are harnesses—large, hopefully hopeless tangles of red and orange straps. There are buckets—five-gallon plastic containers filled with squeegees, rags, bottles of ammonia, and Dawn dishwashing liquid. (It's the secret, says Rolando with a wink.) And there's a roof rig—a cumbersome metal contraption that's supposed to both anchor and suspend us. It's reassuringly heavy and big, but it's in pieces. I try to ask José and Efrain how it fits together, but they just smile and turn up their hands. I hope it's because they don't understand what I'm saying.

We lug all this stuff into the lobby and then into an elevator. First floor: retail shops. Second floor: legal offices. Third floor: life-insurance company. We stop. I hold the door as José and Efrain grunt the gear out of the elevator, through a back door, up some stairs, and out through a narrow roof hatch. I think they're cursing me in Spanish.

Rolando is parking the van, so I take the opportunity to look around. The roof is flat, expansive, and scattered with crushed rock. It's actually quite pleasant up here—a stunning day with brilliant sunshine. It's a lot less cramped and intimidating than I expected. I can stand in the middle and be comfortably far from any edge.

José and Efrain get to work uncoiling ropes, untangling harnesses, and assembling the roof rig. I watch as they tie off the red safety line to the base of an air-conditioning unit. It looks like they used a single slipknot.

There are other workmen up here, too. Three roofers with dirty union jackets are leaning over the edge, beer guts in the dirt, ripping off long sheets of flashing. They curse and spit tobacco, oblivious to the 45 feet of nothingness below them. I can't understand it. One slip, one missed hammer tug, one tiny mistake . . . and they meet the pavement. Do they care? Are they even aware?

A reporter once asked basketball coach Bobby Knight who he'd rather have on the line trying to win the game: a Rhodes scholar or a player with a less-than-stellar grade-point average? Without hesitating, Knight picked the latter. In pressure situations, he explained, intelligence can hinder athletes.

I wonder if the same is true for all human beings. I wonder if there's a certain level of knowledge we reach and then, after that, we start thinking too much. It seems as if a tipping point should exist between naïveté and paranoia. Maybe the way to defeat fear and become courageous is by finding that balance.

I suddenly feel dumb standing with my hands in my pockets worrying about all the things that could happen, so I take a step, and then another, and another. I can still feel the invisible hand pressing against my chest, but with each step the pressure lessens. I continue taking steps until I'm six feet from the edge—72 short inches, 183 centimeters. And I take a breath. Hey. It *is* beautiful up here. I *am* in control. I *do* feel confident. Maybe the hypnosis is going to work. Maybe I *will* be able to do this.

"Joe!"

Startled, I jump.

Fortunately, not forward. It's Rolando coming through the roof hatch. "Okay, let's get moving," he shouts. "I'll show you how it's done, then it'll be your turn."

He checks the roof rig—which, now that it's assembled, looks like a giant catapult. Ropes dangle off its tall front end, while two suitcase-shaped weights counterbalance the rear. Four rubber tires allow it to be rolled around the roof's perimeter as needed. Drop down, clean a row of windows, ride the elevator back up, move the rig, drop down again. That's the drill of a high-rise window cleaner.

I watch Rolando harness himself up, clipping this and that, occasionally chastising José and Efrain in Spanish for some apparent slipup. They just look at me and smile. "This thing here is a bosun's chair," he explains. "It's like a swing. It's what you sit on to clean. Other than that and your bucket, there are only two more things you have to worry about. This yellow clamp here is the jumar, and this black tube is the rope rider. Both are used to control your descent. Come over here, and I'll show you how to work them."

Since Rolando is already just inches from the edge, I hesitate. Instead of moving closer, I giraffe my neck. I try to concentrate on what's being said, but it's impossible when I'm this near open space. My entire focus is on my balance, which I realize makes me more susceptible to losing it. It's like pedaling a bike along a plank. The harder you concentrate, the more you wobble. It's another example of how thinking can interfere with performance.

"You only want to let out a little rope at a time," he explains. "You don't want to drop more than a few feet. Got it?"

I nod, even though I *don't* get it. I feel a sickening need to back up.

And with that Rolando drops off the top—just that quickly, just that effortlessly, just that fearlessly. He makes it look like there's nothing to it, which there isn't, really. I plant my feet on the roof, wrap my fingers around the rig, and peer tentatively over the edge. He's just a few yards below me, looking up, grinning. His boot soles are against the building, his butt in the bosun's chair, his hand on the clamps. . . . He's miraculously suspended in midair and loving every second of it.

"All these people are stuck in their offices," he says, motioning around him, "but I'm outside, way up here. When the weather is nice, like today, it's great. I'm in my glory. Sometimes I'd pay them to let me do this. It's that relaxing."

Relaxing?

"People's windows can get real hazy without them even realizing it," he adds. "I've had people tell me after I'm done that they never knew their windows could let in so much sun. So on one hand, you could say I'm just a window washer; but on the other, you could say I help make things a whole lot clearer."

Rolando slides out of sight. The Window Cleaner of the Year. Maybe he's right. Maybe my windows have grown hazy without my realizing it. Otherwise, why would I be so afraid up here when he's so happy? Here I am, this rich kid with a life full of treasures, yet I can't fully enjoy it because I'm so scared. What is it that I'm not seeing?

Suddenly there's a memory, a flash from my past I had long since buried. I'm eight years old, standing with my dad atop the tallest, steepest, longest slide in the county. I'd begged him to buy two $5 tickets, talked him into standing in line for almost 40 minutes, patiently climbed step after step, my mother waiting at the bottom, squinting up at us. And finally we had reached the top. I unrolled the burlap sack we were supposed to sit on, but instead of seeing an undulating lane of delight falling precipitously away, I saw fright. I told my dad I couldn't do it. I started sobbing and shaking. He said he'd hold me, we'd go down together, nothing would happen. But I didn't believe him. And eventually he just rolled up the burlap, put it under his arm, didn't take my hand, and we walked down every single step we had just climbed, past all the other kids and parents waiting in line. I kept my eyes down the entire time. When we reached the ground, the guy in the booth wouldn't give us our money back, and my mother was pissed.

That's when it must have started. That was my green monster. And all these years of believing it was heights that frightened me when, in fact, it was everything else that was zipped inside that moment: the humiliation, the embarrassment, the disappointment, the anxiety, the inferiority. . . . I had hung all these heavy, negative emotions on it when all I had really experienced was just a little boy's natural, normal hesitancy at being up so high. No wonder I've never been able to look out, let go, and fly. All my life I've been resisting buying tickets and climbing stairs because I didn't want to risk making the same mistake once I got up there. Suddenly, it's all so clear.

As Rolando helps me into my harness and attaches my ropes, I realize I don't fear them coming apart. We've triple-checked all the knots. As he demonstrates once more how to lower myself with the jumar and rope rider, I realize I don't fear their malfunction. These are sturdy, simple mechanisms. As he takes me by the arm and guides me to the edge, I realize I don't fear screwing up. This is a secure, proven system. As he tells me to lean back in the bosun's chair, I realize I don't fear looking down. It's just the ground. And as he prompts me to take that first backward step, to drop off, I realize, unbelievably, that I don't fear doing this.

Rather, as I dangle three stories up, my boot soles pressed against the side of the building, I realize it's not heights that I fear but hurting myself. And now that I understand how to stop doing that psychologically, I guess I need to find a way to surmount the dread of doing that physically.

Because even as I hang here, the apparent master of my height fear, I'm thinking about what it would be like to fall. Of that reality, I'm still scared. Stepping off the edge, I can do. But what about letting go? Would it hurt as much in that instant of impact as it has for all these years?

I look up to see Rolando, grinning.

Are things getting any clearer?

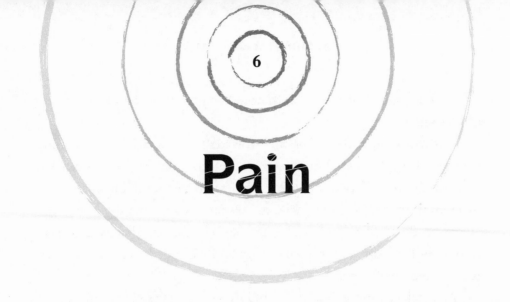

Pain

DEATH MARCHING

It's 0600 hours
at the White Sands Missile Range
in the desert of southern New Mexico.
Approximately 3,200 people, most of them military, stand silent in the darkness—the air so crisp and the sky so black, you can almost hear the stars sizzling. A rock-hard Army sergeant stands at attention beside me, despite having a huge pack strapped to his back. The sleeves of his battle fatigues are rolled up, and there's a spiral of barbed wire tattooed around one biceps. But there's something else on his arms, I notice. They are both covered with gooseflesh. And his chills are not from the morning coolness.

We are listening to the "missing-man roll call," a somber ceremony that precedes the Bataan Memorial Death March. This annual event honors men from the New Mexico National Guard who died along with thousands of others during a 63-mile trek through the Philippine jungle after surrendering to the Japanese during World War II. The name of each missing soldier is called three times, and the list is long. Afterward, a lone bugler plays taps, each note hanging in the air like the spirits of these men.

With that, all 3,200 of us turn toward the east, which is just now starting to brighten. Although we are free to talk, few of us do. We're preparing to march (or run) 26.2 miles through the scrub brush and sage, many of us with 35-pound packs, to commemorate what these men did. We're heading off to personal wars—private battles that will escalate throughout the day and leave us weary and wounded, but hopefully appreciative in new ways.

An artillery cannon booms behind us, signaling the start of the march, and we all surge forward on the leap of our hearts. We're like one giant organism, anxious to begin and, at the same time, be done. Although I have little specific knowledge of the route ahead, I know where it leads—to a world of hurt. I know that before long this crisp dawn will melt into an 85-degree afternoon, that this firm asphalt will turn to ankle-swallowing sand, that the adrenaline that buoys me now will be replaced by lactic acid, and that even my altruistic drive to honor these men will fade into a selfish obsession with my own suffering.

I'm here to face pain, to take its best belly punch, to determine whether some underlying, overriding desire to avoid it could be causing my fearfulness. Indeed, at the heart of every fear is some type of pain—real or imagined, physical or emotional. For obvious reasons, the possibility of getting hurt makes us wary. We'll do more to avoid pain than we'll do to seek pleasure. But I want to see for myself if it's so awful, how much of it I can handle, and whether a pain-free life is an admirable goal or whether it somehow deprives us of being whole. On average, American men die seven years younger than American women. One possible reason is that most guys don't experience much physical pain during their lifetime. Unlike women, who endure childbirth, most men have no counterpart to toughen them and to put things in perspective. When the pain of disease or loss or age finally comes, it's an intimidating stranger. Knees buckle and fortitude crumbles in its unrelenting grip.

I realize I'm being dramatic. I admit that compared to what the original Death Marchers experienced, what I'm doing is chickenshit. But there just aren't many opportunities for middle-age, white-collar guys like me to feel pain, beyond doing something stupid like shooting myself with a stun gun or telling my wife she looks fat. This event is the best I could do, but given my relatively soft existence up until now, I think it's enough. There's meaning here and history, and maybe even a little courage that will somehow rub off.

In the spring of 1942, American and Filipino forces defending the Philippine Islands had been pushed back to the tip of the Bataan Peninsula by the Japanese. They had resisted the invasion for four months, despite being outmanned and poorly equipped. In fact, they used as their rallying cry this derisive song of abandonment and bitterness toward the U.S. government:

We're the battling bastards of Bataan;
No mama, no papa, no Uncle Sam;
No aunts, no uncles, no cousins, no nieces;
No pills, no planes, no artillery pieces;
And nobody gives a damn.
Nobody gives a damn.

With their backs to the South China Sea, no hope of reinforcements, and the exit of General Douglas MacArthur (despite vowing "I shall return"), the battling bastards of Bataan finally surrendered at noon on April 9. But their misery was far from over.

In the Japanese culture at this time, surrender was considered disgraceful. On the battlefield, honor came through victory or death, never capture. In fact, the Japanese soldiers' manual stated, "Always save the last round for yourself." So when they took charge of about 78,000 Americans and Filipinos that afternoon, they treated them not as adversaries but as cowards.

107

None of the prisoners knew what the Japanese were planning to do with them. They were never told where they were going or how long it would take to get there. And such uncertainty made the journey that much tougher. Lacking adequate transportation in the ruined jungle, the Japanese marched their prisoners 55 miles to the town of San Fernando. There, the men were packed into stifling boxcars, transported to the village of Capas, and then made to hobble the remaining eight miles to a prisoner-of-war camp. Twenty-one thousand of them never made it. Some escaped with the help of natives, but most died during the two-week journey. Many succumbed to malnutrition and disease, but many more to the bayonets and boot tips of the guards who herded them northward like cattle.

Each year prior to the Bataan Memorial Death March, the Army ROTC at New Mexico State University presents a seminar in the White Sands Theater detailing all this history. There are photographs, films, mementos and, most stirring of all, survivors themselves. Almost two dozen showed up this year, some from as far away as Minnesota. They stood before the crowd in a crooked but proud line, medals jingling from palsy. One was about to turn 90. Another swept aside the helping hand of a cadet and insisted on shuffling forward unassisted.

After they were all introduced, the audience delivered a standing ovation. More than a few of their hazy eyes blinked. One tried to bow. Somebody gives a damn after all.

When I was growing up during the 1960s, I thought giving your life for your country or even joining the service was the most foolish thing anyone could do. But as I stood there in that auditorium, I surprised myself at how hard I was clapping and what I was feeling.

These men are heroes.

And maybe the reason I'm not—maybe the reason I've rarely even felt courageous—is because I've never had to battle an enemy more obvious than myself. No Japs, no Nazis, no Al-Qaeda terrorists. . . . Maybe when the adversary is outside you instead of in you, it's easier to summon valor, fortitude, and all the qualities we honor and admire.

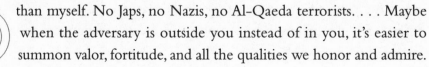

But since most of us will never be backed into that corner, perhaps there's room for two types of heroes. Men like these veterans who faced the inevitable, who did what they had to. And people like these 3,200 who had a choice and opted to do something difficult, something fearful and, yes, something painful.

Maybe there's hope for me yet.

I am determined. I have spent two months training. But still, I am not confident. There are too many unknowns.

There's the pure physical challenge of walking 26.2 miles with a 35-pound pack on my back. Is it possible for me to do this and, if so, how agonizing will it become?

There's the otherworldliness of this missile-range landscape. The liability waiver mentioned heatstroke, rattlesnakes, scorpions, and "unexploded ordnance." What might happen if I wander off course?

There's the machismo of the other marchers. During the first few miles, platoons of soldiers with rucksacks, boots, and canteens run past me, sweating testosterone. How far behind them will I eventually finish, if I finish at all?

There's the loneliness I'm already feeling. I've vowed to walk in solitary silence, because that's what the original Death Marchers did. They were like walking dead. How much does the pain and monotony compound when there's no distraction?

And finally, there's my own fear again. It tightens my stomach whenever I bump up against something big and new, something that pushes me out of my comfortable cocoon. Do I, as doughy and unbaked as I am, possess the crust to withstand?

I ask 81-year-old Lester Tenney this. He survived the Battle of Bataan, the Death March, and three years as a prisoner-of-war in the Philippines and Japan. I ask him whether my generation, which pops over-the-counter pain relievers like M&M's, has guts. He doesn't even pause to think about it.

"No question," he replies. "It's in all of us."

I think about that now as I try to find my rhythm, taking step after dusty step. I marvel at some of the other participants. There's a young woman, dressed entirely in black, wearing a gold lamé fanny pack. Her makeup, nails, and long brown hair are salon perfect, and she smiles at every hunky soldier who passes. There's a guy with a scraggly goatee and a Metallica T-shirt wearing a thigh-to-calf knee brace. It creaks with every labored step he takes. There's a pack of kids from the local high school running around in baggy pants as if this were recess. There's a flush-faced, overweight woman sitting on the roadside, belatedly trying to remove her toe rings. There are a couple of tough-looking characters with bandanas, ponytails, and wallet chains talking in hushed tones and smoking Marlboros. There's a teenager with a flimsy nylon backpack that looks like it was unfolded this morning from a box of Cracker Jack. It's stuffed with bricks.

There is no easy out for them if they can't make it. There's no shortcut. There are aid stations every two miles, but they offer little more than water, bananas, and moleskin. Surrender involves a humiliating ride back to the parking lot in a rescue vehicle. Don't these people realize what they're getting themselves into?

And then there's Private Farley.

I come upon him at Mile 8. We're at the point of the march where the last drop of excitement has just dribbled out of us. I have been walking for two hours and am realizing I'm not even a third of the way done. I have no pain yet, just hotspots—like someone is holding a match to my heels, to my knees, and to the bony parts of my shoulders and back where my pack rubs. I try not to multiply them by three in order to predict my condition at the finish. If pain increases exponentially, I may not make it.

I spot Farley just as we're beginning a four-mile, 1,200-foot climb into a dry, dehydrating wind. He's short, spectacled, and plump, with a loaded rucksack that's bending him into a question mark. Many of the soldiers are marching as teams, and event rules require that all five members finish together. But Private Farley is already struggling.

All conversation has ceased as we collectively reflect upon our gathering aches. It's church quiet, except for the trudge of boot soles on earth and, if you listen real close, the squish of blisters. Farley's sergeant suddenly looks around, spots him 50 yards back, and yells as if from a megaphone:

"FARLEY! GET UP HERE!"

Farley responds instantly, double-timing it up to his teammates. He walks beside them for a while, then slowly begins to drift back again. After about 10 minutes, the sergeant realizes he's no longer there, turns around, and screams once more:

"FARLEY! GET UP HERE!"

This scene repeats itself many times during the next half-hour. Even when I'm well ahead of them, I can still hear that sergeant's voice in the distance booming at Farley, ordering his sorry butt back to the front. I'm embarrassed for him, but also a little jealous. He has his own personal whip cracker.

Lester Tenney, who was eventually awarded a Bronze Star for bravery, recounts the Death March in a cold, matter-of-fact tone. At first, it's hard to believe he can be so unemotional about it, but then you realize that skin isn't the only organ capable of developing scar tissue.

Like many of his fellow soldiers, Tenney had been subsisting on 800 calories per day during the final 45 days of the battle. So even before the march began, he belonged to a skeleton army. Once the march started, fear was added to the fatigue. It hung like humidity in the jungle air and produced a constant sweat. The Japanese were under orders to clear the Bataan Peninsula as quickly as possible and to kill any stragglers who were slowing the process. So if a man stumbled or fell off the pace, even to pee or defecate, he was either beaten or bayoneted. Guards on horseback occasionally used their samurai swords to behead those who faltered.

Tenney hiked from dawn to dusk for 12 days, averaging just one to two mph. His bed was the same road he walked on all day, and his only sustenance was an occasional ball of rice, a stalk of sugar cane, or a handful of dirty water. But his misery didn't end when the march did. While in a succession of POW camps, he was starved, beaten, and tortured. He was hung by his thumbs for a day and a half. He had a strip of wet bamboo tied around his testicles. (It became a vise as it dried.) And he had slivers of bamboo shoved beneath his fingernails and lit. (The flames burned away his fingertips.)

Despite how agonizing this sounds, Tenney claims that physical suffering is not the worst type of pain. In fact, the only time that his voice quivers, the only time his veneer chips, is when he mentions a woman named Laura. They were married shortly before he shipped out, and he carried her picture in his boot. Her memory was steady nourishment through his years of imprisonment. But she didn't wait for him.

"Twenty-four hours after being mercilessly beaten, the physical pain subsides and you're able to get on with your life," explains Tenney. "But emotional pain is different. I tried to pretend that losing Laura didn't matter, but it did. For a while after I got home, I became a drunkard. Emotional pain isn't as severe as physical pain, but it hurts for much longer."

He pauses. He grimaces.

"But remember," he finally adds, "it's not the pain that'll kill you. It's the refusal to fight it."

As I approach Mile 12, demoralized that I'm still not even halfway finished, I hear someone singing. It's coming from somewhere up ahead in the brown hills. It's a male voice, low and mournful, but so strong and clear I can make out every word.

At first I was afraid, I was petrified
Kept thinkin' I could never live without you by my side . . .

Even though my hotspots are wildfires now, the music makes me walk faster. It's as if, in this blasted place, any semblance of life and energy automatically draws you to it. Others are reacting the same way. It's some sort of vague, magnetic promise.

> But then I spent so many nights
> Thinkin' how you did me wrong
> And I grew strong . . .

The music is coming from a soldier with a cassette player duct-taped to his chest. He's plodding along, head down, but his little box is pumping at full volume. There's a small band of marchers around him, all silent, all listening, all refueling.

> Weren't you the one who tried to hurt me with goodbye
> Did I crumble?
> Did you think I'd lay down and die?
> Oh no, not I. I will survive . . .

Although the dust from the trail has powdered the inside of my throat, I start singing along in a hoarse croak. And others do, too. Privately at first, but then louder and together—a tiny group of strangers belting out the chorus of a '70s dance tune on a Sunday morning in the middle of nowhere.

> It took all the strength I had not to fall apart
> Kept trying hard to mend the pieces of my broken heart.
> And I spent so many nights
> Just feeling sorry for myself. I used to cry
> But now I hold my head up high . . .

These lyrics are meant for us. They're a message, a pep talk. I make fists and punch the air with each finishing note. The soldier next to me has his eyes closed, absorbing every tinny vibration as if it were a precious desert water droplet. I feel empowered and stride off, the music slowly receding but still clear.

> Oh as long as I know how to love I know I'll stay alive;
> I've got all my life to live,
> I've got all my love to give and I'll survive,
> I will survive. Hey, hey.

113

The midway point, Mile 13.1, is unadorned. There is no congratulatory message scrawled in the sand, nobody waiting to offer encouragement or applause. Physically, it is a signpost like any other; but psychologically, it is a flashing neon arrow pointing homeward. Shortly after I pass it, the hills part, the trail begins to slope downward, and the white water towers of the army base appear in the distance. My pain suddenly has an end point, and the sight of it makes all the difference. We are now closer to the end than we are to the beginning, and that simple knowledge is invigorating.

The next aid station is buzzing. We've turned the corner, and everyone's spirit is soaring. Never mind that the runners are already finishing. Soon we will be, too. There is chatter instead of groans. There are smiles instead of frowns. And, like a mirage, there are hot dogs.

Now, a hot dog isn't a very extravagant food. But when you've been swallowing nothing but bananas and water for three-plus hours, the site of one plumping on the grill, gently sweating, soft buns beckoning, is irresistible. Somehow, enterprising ROTC cadets lugged a gas grill up here, and they're doing a brisk business. Whenever they open and close the lid, it's as if they're sending smoke signals. Marchers line up fixated. There is moisture in our mouths once again. PowerBars be damned.

Two beefy soldiers dressed in desert fatigues buy three hot dogs apiece. I walk behind them as they eat. A lean woman in a sports bra and visor, arms moving like pistons, passes on our left, makes a face, and says, "How can you eat that?"

"Are you kidding?" one of them mumbles between bites. "This is heaven."

It seems like it takes them only a minute to finish. Then one elbows the other, motions his head down the trail, and they take off running.

Not everyone is so energized, though. A couple of miles later, I come across a limping soldier. His pants leg is ripped, and there's a bandage wrapped haphazardly around his thigh. He looks like he took a bullet and is returning from the front. Since he has no buddies to help him and it looks like the injury is recent, I ask if he needs assistance. He stares at me with bayonet-blue eyes and says fiercely, "I'm fine."

Okay. No problem. I'll be moving on.

Shortly thereafter, I meet another soldier, who's carrying *two* packs. One is strapped to his back, and the other to his chest. I can't believe it. That's at least 70 pounds of equipment. His four teammates surround him, one of whom is carrying only a water bottle. It's obvious he's hurting, and his comrades are doing all they can to help him along. After a while, the soldier with the twin packs asks for a break, but as he's transferring the load, it falls to the ground with a heavy thud. For a few seconds, they all just stand there, looking at it.

"Shit."

It's getting to be a circus out here. With each passing mile, my fellow marchers become simultaneously more entertaining and more annoying. Sergeant Rob Atteberry, a hard-ass Army Ranger who once won the mil-itary-with-heavy-pack division in just over five hours, feeds off this. "I use the other marchers to motivate me," he explains as we walk together for a while. "I tell myself I cannot let that young pup, old fart, or out-of-shape piece of crap beat me! When I start to hurt, I look at everyone sitting alongside the road whining about their aches, and I laugh. Or I think about the guys on the real Death March, and how they'd be shot if they stopped. Before long, I forget my pain. I know it sounds sadistic, but I gain strength from other people's misery."

I notice, disconcerted, that he's looking directly at me when he says this.

Between Miles 20 and 22, there is a sandpit. At this point in the march, with fatigue nearly as intense as the noon sun, it is an inhumane challenge. Indeed, it is designed to break us. The army base is nearby, there are less than six miles remaining, but I'm walking in slow motion—each step sinking in the tractionless grit. Plus, there's a headwind. It feels like the hot air that rushes into your face when you open the oven door to check on dinner. And it bakes me even more.

Psychologically these things are crushing, but so is the physical pain I'm experiencing. The soles of my feet feel seared, as if they've been held to a frying pan. The skin on my shoulders and low back has been rubbed raw by my pack. My hip joints feel like rusty hinges. My hands and forearms are swollen. And despite forcing myself to drink two cups of water at every aid station, I am dehydrated.

When you're barely moving, when you're this close to stopping, when your muscles are screaming—the temptation to quit becomes overwhelming. Although I swore I never would, I start thinking about it. And the possibility consumes me. To end it right now, to throw off this pack, to lie down in the dust would be so simple, so luxurious. I remember what one of the survivors told me yesterday: "After a point, death became easier than life." I understand what he means. But I'm not so far gone yet that I've lost sight of the fact that, ultimately, quitting also hurts.

What is this thing called pain, anyway? It has never been isolated in any lab, it is not a measurable substance, yet I can point precisely to it and tell the doctor where it hurts. Pain is a riddle. I can't hold it in my hand, yet my hand can feel it. Experts claim that it's nothing more than a neurological impulse, an alarm sounded by the brain to call attention to a threat. They can trace its path, from the point of origin to spinal column to thalamus to cortex to limbic system. It's not until the pain reaches the brain that it's recognized and interpreted.

"I had a kidney stone not too long ago," says Tenney, "and it was horrible. But the doctor gave me a shot, and the pain disappeared. That shot didn't do a damn thing to the kidney stone. It was still there. But the drug went to my brain and told it not to feel the pain anymore. I figure if a shot can do that, I should be able to do that. I have control over my brain."

During the Death March, Tenney dealt with his pain in two ways. First, he set short-term goals for himself. Instead of worrying about how he was 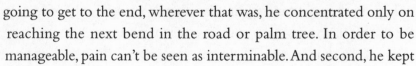 going to get to the end, wherever that was, he concentrated only on reaching the next bend in the road or palm tree. In order to be manageable, pain can't be seen as interminable. And second, he kept reminding himself that no matter how intense the pain became, it's never the pain that kills you. It is merely a by-product, a signal, a nerve impulse. There is nothing to fear in pain itself. Pain and death are not synonymous. It is just a warning that something's wrong. *You* decide whether to back off, ease up, let go, or continue on.

I use Tenney's tricks as I stumble through the sandpit. They work. The pain subsides a bit. It disconnects from my body and starts to drift. I glimpse its separate existence. But at the same time, something strange happens, something I never expect: Instead of feeling relief that the pain is gone, I miss it.

Part of the reason I'm out here trekking through this goddamn desert is to taste pain. Like most Americans, when my muscles ache or my head throbs, I automatically reach for the Tylenol. But perhaps it's not the pain I dread, but rather what I might learn about myself if I experience it. Will I scream? Will I cry? Like the song suggests, will I lay down and die?

Pain is a measure of manhood, a litmus test for cowardice. So it's understandable why I want to avoid it. But when the pain is not razor sharp and debilitating, maybe it's better to let it live. Maybe it's not a sign of strength leaving the body, but weakness. In a book called *Why We Hurt*, Dr. Frank Vertosick points out that "pain isn't synonymous with life, it's synonymous with intelligence." Plants don't feel it, and neither do many other simple organisms. Pain is our teacher. It makes us aware. As Nietzsche wrote: "In pain, there is as much wisdom as in pleasure." I suppose the same can be said of fear.

In all the world's religions, pain and suffering play a central role. It is the way to become enlightened and, ironically, achieve a pain-free existence. It is both the punishment and the reward. Maybe there is something to that. Despite how miserable I feel, there's a dark part of me that's enjoying this. It hurts so *good*. I'm not as conscious of being alive when I feel fine. Pain puts me in the now. It's meditative.

And as I take each agonizing step, as I push onward, I realize that I'm building myself up at the same time as I'm tearing myself down. Pain is full of contradictions like this. There's growth in deterioration.

I eat an orange at Mile 24. It isn't even a whole orange, just a wedge. A smiling volunteer holds out a giant Tupperware bowl of them at the final aid station. They're floating in ice water, and I grab one without stopping. It is candy sweet. I let the juice drip down my chin and onto my chest. I gnaw every last bit of pulp off the rind. It is *so* orange—in appearance, taste, smell, feel. It is the best orange I've had in my entire life. It almost makes me cry.

One of the survivors remembers a rice kernel. He spotted it lying on the filthy floor at the POW camp where the marchers were interred. It must have dropped unnoticed from one of their bowls of meager rations. He remembers reaching down with his bony fingers to pick it up. He remembers chewing it. He remembers it tasting good.

Three guys sit behind a folding table at Mile 24.5. They applaud me slowly and resolutely as I shuffle past. On the table are bottles of Gatorade, in blinding colors, and sweaty cans of soda and beer, just surfaced from a cooler. Such plenty overwhelms me. I would like nothing more than to slug an ice-cold Coke, to feel the sugar and caffeine flow into my veins like electricity. But I'm confused. I don't immediately realize that these drinks are free. I think you have to pay, and I don't have any money. So I nod my head and walk by, until about 100 yards later when I realize. But by then it's too late. It would hurt too much to go back. That's 200 extra steps.

Another survivor remembers the delicious sound of rushing water, and how the droplets tumbled over each other, catching the jungle sun like liquid diamonds. There were artesian wells along the Death March road, but the prisoners were rarely permitted a sip. In fact, the guards would order the parched men to sit in the dust beside them and watch the fresh water spill out. Some men couldn't take it. Some broke down, drank their fill, and then were killed.

There's a row of Porta Potties at Mile 25. They've turned sour this late in the day, and I hold my breath as I take a short vivid-yellow piss. Thank God I don't have to sit down; there's no longer any toilet paper, and the seat is spattered. I use my elbow to lift the latch and push open the door, trying not to think of the bacteria. I must not be totally fried yet. I still have some dignity, some self-respect.

When pressed, the survivors grudgingly admit that after a few days of marching they even lost that. Since stopping for any reason was forbidden, they had no choice but to go to the bathroom while walking. For many men, dysentery made the situation even more humiliating.

At Mile 25.5, a husband and wife are running a makeshift aid station. He's strung a garden hose from his house and is spraying anyone who requests it. I close my eyes and walk through the mist. It awakens me to the fact that soon I'll be finished. I won't have to take another step. He points to a steel tub of ice water and invites me to soak my feet. But when I refuse, when I say I have to continue, his wife hands me a cool towel. "Good job, sir," she says. I wipe my face, trying to make myself look presentable. I want to hug them both and thank them for their kindness.

In the book *Beyond Courage*, one survivor tells the story of an old Filipino woman who brought the marchers water and then darted back into her roadside hut. But the guards dragged her out, cut off both ears and breasts, threw them at the men who accepted her gift, and then left her to die screaming in the dirt.

Teams are regrouping at Mile 26. For their time to be official, all five members must finish together. So they wait for the stragglers. Some will be here for hours. You never desert a comrade. I pass through their vacant stares, but it's the quiet that's most noticeable. Despite the number of soldiers here and their proximity to victory, there is no celebration. Rather, there's a weary, respectful hush hanging over the battlefield.

Tenney remembers men sitting by the side of the road, too. He'd pass them, at first hatefully jealous that they were somehow granted a respite. But then he'd realize they were dead, propped there by sadistic guards to resemble an audience.

There's a white line across the road at Mile 26.2. Someone rips the tag off the number on my chest, another gives me a voucher for a free lunch, and somebody else hands me a commemorative pewter key chain. It's 1:30 in the afternoon, and it has taken me 7 hours, 2 minutes, and 43 seconds to complete this. I limp down the chute and into the shade of the finish-line tent. I don't immediately know what to do. When your body has been performing a repetitive action for this long, it becomes programmed. Despite the pain, I don't know how to turn my body off. But then I notice a hand. It is liver spotted and wrinkled, and it is trembling up toward me. As if in a dream, I take it. I shake it. The grip is surprisingly firm. And then I realize that it is the hand of one of the original Death Marchers. He has insisted on being seated at the finish to personally congratulate everyone who crosses. He's wearing thick, smudged glasses, a red cap and vest hung with medals, and a genuine smile.

"Thank you," he says, pumping my arm. "Thank you."

Despite how much I hurt, I feel such a wave of emotion that I choke up. I have no reply. I can't even look into his eyes. But if he had asked me to do another 10 miles, I would have adjusted my pack and started all over. This thing called spirit. . . . It never dies. It never tires. It fears nothing.

The area where the march began, where I listened to the missing-man roll call this morning, is now the site of a huge party. There are people everywhere, plus food tents, elaborate tailgates, and a disc jockey.

I drop my pack and sit on the grass with my back to a bank of speakers. I let the vibrations massage me. Nancy Sinatra is belting out "These Boots Were Made for Walkin'," but no one is even thinking about dancing. It feels too good to sit, to not move a single muscle, to bask in the afterglow of achievement.

"Everyone is feeling the same pain," says the soldier next to me, as we watch people walk tenderly past us, as if they were barefoot on hot asphalt. Indeed, it looks like the aftermath of war—bodies strewn about, an occasional groan floating up, even a busy medic tent.

Seeing everyone else's pain takes the edge off mine. Sharing dilutes it. And watching so many people stream in after me is a potent anesthetic. I wasn't last. In fact, there are thousands still out there.

I sit there for close to an hour listening to the music, watching the rest of the world go by, content to remain blissfully stationary. I watch a chubby girl fly by repeatedly on her chrome scooter, laughing. I witness a boy, no older than six, run up to his father, hug him around the leg, and yell, "Daddy! You made it!" I feel their exhilaration, their joy. I am aware of *everything*. It's as if the pain has sharpened my consciousness. It's life I feel, and I am deeply appreciative for it.

I'll be honest: I was scared of this event. Like I said, I wasn't sure I'd be able to finish. Fear springs from doubt. It mushrooms as we question ourselves. But we are capable of so much more than we think. It's not just our chests that expand with courage; it's our potential.

Over by the food tent is Farley, plate loaded with hamburgers and potato salad. Somehow, he made it. Fanning herself beneath a tree is the woman in fashionable black with the gold lamé fanny pack. And nearby are the high-school kids with the baggy pants, still running around as if it were recess. I spot the overweight woman with the toe rings, too, and the tough-looking characters with the ponytails, still smoking Marlboros. There's the guy with the creaking knee brace, the grim soldier with the leg bandage, the guy with the cassette player duct-taped to his chest, the two hot-dog eaters, the woman in the sports bra, even the guy who was carrying two packs (and his hobbled teammate). They're all here. They all made it, despite how unlikely it seemed. They're all heroes.

I'm no longer afraid of this pain. Although it hurts and I'll be sore for days afterward, the accomplishment, perspective, and pride I'll derive will tranquilize it. My abrasions and my blisters will become my medals. It's the same reason mothers choose to become pregnant again. Some pain is worth it.

But I'm not so arrogant as to think I've mastered pain. I've merely toured one of its subdivisions. I can see now there are many other types, and I'm less certain of my ability to handle them. For instance, the pain of terminal illness still scares me because it is so pointless. For bravery to exist, don't you at least need a chance? And what Tenney

121

mentioned—emotional pain—that would be devastating. I don't think I could endure losing my wife or children.

What all pain has in common (but especially those last two) is the reminder that we're mortal. It's an elbow in the ribs, a finger bent backward by a bully, a clear sign that we're not only vulnerable but also insignificant. Pain is the message—sometimes loud, sometimes whispered—that there is something bigger than us, and we are ultimately powerless against it.

To get to the root of my fear, I'll have to find a way to stand before that next.

GOD

(AUTHORITY)

CHASING TORNADOES

"Everybody in the vans—NOW!"
screams David Gold, his voice barely discernible
above the thunder and wind.

Doors slam, tires spin, and in seconds our entire caravan is hurtling down a two-lane country road somewhere in south-central Iowa.

"This is not the best of situations," says Gold, simultaneously scanning the black sky, reading roadmaps, and downloading the latest storm data to his laptop. "To get ahead of this thing, we'll have to punch the core and then blast east. Prepare for a terrible beating!"

"Core punching" is to storm chasers what "up the middle" is to the Green Bay Packers. It means you're going right at the very spot where your opponent is strongest. And there's a good chance you may not make it.

"Get ready for 70-mph winds and hail," warns Gold, our quarterback. And then the wrath of God Himself is upon us.

Our big passenger vans are buffeted by powerful crosswinds that force the drivers to tack into them. The sky is a sickening shade of dark green—

like bile—and the lightning is almost continuous. We're in the gut of the storm, surrounded by detonating primeval forces. It wouldn't surprise me to look out the window and see a dinosaur. It's that prehistoric.

Then comes the hail, hesitant at first but eventually a shotgun-blast's worth. The sound of the pellets hitting the roof makes talking impossible. Fortunately, they're small and short lived, but the rain that comes next is terrific. It doesn't fall; it sweeps across the earth as if some giant custodian is power washing us from overhead.

A high-pitched scream cuts through the din. It momentarily freezes everyone, until we realize it's coming from the radio. It's a warning, not a test, from the Emergency Broadcast System. The National Weather Service has issued a tornado warning for Baxter, Iowa, and surrounding counties. Doppler radar indicates an area of rotating wind and rain not far from where we are.

"This is a dangerous storm," says the announcer. "Take cover immediately."

I don't know what's worse: fear or shame.

Fear pushes me out of bed on humid summer nights after being awakened by the growl of an approaching thunderstorm. I close all the windows in the upstairs bedrooms, jealous of how deeply and peacefully my family is sleeping. As the first fat raindrops smack the back of the house and the wind frisks the locust trees, I pull spare sheets and pillows from the linen closet and lay them in the hall, so I won't be near any windows.

Before long, the rumbles become explosions and the lightning turns to flashbulbs. I close my eyes, plug my ears, and pray I won't be struck dead. I curl myself into a tight ball in order to be less of a target. But at the same time, I try to stay attuned to the atmosphere in the house. Just before lightning strikes, you're supposed to smell ozone, feel your skin prickle, and see the hair on your arms stand on end. Maybe that's why I overreact when something brushes my leg. I flinch and yell. Is this the end? But it's only my 16-year-old son, with a full bladder, heading for the bathroom.

"What are you doing here?" he asks, sleepy eyes suddenly wide. "I almost tripped over you."

I don't reply because I know he knows the answer. This isn't the first time he's caught me here.

Instead, I warn him about being in the bathroom during a thunderstorm. Metal pipes and water are electrical conductors. But he just shakes his head and steps over me. He takes a long, powerful piss—the kind of relief I miss—then heads back to bed without saying good night.

Shame pushes me into my own bed, disgusted by the example I just set. What will be the effect on my boy of witnessing that? As NBA coach Pat Riley said: "Being afraid is okay, if you're afraid with dignity." Why can't I rise above this? Why do I feel so helpless? If it's just angels bowling, like my mom used to say, why does it seem I'm the lead pin?

Most of it probably stems from almost being hit by lightning when I was 15. It was a searing bolt that turned my parents' backyard bright white. I felt the heat of it and, without a second's lapse, the concussion. Just that quickly, I realized I was no longer invincible, and it sent me running. Ever since, I've been cowering. When the weather report is foreboding and the sky darkens, I get this dread that's beyond the pit of my stomach. It's in my bones. And I become quiet and withdrawn.

But part of it also stems from looking upon every storm like God Himself created it—infusing it with all the vindictive wrath and fury promised in Revelations. *Say your prayers. It's the end of the world. You've sinned, human, and now it's time to be punished.* (Can you guess I went to 12 years of Catholic school?) To me, a thunderstorm isn't just an imbalance of electrical charges in the atmosphere; it's the raw collective potency of the universe. It's the Almighty, the Supreme Authority, throwing a temper tantrum.

I suppose if I lived in Miami, I would feel the same way about hurricanes, or in California, earthquakes. But because I live in a quiet valley in southeastern Pennsylvania, where there's comparatively little for God to be pissed about, it's severe thunderstorms. They are the most powerful, uncontrollable force I routinely encounter, and the experience never fails to make me shudder.

Which is why I've signed on for a 10-day storm-chasing adventure with David Gold and Silver Lining Tours. His trips are led by a respected team of meteorologists, who scour the Midwest in search of violent storms and tornadoes. Their goals are twofold. First, to educate people about how storms work (which should help, I figure, with my Zeus complex). And second, to get them as close to the action as possible without getting hurt. It sounds maniacal, but some people consider it the ultimate thrill.

Is it wise, I wonder, to play chicken with God?

Storm chasers are like pirates—a bandit breed that sails the nation's highways in ships bristling with antennae and satellite dishes. They are voracious—devouring truck-stop burritos and data downloaded by onboard computers until they're able to pinpoint a target area and close in upon it. When the hunt is on, they swarm. Vehicles often appear from nowhere, creating traffic jams and dust storms on quiet country lanes. And although their adversary is never really vulnerable, they bravely take measurements, photographs, and video footage. They try to capture the storm's spirit. Usually, a tenacious battle ensues, complete with shifting strategy, thunder and, if they're not careful, wounded. Sometimes they're able to sell their booty for thousands of dollars to television stations. And then, just as quickly, they're gone.

Gold is one of them. He's 31, on the brink of earning a doctorate in atmospheric science from the University of Texas, but often still a boy—obsessive, pouting, and highly excitable. Silver Lining Tours is his business, founded when the idea of commercial storm chasing was considered lunacy. (Not that it has outgrown this cachet, but at least today it's regarded as feasible.) Gold comes from a family of doctors, so he has an analytical mind. Data is his morphine. But his real high comes not from the numbers themselves but from seeing a pattern in them that no one else does, then having the guts to pursue—and, ultimately, witness—their confluence. He's addicted to that.

During a chase, Gold's personality intensifies with the storm. He becomes more talkative and animated. When he spots a funnel or anything else spectacular, energy is transferred from it to him. You can see where the term *cloud nine* comes from. However, if the chase is fruitless—if, as he puts it, "we get jerked around by the atmosphere"—then his mood collapses as quickly as the dying storm itself. He becomes silent, morose—suddenly aware of his hunger, exhaustion, and the cruel fact that no matter how smart you think you are, everyone is an amateur when it comes to predicting the weather.

Nonetheless, he has participated in hundreds of career chases and seen dozens of twisters. On the door of one of the vans, like notches on a gun belt, are tiny black-masking-tape tornadoes—six in all. That's how many he's spotted so far this year.

But despite his reputation and all his sophisticated equipment, I'm nervous. A tornado is the most violent force on earth, packing winds and concentrated destructive power even greater than a hurricane's. It is nothing to toy with. Yet here am I in Oklahoma City, in the middle of Tornado Alley, in a town that has been hit by more twisters than any other in the world, to essentially begin a sightseeing tour. Fortunately, I'm not alone in my foolishness. Fourteen other people have paid $2,400 apiece for this "privilege." In fact, Gold had to turn some away.

So where do we play?

That's the question that begins every day.

It's 9:00 A.M., and our entire group is packed into a vacant room at the Oklahoma City Holiday Inn. Gold has plugged in his laptop and is giving us our initial lesson in weather prediction.

"The first thing I look for is low-level moisture," he explains. "You need surface dew points of 65 degrees or greater for big storms to form in the south-central plains."

He connects to a meteorological Web site and the screen becomes a maze of squiggly lines and tiny numbers. Gold takes off his glasses and squints at them, explaining that often the fuzziness gives him a better sense of patterns. "See this?" he says, although none of us does. "There's a pool of juice sitting over Texas. That's good. What we need to look for next is a developing southerly wind that will bring this humid air to us."

He calls up another screen that's a mass of tiny arrows denoting wind direction at various weather stations across America. "There's a strong northwesterly flow carrying cool, dry air aloft," he says, pointing to a channel of synchronized darts, "so if we can get that southern moisture up here, we're in business."

Next he checks weather models from the National Storm Prediction Center in Norman, Oklahoma, for the coming 6-, 12-, and 24-hour periods. Sure enough, it looks like that Texas moisture will waft northward, causing a convergence of differing air masses and winds. That's exactly the type of volatility needed for storm generation. The more powerfully diverse the energies, the more potential the atmosphere has for eruption. In fact, the purpose of a thunderstorm or tornado is quite simple: to eliminate such imbalances.

"Northern Kansas to southern Minnesota looks good for tomorrow," he concludes, snapping shut his laptop. "So we need to get in position. Everyone should be in front of the hotel, ready to roll, in 45 minutes. We'll head to Omaha, then reexamine the data."

That's Omaha, as in Nebraska, as in approximately 400 miles away. Distance is nothing to these guys. Gold's driving record for a 10-day tour is 7,200 miles.

At 11:00 A.M., right on schedule, we leave Oklahoma City, heading north on Route 35. Besides the paying customers and six tour guide/drivers, there's a TV crew from Des Moines, a reporter from the BBC, and three guys from The Weather Channel. To transport us all, there are five vans, an SUV, and The Weather Channel's million-dollar StormTracker truck. I had expected a nimble strike force, but this is a lumbering caravan. Heads turn as we move along the interstate, radioing information between us. We're like an invading army.

More twisters occur here in Tornado Alley—the general area

encompassing Texas, Oklahoma, Kansas, and Nebraska—than anywhere in the world. During spring, warm moist air shoots northward from the Gulf of Mexico and hits cool, dry air racing eastward off the Rockies. Since the cool air is naturally lighter, it overrides the heavy, humid stuff—acting like a lid on a boiling pot. When the pressure in this pot becomes too great, when the steam must dissipate, the lid is literally blown off. That's when storms form. Big storms.

Seventy percent of all tornadoes occur in the United States from March through June, with May being the most active month. That's when the most pots are boiling. Yet despite how numerous tornadoes are at this time of year, the Great Plains are so vast that it's exceedingly difficult to catch one. In fact, Gold makes no promises. While the odds of witnessing a violent thunderstorm are good, tornadoes are fleeting and surprisingly fragile. They can form and disappear in seconds, leaving just a few telltale wisps. Gold tries to keep our expectations realistic, but at the same time he feeds us tantalizing possibilities. His personal record is nine tornadoes in an unforgettable eight-hour span, and just a day before our tour began he spotted one near Ardmore, Oklahoma. I saw his footage on The Weather Channel.

Before long, we pass into Kansas, the home of the most famous tornado of all—the one that swept Dorothy and Toto into the Land of Oz. I feel like I'm heading some place similar. I've never seen the Great Plains, and they are amazingly blank. It's country you forever pass through on the way to somewhere else—flat and spring green, with only an occasional farmhouse, John Deere dealer, or cluster of cattle.

Unlike all the other vacationers in America, we're purposely driving away from the blue sky that's overhead. I'm finding that pretty ironic. For the next 10 days, we'll be hoping for bad weather and feeling disappointed if the sun persists. I didn't even pack any SPF.

Despite my underlying fear, I'm getting caught up in the anticipation. With nothing else to look at, I'm yearning for entertainment. And at 4:40 P.M., Gold notices a "rapidly developing storm" in the vicinity of Russell, Kansas. So we pull off the interstate, climb out of the vans, and squint at a high cirrus–cloud layer barely visible to our west. After downloading fresh data, Gold decides to chase it. Even though it's 135 miles away and not much of anything yet, it shows promise. And just that quickly our plans change. We make a U-turn.

But by 4:53, after looking at more radar images, Gold determines this particular storm will quickly fizzle. However, there are others popping along a rapidly forming moisture ridge in the same vicinity. He didn't expect this. He thought the dew points would be too low to produce anything substantial today. But in this business, surprises are routine and flexibility essential. We're driving faster now, upwards of 80 mph, blowing past the Knute Rockne Memorial Service Plaza and (a good sign?) the Chase County line.

By 5:30, we're aiming for what Gold describes as "the most intense storm in the U.S. at the moment." It's in southern Nebraska, heading toward us at approximately 40 mph. While it doesn't look tornadic, it could produce baseball-size hail. We plot a course for intercept.

We're chasing a supercell, the king of all thunderstorms. On radar, it's easy to see how it gets its name. It looks like an isolated amoeba with a central red nucleus that represents the most intense area of disturbance. In this part of the country, you can actually see a supercell being born. When that cool–air lid gets blown off the atmosphere, it's like watching a nuclear bomb silently detonate. All the hot, moist air rushes upward and condenses, forming a billowing mushroom cloud that can be a mile tall. Upper-level winds eventually shear off its top, making the storm resemble a huge black anvil.

Although it looks solid from afar, each supercell has a rotating core. Deep in its soul is what's called a mesocyclone. This spinning column of air helps organize the inflow and outflow of moisture, and it's the turbine that generates tornadoes.

A supercell on the Great Plains is an awesome sight. If conditions are right, it can explode in minutes and quickly grow to a diameter of 5 to 10 miles. Once established, it can travel for upwards of 300 miles, devouring smaller storms forming around it. But despite its intimidating appearance and incredible power, it is actually quite delicate, built of nothing more than air molecules and water droplets. If the upper-level winds aren't strong enough to move it along and form that anvil, the storm eventually rains itself out. It extinguishes its own furnace. Almost before your eyes, it collapses and vanishes.

By 6:30, we're in Alma, Kansas, and things looks ominous. A solitary cross atop a white church steeple is silhouetted against a black sky. It seems like a prophecy. But this storm, which came barreling out of Nebraska with so much promise, is already gasping. There isn't enough moisture in the atmosphere here to sustain it, explains Gold, disappointed. Now it's turning into "junk," the storm chasers' derisive term for a time waster.

However, 120 miles farther west, another big supercell has formed, and this one looks like it may be tornadic. Gold is pissed. He apologizes to the group over the radio, calling his morning forecast "amateurish." He let us get sucked too far east. If we chase this one, the same thing will happen. By the time we get there, it will be sputtering. We're too far out of position.

"It's time to cut our losses and set up for tomorrow," he says. "It's looking like the greatest area of instability will be in Iowa, South Dakota, and Minnesota. Let's head for Omaha."

By 10:45, we're eating pizza in the lobby of the Comfort Inn there. Twelve hours on the road, 515 miles on the odometer, and nothing to show for it—not even a photograph. I'm trying to figure out whether to be relieved or disappointed.

We're back in the vans by 10:20 the following morning. There was no briefing; Gold wanted to study the data privately. He needed to concentrate, squint at his computer screen, and get in touch with his instincts. Although there were no confirmed reports of tornadoes yesterday, he refuses to get caught out of position today. He wants to get north as quickly as possible, then work west as the front develops. He's like a general, barking commands over the radio, marshalling his troops for the attack.

A road sign welcomes us to Iowa. Gold explains that during the summer, when this entire state becomes a cornfield, the perspiring vegetation makes its own weather. Rising moisture from the crops produces popcorn thunderstorms that can become quite powerful. But there's no chance of that happening today. The fields have just been furrowed. In fact, as we get closer to the Minnesota border, there are still puddles from snowmelt.

As the day progresses, our target zone condenses. "Iowa is mixing out," concludes Gold around three o'clock. "Dews in the 60s won't make it up here. The moisture is too shallow. Southern Minnesota looks better. A severe thunderstorm watch has been issued for the region. Redwood Falls is our new target city."

Because our caravan is so large, townsfolk understandably get a little apprehensive when we turn onto their Main Street. It's like a band of outlaws riding in at high noon; it can only mean trouble. Sometimes, the sheriff himself comes out. He'll either tail us as we pass through town or, if we're stopped, amble over to peer at our antennae and ask what the hell is going on. Gold is always respectful. He knows how much hassle the law can rain down. In fact, he tries to help the police and local storm spotters whenever possible, relaying information about approaching weather so they can do their jobs better. Most times, they're appreciative. But on other occasions, it's obvious they prefer we move on. Not all storm chasers are as considerate. Many are road rogues out for a thrill. They drive dangerously fast and cause traffic jams that thwart emergency vehicles. Not long ago, the state legislature in Texas tried to make storm chasing illegal.

The sky is looking increasingly unsettled, like a big, swirling gruel that's approaching the boil. We endure numerous false starts. At 3:30, just south of Albert Lea, Minnesota, we spot some spectacular mammatus clouds. These are rounded protrusions, resembling intestines that form along the underside of a cloud. They're an indicator of turbulent winds aloft, but rarely produce severe weather. At 4:30, outside of Otawonna, we spot a cumulus cloud deck, then a condensing updraft, but the formation isn't sustainable and it eventually collapses. All this activity is promising, though. As the evening progresses, the storms should be able to gain traction and grow stronger.

At 5:30, we stop in New Ulm to gas up—both our vehicles and ourselves. Full tanks are a necessity for storm chasing. You don't want to run out of fuel in the path of a monster twister, or have your judgment impaired because you haven't eaten for 12 hours. Bags of chips, microwave pizza, ice cream sandwiches, Slim Jims, diet Coke . . . the group devours the junk food like wolves.

We chase and abandon a series of small storms, zigzagging across the countryside without a firm plan. A tornado is reported 40 miles north of us in Young America, but Gold is skeptical. He says that local storm spotters are often poorly trained and highly excitable. His radar images don't support their claim. The storms are becoming multicellular, which means they're banding together. This is bad news for chasing and tornado formation. The disturbances are too broad and encompassing. Focused energy is what we need.

Looking to salvage what's left of the day, Gold directs his drivers to turn southeast, away from these frontline skirmishes and into the war that is an already mature storm. We're going to core-punch one of the multicells "for some entertainment," he says. Although it's unlikely to contain a tornado, it'll be fat with rain and veined with lightning. We head toward the blackest part of the horizon, headlights on despite the fact that "6:40" is glowing on the dashboard clock.

Just outside of Ellendale, we get hit with some mushy hail and then a deluge of rain. For a few minutes, it's as if we were in a car wash. Then comes the lightning, and it's like nothing I've ever seen. The bolts are miles long, and they don't always travel up and down. Sometimes they shoot horizontally across the sky, like electric whips. The cracks are instantaneous. I sit in the van, my nerves and seat belt taut, being careful not to touch any metal.

We pull into a truck stop along I-35, lining our vehicles up in a neat row as if we were at a drive-in movie. There are lots of tractor trailers here— engines rumbling in the same octave as the now-continuous thunder.

"If you leave the vans," Gold warns over the radio, "be careful of lightning."

Be *careful* of lightning? What the hell does that mean? It's not like it's a downed electrical wire you can cautiously step over. My trust in him diminishes. Why does no one else appear the least bit apprehensive? Two guys from another van have actually run under an overhang, where they're videotaping everything. And in order to keep their cameras steady, they're leaning on gas pumps. Meanwhile, one of the guys in my van opens the sliding door because "it's hot in here."

"Is that a good idea?" I whisper to the driver.

"No, that's probably not a good idea," he replies, but he makes no move to close it.

What are these people thinking? Are they stupid? Do they have a death wish?

You know what really scares the hell out of me? Ignorance, and the threat of dying foolishly. But because I don't know these people, I bury my anger and my fear. I guess that's a good sign. If I can stifle it and not become irrational, then I must still be bigger than it. I watch as another guy comes walking back to the van sipping a jug of Gatorade. He's looking around at the flickering sky as if he were out for a stroll on a starlit night. How can he not be intimidated? What's wrong with me?

Suddenly, Gold's voice is yelling on the radio: "35 North NOW! Let's GO!"

Like a SWAT team, we peel out. The storm is still raging, visibility is practically zero, and cars are off the road, but we're hurtling along at 70 mph. Hydroplaning. Ironically, we pass the exit for the town of Hope.

My fear of lightning is quickly replaced by the fear of getting killed. Now *this* is dangerous. If I die in a long, wet, sickening skid, people won't call me adventurous. They'll think I'm brainless. I have no idea what we're chasing, but even if it's a tornado, it can't justify this.

But then, we're free of it. The rain eases, the sky brightens, and an orange setting sun peeks out from under an ascending black curtain, as if it's checking to see if it's safe to come out. And not far away is a rainbow, equally tentative, but growing stronger with each passing second. Just that quickly, the world has gone from gloom to glory. If fear has a silver lining, it's that life afterward seems almost holy.

Gold cancels our mission. He thought he saw something forming on radar, but he was mistaken. Dinner is a 10:30 omelet at Perkins. But there's no time for dessert. In order to be in the best position for tomorrow, we need to get to Sioux City, Iowa, tonight. When we pull into the parking lot of the Super 8 Motel at 3:00 A.M., the day's mileage is 825.

Our caravan parks in front of the Kmart in Carroll, Iowa. Even though it's midafternoon, I'm still hungover from all the driving we did yesterday. All I do is sit, read, take notes, and highlight maps, but I'm exhausted. When I try to stretch, my ligaments feel like bridge cable.

"Okay, let's grab some lunch," says Gold.

I've been to Kmart before. In fact, it's one of my favorite discount department stores. But I was unaware you could dine there.

"Oh sure, lots of good stuff," he says. "Much better than Wal-Mart."

We slip through the sliding glass doors and, sure enough, there's a mini-restaurant serving hot dogs, nachos, pizza, soft drinks, and hot pretzels. Much of the food is revolving—the hot dogs on rollers, the pizza on a carousel, and the pretzels on hooks in a glass box. It takes a few stabs by the dizzy young blonde behind the counter to get me what I want.

We hang out for almost an hour—milling about, killing time, waiting for blue-light specials. Just when we're starting to think today may be a bust, Gold explodes through the sliding doors and yells: "We have to hurry! There's a nuclear bomb out there! My God, what a specimen. It's going crazy!"

We jump from our booths and scatter toward the vans, triggering

135

a near panic among the gray-haired customers in women's hosiery. Our real blue-light special is going off about 10 miles away. In fact, it caught us sleeping. The supercell formed in less than 30 minutes, practically on top of us, and it's already moving away.

"The only way to get ahead of it is to punch the core," radios Gold. "Hang on!"

We hurtle east on Route 30 toward a sickly green curtain that marks the boundary of the hail band. Its unearthly color comes from the reflection of millions of ice particles. In minutes, we're bombarded, producing a din like a hundred school kids hammering tin. Torrential rain and wind come next. For a while, the only things visible are the twin taillights of the van ahead. Then it subsides, the sky brightens, and we emerge into relative calm. We're in front of the still-developing storm.

Using his global positioning system, Gold maneuvers us into optimal position, occasionally jogging south on two-lane farm roads to develop better angles. We're flirting with the storm now, staying just ahead of it, trying to peek up its skirt. We're at the converging edge of two powerfully different air masses, and I can feel it. Every now and then, Gold pulls off the road to let us sightsee. When we hop out, cameras in hand, the air feels thick, hot, and poised. But before long, there's a lick of coolness, a tentative finger of lower humidity on the backs of our necks, followed by increasingly stronger puffs of wind. It's a volatile place to be, so we don't linger. It's back into the vans, more hurtling and maneuvering, until we're safe again. This is the essence of storm chasing—playing an almost inconceivable game of cat-and-mouse with the most destructive force on earth.

Gold is furiously downloading weather data. He knows how big this storm is, how fast it's moving and in which direction. He knows where the lightning is, the hail, the wind, the rain. He points out all the textbook supercell features as if it were a diagram on a classroom chalkboard. He's slowly getting into its psyche, trying to anticipate what it will do next. But he's careful not to let his enthusiasm cloud his respect.

A storm like this is predictable only to a point. You can't ever let yourself forget that. As soon as you do, it inevitably turns on you.

We're back on 30 East, paralleling the storm—heading in the same direction at about 40 mph. The van window frames the whole scene, as if it were an oil painting. But while I'm studying its detail, searching for some personal meaning, the few people who live in this surreal gallery seem oblivious to what's happening. A guy is mowing his lawn. Laundry still hangs on a line. A farmer is casually driving his tractor, petting a lazy dog on his lap. Kids are warming up for baseball practice. Traffic proceeds uninterrupted. There's absolutely no sign of panic, despite this potential twister producer looming in the distance.

As hard as it is for me to fathom, I guess when you live out here you become accustomed. Or maybe this storm isn't as bad as it looks to us. Perhaps Gold is compounding the drama for his own benefit.

"Tornado!" someone yells from the back of the van, nearly causing our driver to swerve off the road. "Over there!"

We follow the trembling finger until we spot what resembles a Tasmanian devil whirling across a distant farm field. In fact, there are a number of them, sucking dirt and debris into the air as they scour the earth.

"Those are gustnadoes," Gold explains. "Lots of people mistake them for tornadoes. They form along the gust front of a storm, developing on the ground and sometimes rising as high as 2,500 feet. But compared to tornadoes, they're weak. Those over there probably have winds of only 50 to 60 mph."

Our original storm has birthed a new one, and together they're intensifying as they head into an area of stronger upper-level winds. We're fighting to stay ahead of them—turning south, then east, then south again—occasionally having to dodge into the rain to gain better position. Things are developing fast. A wrong move could cost us a glimpse of a tornado—or worse. So we stop to assess the situation. Download more data. Always more data.

And that's when we get caught, when the two storms sandwich

137

us like a piece of lunch meat. Gold yells at us to get back in the vans, and this time we almost don't make it. Seconds later, we're hit by 70-mph crosswinds that toss us about as if we were riding in Matchbox cars.

This is a special weather bulletin from the National Weather Service. A tornado warning has been issued for Baxter, Iowa, and surrounding counties. Doppler radar has detected an area of rotating wind and rain. This is a dangerous storm. Take cover immediately.

The radio announcement leaves us hanging, caught in a temporary indecisive moment between gloom and glee. This is what everyone came to see, the thrill ride for which we've all bought tickets. But now that we've been told to secure our lap belts, we're not so sure we want to participate.

There are few sounds more chilling than a tornado siren wailing across the prairie. It makes the hairs on your neck stand on end. It is the no-nonsense sound of impending doom, the doorbell of the apocalypse. The siren in Baxter has been blowing for some time when we arrive at 5:45, and it has done its job. The place is deserted. The only signs of life are some rocking chairs on a nursing-home porch that are still rocking, as if the devil and a few friends have gathered to watch the destruction.

The most devastating tornado to ever strike the United States occurred on March 18, 1925. It opened a 219-mile gash across Missouri, Illinois, and Indiana, killing 695 people. Whereas most tornadoes survive for 8 to 10 minutes and travel at 30 mph, this one lasted for nine hours and averaged 73 mph. Its winds were estimated at over 260 mph.

The power of a storm like this defies comprehension. An entire house can be splintered in seconds. Buffalo and steer can be flung through the air. Live chickens have been plucked. The water has been sucked out of wells. Half-ton I-beams have been wrenched from garages, carried a quarter-mile, and sunk eight feet into the ground like crude javelins. And there's one unforgettable photograph—maybe you've seen it—of a single twisted dinner fork stuck into a tree so deep that its tines are barely visible. Stuff such as this makes you want to shudder and laugh simultaneously. Fear does that to you occasionally.

We're back at the front of the storm. It's no longer raining, and the wind is momentarily calm. But the sky is purple and black, like it has been punched repeatedly and is finally getting ready to strike back. There's a thick tension in the air. Yes, it *does* feel like God is pissed.

We pull off the road on a little rise at the edge of town. The drivers leave their engines running in case a quick escape is necessary. Gold says we can get out and look if we want. I don't immediately know what to do. On one hand, I can see perfectly well from my seat by the window. But on the other, I am here to face my fear, and I'm not doing that by sitting here. So I slide the door back and step shakily onto the gravel shoulder. What I see above me makes my jaw drop and my legs wobble even more. The clouds overhead are rotating in a big, slow counterclockwise circle.

Gold is beside himself with excitement: "This could throw a hose at any moment!" Everyone's gaze is turned upward, as if we were all extras in a sequel to *Close Encounters of the Third Kind.* A tornado forms when the rotation we're witnessing accelerates and pushes down a nipple of cloud. That's the beginning of the funnel. However, it doesn't just elongate until it reaches the earth. Rather, a separate dervish forms on the ground below and jumps to meet it.

The sound of a developing tornado has three octaves. At first, it's the hissing, whistling buzz of a million swarming bees. Then, as it approaches maturity, its voice deepens into the rush of a giant blowtorch. Finally, as a full-fledged twister, it speaks in a deafening roar, like the voice of Jehovah.

All I can think of is that I am underneath this. I am so close I can see the rivets on the front of a barreling locomotive. I note a grassy gully beside the road. I'll dive in there if I have to. But I have no other logical thoughts. I am paralyzed by the pure spectacle of it. Fear and awe have become one.

"Be ready to move!" yells Gold. "Stay close to the vans!"

The rotation continues—a magical dance that's ever threatening, ever changing, ever fascinating. It's the spiraling intro to a *Twilight*

Zone episode. I could watch it forever. It's that entrancing, that terrifying, that beautiful.

A few people have actually seen the inside of a tornado and lived to talk about it. They weren't just sucked up, spun around, and thrown down miles from home. Rather, through some freak twist of nature and fate, they found themselves in an eddy under the vortex and were able to briefly look up into the room of doom. And all their reports are remarkably similar. What they saw was the interior of a swaying, spinning tube that widened as it stretched skyward. Its walls were smeared smooth by the high speed of the cloud rotation and scarred by varicose veins of lightning. Everything had a flickering, fluorescent blue hue. Baby funnels kept appearing and disappearing higher up. And in the center, like a vigilant mothership, hung a single, bright, shimmering cloud—real but inexplicable.

Gold orders us back in the vans, and we drive slowly along, trying to stay under the rotation. More than once, he tells his drivers not to go any farther; it's too dangerous. But they're inevitably lured forward, heads craning out windows, dashboard video cameras on. Rarely do you get this close to a tornado when it forms. If one erupted, it would be the experience of a lifetime.

I don't recall how long we spent like this. We became suspended. I stopped taking notes, snapping photos, and glancing at my watch. I surrendered, although I don't know to what. But in the end our storm was not quite strong enough. It tried, but a tornado never materialized. The rotation gradually disintegrated, leaving just a contorted wormball of menacing clouds. Despite all their scientific brainpower, meteorologists still don't know what triggers a tornado. Although it can be right over your head, it is still utterly mysterious. Perhaps that's another reason people chase it and, in my case, fear it.

Disappointed yet relieved, we call it a day and head south through steady rain. The storm is vast now, consuming all the available energy in the atmosphere, wringing it dry. I can't believe we saw all this begin as a puff of cloud outside a Kmart. We eat dinner, then drive toward Platt City, Missouri. Distant, thunderless lightning plays on the night sky. I find myself thinking what it must have been like for the pioneers hundreds of years ago. They had never experienced anything like this and were virtually unprotected. They must have thought it *was* the end of the world when one of these storms hit. They had a right to be scared.

I feel safe and snug by comparison, tucked into a sturdy van with a full stomach and a known destination. But most comforting is that there's an ember of confidence glowing inside me. I can look at the lightning in the distance without cringing. I can appreciate its reason for being and, thereby, its beauty. I'm learning.

"Not being able to understand storms is what was haunting me," explained Bill Hopkins of Austin, Texas, who also went on a storm-chasing trip to face his fear. "Knowledge helped me take control. The tables turned. Just the simple act of chasing instead of being chased changed the whole thing for me. I was no longer being hunted. I was hunting."

The rest of the tour is anticlimactic. A "death ridge" builds in over the Plains, but this isn't as ominous as its name. It's a huge area of high pressure that chokes off severe weather—a giant bubble of cool, dry air that squats over the Midwest and squashes all hopes of storm formation. Although we punch deep into central Minnesota one day and drive the length of South Dakota (and back) on others, the search for a respectable supercell proves futile.

By the tour's final day, we're back in Oklahoma with 4,800 total miles on the odometer, desperately looking under every cumulus cloud for some bit of bad weather to punctuate our trip. For a while, it looks like something might pop along a weak low-pressure front creeping out of Colorado and New Mexico. But although the clouds look impressive at times, they never develop into much.

"It's a dead horse," says Gold at 7:30 P.M., sounding the death knell.

Back at the Oklahoma City Holiday Inn, we gather in the lobby lounge to exchange e-mail addresses and clink beer bottles.

We reminisce about the cores we punched and the tornado we almost saw. We boast to the other patrons that we're storm chasers, brandish our Silver Lining T-shirts, and boldly ask the bartender to click from ESPN to The Weather Channel.

And that's when we notice that the energy we were tracking earlier in the day has finally coalesced. Radar shows a thick line of yellow and red advancing from the west. Severe thunderstorm warnings have been posted. But there's nothing we can do but shake our heads. Chasing at night is impossible.

And maybe that's why the old fear returns when I'm awakened at 3:18 A.M. Since there are no windows to close or children to check, I lie in bed and again feel that familiar dread. It's the worst storm of the trip. The rain is drilling my door and window, and the thunder is pounding as if it wants in. Alone in the dark, I personify the maelstrom—suffusing it with vengeance, giving it anger, believing it on a mission to reassert dominance. Curled up in the sheets, I feel twice as pathetic and ashamed as before. To have spent all this money and wasted all this time, but still be quivering, is the epitome of frustrating. Although tornadoes rarely strike at night, when one does, it is doubly devastating because no one sees it coming. I feel trapped, like my room is a cage. There's nowhere to run, no data to download, no plan from Gold to get ahead of this one.

The tables have turned. I am back to being the hunted.

In the midst of this dark thought comes a bolt of illumination: *Check that thinking.* I feel insignificant and small during a storm because I *am* insignificant and small by comparison. My brain is not malfunctioning; it has made an accurate assessment. God or Mother Nature or whatever deity sits in the control tower can't see me. From up there, I'm just another soldier ant. It's only my ego, my inflated perception of myself that has singled me out and made me a supposed target. My fear is merely the result of thinking that I matter.

Maybe before you can be fearless, you must be humble. Maybe before you can be courageous, you must surrender. Maybe before you can have pride, you must swallow it. The ego obscures reality just as the clouds do the sun. Maybe that's why intelligent people seem more prone to phobias. It's not because they're smarter, it's because they feel more self-important. Conceit is what worry and fear feed on.

Thanks to this trip, I know more about thunderstorms than I ever did. The knowledge of why they exist and the perspective I've gained on the relatively puny ones in Pennsylvania has helped me surmount a key element of this (and all) fear: ignorance. But that doesn't mean I no longer sweat when a storm peeks its furrowed brow over the horizon. That doesn't mean I'm able to sleep in my bed next to the window when one rages. That doesn't mean I'm no longer ashamed of my inability to stand up to this. It just means that I accept the anxiety in a way I never did before. I see that without it I might grow too big. This fear of storms, which ironically set in when I was a cocky teen, is not the fear of being struck down by my God, but by my own vanity. It's my instinct, my own good sense, warning me of that lethal and never-ending possibility.

And I realize now how chasing that potential twister could have been so terrifying *and* so exhilarating. It's because within every black wormball of cloud, there really is a silver lining.

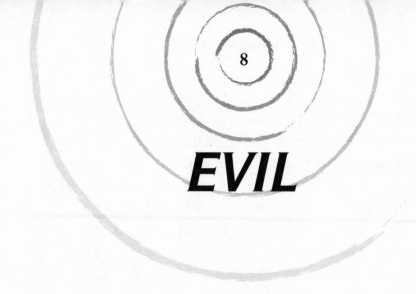

EVIL

CHALLENGING LIZZIE BORDEN ON FRIDAY THE 13TH

The incessant beep of the alarm clock
is six inches
from my right ear.

It gets increasingly louder.

Five A.M., Friday the 13th.

Time to get up on the wrong side of bed.

I crawl over my still-unconscious wife. We've slept together the same way—I on the right and she on the left—and we've gotten out of bed the same way—I on the right and she on the left—for 17 years. Seventeen extremely lucky years, I might add. No major illnesses. No broken bones. Two healthy kids, prosperous careers, a nice home.

WHAM!

I hit my head on the ceiling as I try to stand up, forgetting that it slopes sharply downward on her side of our loft.

"Damn!" I yell, rubbing the top of my skull. As I stagger around in the dark, I whack it a second time, just as hard.

I crumple back onto the bed, wounded. Maybe I shouldn't be messing with this. If the whole day goes this way, I could end up dead. My plan is to break as many superstitions as possible on the unluckiest day of the year, then spend the night in Fall River, Massachusetts, in the house where Lizzie Borden allegedly murdered her parents with an ax. I'm tempting fate, thumbing my nose at that fuzzy gray plane of existence called the supernatural. I'm deliberately challenging those big bad evil spirits to come get me and see what they're made of. If God isn't the source of my fear, then maybe it's the alternative: Satan, ghosts, Hell, and all that my Catholic upbringing says I'll be condemned to if I'm not careful.

"Are you all right, dear?" asks Maria, sitting up.

"I think so," I answer dimly.

According to a recent national survey, most Americans are superstitious in some way. More than 50 percent are "optimistically superstitious," meaning they believe that avoiding sidewalk cracks and knocking on wood brings good luck. More than 40 percent are "pessimistically superstitious," meaning they believe that opening umbrellas indoors and walking under ladders brings bad luck.

At first, I found these numbers hard to believe. Never have we understood the world or ourselves in finer detail. Yet the vast majority of people surveyed admitted to harboring some belief in a force—whether benevolent or diabolical—that makes Providence either smile or frown upon you.

The more I thought about it, though, the more I realized I wasn't being honest with myself. Although I wouldn't immediately call myself superstitious, I wore a St. Christopher medal around my neck for more than a decade. I think twice when a black cat crosses my path, I don't walk under ladders, and I knock on wood after mentioning something good.

Indeed, the closer it got to Friday the 13th, the more apprehensive I became about violating its sanctity. On Thursday the 12th, I mentioned my plan to a coworker. She's young, well-educated—a woman who prefers business suits, salads, and logic. So I was surprised when she gave me a genuinely puzzled look and said, "Why would you ever want to fool with something like that?"

She was right, of course. I've been blessed. My wife was a blind date, for God's sake. Why do I want to put it all at risk? Why *am* I fooling with this?

And that's when I started to get scared—not a roiling panic or a pounding heartbeat, just a simmering dread and an annoying unsteadiness. These superstitions weren't born from nothingness. More than a few people must have gotten up on the wrong side of bed and had horrible things happen for the belief to become so widespread.

I walk carefully downstairs, let the dog outside, and watch as she takes a shit. You're supposed to get a sty in your eye if you witness this. Once she's finished I step on all the sidewalk cracks to "break my momma's back," then set the chairs on our deck to rocking so evil spirits will come sit. Next I head for the garage, where I rip the tag off an old mattress and set up the extension ladder so I can walk beneath it. Back inside, I open an umbrella and set it on the floor, thereby inviting bad things to rain upon my home. I sweep over the front threshold with a broom, brushing all the good luck out of the house. I set a garden hoe in a corner of the hall, where it will supposedly cause many furrowed brows. And, of course, I spill some milk and dump the salt.

"Maria, I have a present for you."

"You're kidding. How hard did you hit your head?"

"No, I'm serious. Here."

She opens the long, rectangular box and lifts the tissue paper.

"It's a . . . knife? How . . . nice."

"It's supposed to be bad luck to give one to your spouse," I explain. "It severs the relationship."

In the bedroom I hang some clothes on a doorknob, place a hat on the bed (then wear it backward), put a pair of shoes on a table, thread a button through the wrong hole, and walk with one shoe on and the other off. Finally, I throw back my head and laugh. Not at all of this foolishness, but because doing so before dawn supposedly guarantees ill humor the rest of the day.

And that's it for my morning checklist—20 superstitions down, with only a couple of lumps on my head to show for it. Now comes the bold part—getting behind the wheel of an automobile (thank God it's a Volvo) and driving 300 miles. Hurtling through New Jersey, across the Tappan Zee Bridge, through New Haven at rush hour, then along Route 95 into Massachusetts. That's five hours of 70-mph jockeying with crazed New Yorkers trying to get a jump on the weekend.

Before backing out of our driveway, we double-check our seat belts.

The Lizzie Borden Bed and Breakfast Museum is located 50 miles south of Boston in the town of Fall River. The house was built in 1845 and later purchased by Andrew Borden. He was a wealthy entrepreneur who chose to live as a commoner. The house at 92 Second Street—which he shared with his daughter Lizzie; Lizzie's older sister, Emma; and their stepmother, Abby—was a modest one-family unit that lacked plumbing and even a serviceable icebox. Although they had a housekeeper, Lizzie loathed living so far below their means. She wanted a home on "the Hill," where the socialites lived.

Judging from the few pictures I've seen of Lizzie, I would have never wanted to mud-wrestle her. She had a bulldog build, a bloodless complexion, curly red hair, and eyes that looked like they belonged in someone else's head. As she advanced into her thirties, she gained weight and generally wore the pained frown of a tightly corseted spinster who desperately needed to get laid. She had no job, no skills—essentially nothing to do. Personally, I have no trouble imagining her swinging an ax while suffering from PMS. But the crime was not that straightforward.

On August 4, 1892, stepmother Abby was on the second floor making the guestroom bed when someone repeatedly hit her in the head with an ax. Crime-scene photos show her facedown in a pool of blood. A few hours later, Andrew returned from his morning banking and settled down in the sitting room to read the paper and take a nap. But he never got quite that relaxed. Someone repeatedly hit him in the head with an ax. Crime-scene photos show him reclining on the divan missing most of his skull.

The puzzling thing about the murders is that despite their brutality, no screams or struggles were heard. The maid claimed she was outside washing windows and chatting with neighbors, while Lizzie (who found the bodies) insisted she was either in her room or in the barn behind the house. (Emma was away on a trip and their houseguest, Uncle John Morse, was out on business.)

Once news of the crime became public, throngs of curious people gathered on Second Street. There were no immediate arrests, and the bodies remained in the house for two days until the authorities completed their investigation. No definitive murder weapon or bloodstained evidence was found. Uncle John Morse, when he returned, had an ironclad alibi and witnesses to his whereabouts. Reports of a stranger, a messenger, seen in the area around the time of the murders could not be verified. And because Lizzie and her maid were upstanding citizens—fragile women in shock—they were treated with deference. And besides, how could either possibly be capable of something so heinous?

But if not them, then who?

As the investigation continued, certain facts about Lizzie surfaced that cast doubt on her innocence. A local pharmacist reported that she had recently tried to purchase prussic acid, a lethal poison used to kill rats. When he refused to sell it to her, she stormed out of his store. Under intensive questioning, Lizzie changed her story frequently. At first she was here, then she was there—the constant flip-flopping made the authorities suspicious.

When she was arrested and officially charged with the murders, the townspeople went into an uproar. They couldn't believe it; but then again, maybe they could. Lizzie was always a strange bird. The ensuing trial was every bit as big in its day as O. J. Simpson's was in ours. Lizzie spared no expense in her defense, spending thousands of dollars on Boston's best lawyers. And they did their job. Presented with only circumstantial evidence, the jury deliberated for just one hour before returning a verdict of "not guilty." It's understandable. They all had doubts.

But if not Lizzie, then who?

No other arrest was ever made. The murders remain unsolved to this day. The house was meticulously restored by new owners and opened as a bed-and-breakfast museum on August 4, 1996—the 104th anniversary of the killings. You can sit at the dinner table where the family ate their last breakfast. You can browse through Lizzie's room and see many of her personal possessions. You can have your photo taken on the divan where Andrew Borden was found. And you can even sleep in the bed that Abby Borden was making when she was struck dead.

That's the room I've reserved—the John Morse Guestroom. It's a perennial pick for Halloween lists of the creepiest places to stay. Supposedly, the entire house is haunted and on certain days of the year—like the anniversary of the murders, full moons, and Friday the 13th—the spirits become more active. Of course, I'm skeptical of all this. But if there's a place that deserves to be spooked, then this is it. And if there's a guy who deserves to be worried, then he's me.

Fortunately, the drive to Fall River is without incident. In fact, it's pleasant. The day is sunny and cool, and traffic is surprisingly courteous. Maybe everyone is being a little more careful given what date it is. Since it's too early to check in, we visit the headquarters of the Fall River Historical Society. The keepers of this restored mansion claim it contains "the largest and most important collection of artifacts relating to the life and trial of Miss Borden." And they're not exaggerating. An entire room is filled with memorabilia. There's the head of the hatchet that may have done the damage. There are pillow shams from the bedroom where Abby was murdered. There's the braided hairpiece she was wearing when attacked. There's an original copy of the $5,000 reward that Lizzie and Emma posted. And most fascinating of all, there are the skulls of Andrew and Abby, which were used as evidence in the trial. The huge holes in each convey the viciousness of the murders. To be able to shatter bone like that required strength fueled by rare fury. This was no crime of happenstance. This was a crime of vindictiveness and hatred.

As I look at all this stuff, I feel myself getting drawn into the debate, wondering if and why and who. It's been going on for more than a hundred years and likely will continue. There's been a made-for-TV movie starring Elizabeth Montgomery. There have been documentary specials produced by A&E, Discovery, and the History Channel. There was even a popular Broadway show tune: "You Can't Chop Your Papa Up in Massachusetts."

There's a subtle creepiness to this town, as if there were barely discernible organ music playing in the background. It reminds me of a scene from one of my favorite movies, *Blue Velvet*. A guy is watering his suburban lawn. There's the pleasant chat-chat-chat of the sprinkler, the giggles of children, the prettiness of the azaleas. . . . Then the camera slowly pans down into the ground and you see the worms and the bugs and the ugliness that exist just a few inches below it all.

It's the same thing here in Fall River. On the surface, everything is prim and proper. The people are polite. The summer sprinklers are on. But beneath this veneer is astonishing ugliness. This room is filled with proof that it exists, that it can surface again, and that anyone can be its victim.

There's a boy in my neighborhood named Eric. I love him, because he's had a lot of misfortune. And he's only eight. Other kids have skinned knees at his age; Eric already has scars on his heart. His parents are divorced, but when they occasionally try to get together on his behalf there's inevitably alcohol, arguing, and fighting. He hangs out at our house. He rides his bike over to see me.

A few weeks ago, I mentioned this trip. His eyes grew wide when I told him the story of Lizzie Borden and what she supposedly did.

"Yeah, I saw a show on TV about that once," he said, nodding his head. "But my dad made me turn if off."

And that's when I saw it. Beneath his innocent face was a dark thought. He had glimpsed the way out and a part of him liked it. He was imagining hammering his parents to bits while they were cursing and fighting. He was sensing how good it would feel to finally let his frustration and rage boil over—to get their attention and make them listen. I heard the chat-chat-chat of the sprinklers, the giggles of my kids upstairs in the house, and realized it's in all of us. And that's why it's so fascinating and frightening when it gets out.

Maria and I sit around a quiet fountain in the mansion's courtyard. I look at my reflection in the water and toss in a pebble. It's supposed to disturb a calm spirit. I reach down into the pool and pick out a penny that's tails-up—another precursor of bad luck. I yawn deeply without covering my mouth, thus giving my soul an escape route. And when I sneeze, I cut Maria off before she can say, "God bless you."

On our way to lunch, we stop to kiss over a gate, which is supposed to be another way of jinxing a relationship. Something about building fences. And I step on an anthill, grinding the little buggers into oblivion, so bad luck will reign.

The waitress in the restaurant looks harried. She overfills a water glass and confuses our orders. "I didn't start out having a bad day," she says, apologizing, "until I realized it was Friday the 13th."

Maria and I exchange knowing smiles. That's it, isn't it? If you fear that misfortune will come, you're already doomed. The mind fulfills its own prophecies. But if you remain optimistic, then you won't be affected. Maybe the secret to being courageous is just being positive.

"What time is it?" I ask, suddenly remembering.

"Ten after one."

"Aw, man, we need to get out of here *right now*."

"Why? What's going on?"

"In three minutes it'll be 13:13:13. Give me your compact."

"My compact? What for?"

I grab the little makeup mirror from Maria and hustle her out the door.

"What time is it now?"

"One twelve. Look, what are you doing? People are looking."

"Do me a favor and start counting once it's 1:13."

I look for a suitable spot—a window ledge, a concrete bench, a big rock, the corner of that step.

"One, two, three . . . "

I squat down. Maria was right. People at the window tables are watching us curiously.

"Seven, eight, nine . . . "

Almost time. I open the compact. Look at myself in the glass.

"Eleven, twelve, *thirteen!*"

I smash it against the step again and again, shattering the glass.

"What are you doing? That's my compact!"

The superstition that breaking a mirror brings seven years' bad luck has two origins. One stems from the fact that mirrors were once rare and valuable objects that could be repaired only at great expense. So to encourage more care, someone invented a good scare. It was especially effective with children. The other has to do with the belief that the image in a mirror is a reflection of the soul, just like your face in a quiet pond. Shatter it and part of you disintegrates. And to do so at 13:13:13 on the 13th day of the month is the most onerous.

"You're crazy, you know," says Maria, but this time she's serious.

We pick up the shards together and throw them in a wastebasket.

"You don't really believe in this stuff, do you?" I ask.

"I didn't think I did. But breaking a mirror—that's a big one."

We walk slowly back up the Hill, in silence.

There's one more thing I have to do: Visit the Oak Grove Cemetery, where the Borden family is buried. It's only a few blocks from the Historical Society, but it's vast (47 acres). We wander for half an hour before finally noticing the white arrows painted on the walkways. Evidently, we're not the only ones who come looking for the graves.

A 15-foot-tall cement monument marks the spot, with A. J. BORDEN embossed in stern letters across the bottom. It's a suitable memorial for a man of his stature. The particulars are carved on either side: the years of his birth and death, and similar statistics for his children and wives. But there's no mention of how he died, no quote to sum up his 70-year life, no hint of the attention his unfortunate family brought upon

153

their community. Nearby are two squat grave markers, set in the ground so the names face upward (toward Heaven?): Lizbeth, as Lizzie preferred to be called, is next to Emma, her sister. There are no candles or bouquets, just a patch of worn earth and some flowering clover growing unassumingly. Indeed, Lizzie's plot looks remarkably innocent, like she's resting peacefully—like she didn't do it.

I stand on her grave and spit. I figure if this doesn't piss her off, then her ghost must no longer exist—if it ever did.

Although not as quiet as Oak Grove, downtown Fall River is every bit as funereal. Its main thoroughfare is perched high above the river and walled by reddish brown brick buildings built in the 1800s. It's as if the whole town were rusting, like the hulls of the cargo ships moored below it. There aren't any Eddie Bauer outlets or Gap stores on this New England Main Street. Instead there's Facchiano's Shoe Repair, Bill Aguirre's World of Self-Defense, and Pawtucket Pawn Brokers. From their open doors leaks the smell of damp carpet, mothballs, and lost prosperity.

Maria and I squat on the steps of a church, as I try to light three cigarettes with the same match. It's a superstition that stems from the Boer War, when British soldiers learned that such thriftiness enabled Dutch snipers to pick them off. Since I don't smoke, lighting even one cigarette is challenge enough.

"Do you notice anything strange about this place?" asks Maria, taking a puff and making a face.

"What, besides just general weirdness?"

"There aren't any children. Up on the Hill, downtown, I haven't seen any."

She's right. It's the middle of July, and I've yet to spot even one kid pedaling a bike or a mother pushing a stroller. What's going on here? What does it do to the soul of a town when the thing it's most renowned for is an unsolved, double ax murder? What kind of pallor does that cast over the citizens, let alone the chamber of commerce?

I know I wouldn't want to live here.

Four o'clock.

Time to check in.

But the famous Lizzie Borden House looks disappointing. The photos in the brochure were expertly cropped so as to block out a bus station across the street, plus a print shop and beauty parlor immediately adjacent. Big Greyhounds maneuver and wheeze just a few yards from the front door, and many of the passengers they swallow and discharge look like potential ax murderers themselves. Perhaps it would be more harrowing to spend the night in the terminal.

I press the doorbell two or three times, examining the home's nondescript brown shutters and tan siding, before I hear some deadbolts sliding.

"May I help you?" asks a pleasant woman in her fifties.

"Yes, we're the Kitas. We have reservations for tonight."

"Oh yes, the Kitas. Come in. My name is Eleanor. You're the first guests to arrive. And if I remember correctly, you're in the murder room. Right?"

"Uh, right."

"Yes," she says, checking her book. "You reserved the John Morse Guestroom. That's where Abby was killed. Such a shame. Come along, I'll show you to it."

We grab our bags and follow Eleanor up to the second floor, past a sign on the landing that warns: "Low ceiling. Be careful. We've already had two serious head injuries here." Well, at least they have a sense of humor.

Eleanor guides us matter-of-factly, as if she were a Hilton bellman and ours were just another routine check-in. She opens the door to a small room that overlooks the bus terminal. It's decorated as it would have been in the late 1800s—dark, heavy furniture; flowery carpeting; patterned wallpaper. It looks comfortable and cheery, although a bit noisy—a typical room in any Victorian-era bed-and-breakfast in America. But there are a few notable differences. In the corner behind the door is the green velour dress that Elizabeth Montgomery wore when she played Lizzie in that made-for-TV movie. And hanging on the wall between the bed and dresser is a black-and-white photograph of Abby as police found her after the murder. She's facedown on the ground in a white housedress, with blood pooling from what's left of her head. She appears to be kneeling or, perhaps more precisely, saying her prayers. The perspective is such that while you're looking at the photo, you're in the exact same position Abby was in when the killer snuck up behind her.

Eleanor taps me on the shoulder.

"This room doesn't have a private bath," she says. "You'll be sharing the one in the hall with the guests next door. And don't forget about tonight's tour. Meet downstairs at 7:00. I'll answer all your questions. There will be snacks afterward. If there's anything else you need, just holler."

She leaves without giving us a key, a crucifix, a string of garlic, or anything else to fend off evil spirits. Just holler, she says, evidently forgetting that approach failed the Bordens.

I kill time by clipping my fingernails, which you're never supposed to do on Friday. Then I open the window and scatter the parings outside, daring a witch to collect them and put a curse on me. As I try to whistle and piss at the same time (another harbinger of bad luck), I look at the Lizzie Borden towels hanging in the bathroom. They're available for purchase (the card says) in the gift shop. They sport little bloody hatchets.

Since the tour is still hours away, I decide to take a nap. The sheets are wonderfully fresh, which is a good sign because a bed changed on Friday supposedly brings bad dreams. And as I lie there, I sing. Not because I'm happy, but because of what it's supposed to bring:

Sing while eating
Or sing in bed,
Evil will get you
And you'll be dead.

I drift off. I hear buses coming and going, the rest of the guests checking in, Eleanor talking on the phone, Maria turning the pages of her book and clearing her throat. . . . But it's all in the distance, enveloped in a gauzy thickness. I'm aware, but I'm not totally here. Is this what it feels like to be a ghost?

And with that crystalline thought, I wake up. Eyes wide, head clear, as if I'd been dozing for minutes not—two hours!

"You're never going to be able to sleep tonight," says Maria.

"Why didn't you wake me?"

"You were sleeping like the dead."

Indeed, I feel dangerously refreshed. What a condition to be in heading into a long night in a haunted house. I'll be lying in bed, worrying over every little sound. Maybe this is part of Lizzie's plan: Keep me up and slowly drive me nuts.

Eleanor is waiting for us in the parlor, as are six other guests. There's a middle-age daughter and her elderly mother, who live about 30 minutes from Fall River. They're staying in Lizzie's room, which is right next to ours, and sharing the bathroom. On the couch watching a video about the murders is a family from Brooklyn—mother, father, and two kids about eight and 11. The youngest looks worried, although he's trying not to show it. They're staying in Abby and Andrew's suite at the rear of the second floor. One other couple has yet to show. In fact, they haven't even called, and Eleanor is getting nervous. That's reassuring. In a place like this, you need someone counting heads.

The house itself is a maze. Although it looks small from the outside, it has 17 rooms. On the first floor, there's a kitchen, dining room, parlor, and sitting room. The last is where the second murder occurred. In fact, the settee where Andrew was found looks remarkably like the original. We all take turns lying there like the dead man and snapping photos. Meanwhile, Eleanor sets the stage.

"The Borden family wasn't feeling too well that morning," she explains. "The house had no refrigeration, and the mutton they ate for dinner the previous night might have turned. Andrew, Abby, and Uncle John Morse just picked at their breakfasts here in the dining room, while Lizzie didn't even come downstairs. That was not unusual for her, though. She generally avoided her stepmother, whom she disliked, and often slept late. Afterward, the maid went outside to clean the windows, and Andrew and Uncle John left on business."

Eleanor motions the group up the stairs to our room and explains the scenario, going so far as to act out the actual murder by swinging an imaginary ax over her head. "That famous ditty, 'Lizzie Borden took an ax and gave her mother 40 whacks' isn't accurate," she points out. "Those who did the autopsy estimated Abby only got hit about 18 times. Underneath the carpet where she fell, the wood floor is still stained with blood. We've scrubbed and scrubbed, but it doesn't come out."

In Lizzie's room, there's a collection of her books and other belongings. It's fascinating to look at them, to try to see into her mind, to imagine her lying on the fainting couch afterward, struggling to regain her composure. Then there's Emma's room, which is much smaller and back still farther. It was empty that day because she was on holiday. An ironclad alibi.

"Some people say Lizzie hid the dress she was wearing in Emma's closet," continues Eleanor. "In that day and age, the police wouldn't dare go into a young lady's wardrobe. The dress was specked with blood, and they say Lizzie eventually burned it in the stove."

Back even farther is the Bordens' bedroom. It now has a private bath and a separate air conditioner. It's the most spacious and expensive room to rent and is connected to the kitchen below by a narrow, winding staircase. As we look around and Eleanor rambles on, the boy from Brooklyn disappears for a few seconds and returns with a half-empty bottle of vodka.

"Where did you get that?" exclaims his mother.

"I found it under my bed."

Eleanor is equally perturbed. "I'll have to speak to the help about this," she says.

With the booze in her hand, she leads us up to the third floor. This is where the tardy couple will be staying, if they ever get here. Actually, I'm beginning to doubt their existence. Maybe they're a seed that's been planted so comfort will sprout when we hear strange voices and creaking hinges later this evening.

The Bordens' maid lived up here in this small, well-appointed room with a severely sloping ceiling. It's warm and stuffy, about what you'd expect from a converted attic. After the murder trial, the maid fled and was never heard from again. It was all too horrific.

Down a narrow walkway on the same floor is a bigger room that's used for storage now. "Damn light bulbs are always burning out," complains Eleanor, flicking the switch. "I can't tell you how often we have to change them in this place. It's so strange."

We all peer into the room, giving our eyes time to adjust.

"What's that?" asks the boy, pointing to some dark stain on a plaster pillar.

"We don't know what that is," says Eleanor. "We wash it off, and it keeps coming back. Some workmen took a look and said it was water dripping down from the roof."

"It looks like blood," says the boy.

"Yes, it does, doesn't it?" Eleanor replies.

I begin wondering if she'd part with the vodka.

"Actually, there are two ghosts we sometimes see up here," she adds. "They're children, about you and your sister's age. Supposedly, they were killed at the house next door. Their mother threw them down the well. Some guests say they hear them crying or see them walking around up here."

Silence. The boy's eyes are as wide as nickels.

Back in the kitchen, munching on cookies shaped like miniature hatchets (complete with red icing tips), it's time for some blunt questions.

"So Eleanor, do *you* think Lizzie did it?"

"No, I don't," she says, in a matter-of-fact tone. "We had a couple of psychics stay here at different times, and they both reached the same conclusion. They saw two men arguing right here in the kitchen. One hit the other, dragged him over to the couch, and finished him off. Few people know this, but Andrew had an illegitimate son named

Billy. He was never questioned in connection with the murders, but he later hung himself. I think that's who did it."

"Have you ever *seen* anything weird?"

"Sure, lots of times. I was sitting over there in the parlor once—right in that chair, waiting for guests to arrive—when I saw smoke coming out of the kitchen. At first I thought there was a fire, that I'd left something on the stove, but then I realized it wasn't that kind of smoke at all. It was a thick white mist, and it was very deliberate. It moved along the ceiling, into the sitting room, and hung right above where they found Mr. Borden.

"On other occasions I've heard footsteps overhead even though I know there's no one in the house," she continues. "And sometimes I feel this presence, as if someone is here with me. I can't describe it any better than that. But there's no doubt in my mind that there's someone here."

"How about the guests? Have *they* ever seen anything?"

"Some people sure want to," says Eleanor, smiling. "They come here on Friday the 13th, like you all did, or August 4, the day of the murders. That date is booked out years in advance. Some people even sleep on the floor in the exact spot where Abby was found. I'll never forget one couple who swore their bed lifted off the ground. They packed their bags and checked out in the middle of the night."

"What room were they in?" I ask hesitantly.

"Why, the John Morse Guestroom. The same one as you."

I want to be skeptical, to think positive. I want to be like the boy's father, who has left all this nonsense and is now in the living room watching Jay Leno. I want to be able to say to Maria, "Sure, let's take that Ouija board down from the shelf and dare it to speak." But I can't. I've broken more than 40 superstitions today, and as the night settles in deeper and these ghost stories become creepier, I could use a shot of that liquor.

Finally, after there's nothing left to talk about, after we've delayed the inevitable as long as possible, we all climb the stairs to our respective rooms.

Except the boy from Brooklyn. He's hanging back.

"Come on," says his mother. "It was *your* idea to come here."

It's interesting to observe the fascination children have with fear. Whether it's movies, books, or Halloween, part of them wants to be scared at the same time another part doesn't. It's like being tickled. There's delight in the fright. Perhaps it's their way of learning about fear, of gradually coming to know the difference between what's real and imagined. It's a knack that takes continual practice. But as we mature, society convinces us that fear is a weakness, and we stop exploring it. Sure, we may still go to horror movies and read Stephen King novels, but we no longer engage fear like we used to. And as a result, we lose our perspective. Instead of flinching and then giggling when someone says, "Boo!" we slide further into our cocoons.

The John Morse Guestroom seems far less safe and pleasant than it did this afternoon. I try turning on a little desk lamp as a nightlight, but the damn bulb is burned out. And the door has no deadbolt. So I feel my way into bed and lie with my wife in the blackness. All I can think about is being less than two feet from where a woman was brutally murdered. Her blood and pieces of her head must have splattered this bed. The walls and furniture were witnesses.

"You awake, Maria?"

"Yes."

"Do you think we'll be okay?"

"Sure, it's just a ghost story."

"Love you, dear."

"Love you, too."

This is how it all ends, doesn't it? This is how we're destined to spend forever, lying side by side on our backs, man and wife, six feet below ground.

The incessant beep of the alarm clock is six inches from my right ear. It gets increasingly louder.

Seven A.M., Saturday the 14th.

I'm still here . . . and nothing happened.

Nothing.

I am at once tremendously relieved and deeply disappointed—like I somehow didn't get my money's worth. Not one weird sound, not a single nightmare, not even a sizeable goose bump. I slept soundly, and so did Maria. And as far as I can tell, there's nothing overturned or missing in the room. No sign of an intruder.

I almost can't believe it. I stuck my tongue out at fate, dared it to come get me, taunted the biggest of all bullies, and it didn't so much as look at me. This is what it must be like to walk away from a plane crash. Somehow, I got lucky.

I lie awake in bed for a long time, thankful.

But then a fresh thought, as bright as the sun streaming through the window: Maybe fate is setting me up. Maybe it has a cunning plan to get even. Since time is of no consequence to it, maybe the stalking will take decades. Its revenge will be my nervous waiting for a new ax to fall. And one thing is certain: Sooner or later, misfortune *will* come—something *will* happen to either me or someone I love. And then I'll know whom to blame. Then I'll wonder if it could have been avoided had I not fooled with this.

If fate is anything, it's devious. It twists.

I better start making amends right now. I better commence pacifying the devil.

I throw the covers aside, slide my feet onto the floor and, very deliberately, get up on the *right* side of bed.

9

Change

TRYING TO GET FAT

I'm sorry.

Somehow

I got sidetracked.

The wrath of God. The fiendishness of Beelzebub. What was I thinking? Although I respect what each represents, neither is the one, true source of my fear. That much is clear. Rather, I need to go back to something I learned earlier about conceit—about how we can manufacture fear by thinking we matter, about how paranoid we can become protecting this grandiose image of ourselves.

Think of it this way: Our ego is like a Tinkertoy scaffold. The older we get, the bigger and more intricate it becomes. But at the same time, it grows more fragile. It teeters. We realize that despite our best efforts to prop it up, it lacks integrity. To our credit as architects, most of us make it through our entire lives without it collapsing. But it makes for a stressful, scrambling, look-over-the-shoulder existence.

What I need to do is knock the foundation out from what I've built, from what I'm most proud of. I need to challenge my very ego, my own façade of self-importance, the image I present to the world. This is different from humiliation or rejection. You can rebuild after embarrassment or eviction. What I'm talking about is removing the key piece of what holds me together, of sending the whole thing crashing down, in order to see what's left. It should either be the root of my fear or just the ruins of what I am not.

So rather than look toward authority or evil for the answer, I need to examine something far more banal. Like, for instance, a hot dog.

That's right, a hot dog.

I haven't eaten one in 15 years.

To be honest, it scares me. Not so much what it's made of, but what it represents. In it, I see me as a fat man.

When I was a senior in college, I weighed 200 pounds. I had no concept of exercise or nutrition. I thought cholesterol was an arena in Philadelphia where the Big Five played basketball. I ate whatever I wanted, whenever I wanted, in whatever quantities were available. And in particular, I ate hot dogs. A typical lunch was five with chili and cheese from Potts Doggie Shop in Bethlehem. I'd eat them in my car, with a carton of iced tea, in less than 15 minutes. And I'd visit three or four times per week.

But after graduation, I eventually took a job with health-and-fitness publisher Rodale Press. Everyone there was lean and organic. I started feeling guilty about sitting in my office eating a submarine sandwich when the lunchtime sign-out board was filled with people running, cycling, and visiting the co-op. This lifestyle began to infect and change me. I learned that hot dogs are essentially made of waste products (hearts, kidneys, livers, and assorted muscle tissue). Each one of those chili-cheese dogs had 426 calories, 27 grams of fat, and 1,100 milligrams of sodium. No wonder I had barely pulled a C in my postlunch economics class.

Almost 20 years later, I weigh 165 pounds, have run marathons, and prefer soy milk with my granola. I have become obsessive about health. I know my blood-lipid levels, body-fat percentage, blood pressure, bone density, resting heart rate . . . Every two years, I travel cross-country and pay $700 for a high-tech CT scan that lets me look inside my body to see if any tumors, polyps, or plaque is forming. So far, I'm relatively clean. I'm not planning on dying by my own doing.

Along the way, fat has come to symbolize everything I do not want to be. It is my mortal enemy. Every morning I step on my bathroom scale to assess the war. If the needle is creeping upward, I know I must immediately adopt evasive maneuvers—cut out the cookies at lunch, refuse all second helpings, go for a long run. As I've gotten older, the battle has escalated. As my metabolism naturally slows, I've become even more vigilant about what I put into my mouth.

Why do I do it? Obviously to feel good, live long, and remain young. At 42, I'm in better shape than most men half my age. A few years ago, for another book, I tried out for my high-school basketball team and made it. I kicked some adolescent ass. This healthful lifestyle of mine is not just how I make a living, it's who I am as a human being. It's the example I set for my kids, the spark in my marriage, my very self-worth. It is an obsession to be sure, but one that imparts measurable rewards. The denial and self-control can even be fun. I like being the boss, if only of a hot dog in a bun.

But there's another reason I do it, one that's more difficult to admit. I'm afraid of getting fat. Obesity and its relatives (diabetes and heart disease) run in my family. I know the shame of wheezing atop a single flight of stairs, of growing out of my pants, of having a girlfriend pat my belly instead of my abs and laugh. Once, I spent three days with a 600-pound man named Kevin Miller. He's so big he got stuck in an amusement-park turnstile. His life pendulums between challenge and mortification. I got the sense that if he were ever diagnosed with a fatal disease that would cause him to waste away, some part of him would secretly be relieved. (I'll introduce you to him later.)

For me, the terrifying irony of getting fat is this: At the same time there would be more of me, there would also be less. I'd lose the person I'm comfortable with, the skin that fits me so well. My kids would lose their father, my wife her husband, my life its focus. It's a twisted perception, I know. How my body looks should have no influence on what I am. Appearance and health should not determine moral worth. But it does. We all know that.

The fear of getting fat is second only to the fear of public speaking in this country. In fact, it ranks significantly higher than even the fear of death. So what would happen, physically and psychologically, if I stopped exercising and returned to my old way of eating? What would result if I suddenly turned my back on nearly 20 years of healthful living? What if I removed this key support right here and deliberately tried to get fat?

I feel strangely free. While driving to work I spot a billboard advertising the new Wendy's Bacon Double-Swiss Burger and realize I can have one, or three. DoubleStuf Oreos, french fries, Häagen Dazs, nacho-cheese Doritos . . . the ban has been lifted. Make no mistake; I love to eat. It's just that I've been ordering off a different menu for the past two decades. Instead of steak, I get the tuna cooked medium rare. Instead of blue-cheese dressing, I dribble a little balsamic on my salad. Rather than white rice, pasta, and breads, I buy the whole-wheat versions. But I do miss all those other less-healthful foods. There's a Pizza Hut I run by almost every day at lunch. It smells *so good*. I want to stop, to gorge myself, to suck the cheese out of the stuffed crust, but I keep running—always. I'm one dedicated son of a bitch.

Today is going to be different, though. I won't be exercising. Instead I'll be driving to Potts for the food I'm most nostalgic about. You would think I was planning a lunchtime tryst with Lola from accounts-receivable—my anticipation is that palpable. In fact, this is just the beginning: today chili dogs, tomorrow a Big Mac, the day after that a Cinnabon, and on Friday the Pizza Hut lunch buffet. The possibilities are endless. Temptation is about to become indulgence.

Strangely, I feel no fear. While I dread the result, it looks like I'm going to enjoy the process. No doubt one reason obesity is so prevalent (affecting about 60 percent of Americans) is because it's extremely pleasurable getting there. In that respect, it's no different from developing lung cancer by smoking cigarettes or AIDS by having unprotected sex. It's tough to say no to all the savory morsels when the end fear is so distant.

I haven't set a time limit for this. I'm going to keep eating and not exercising until I either explode or go nuts. I honestly don't know if I'll last a week, a month, or whether I'll have so much fun I won't want to stop. Maybe fat is really where I'm at. To objectively gauge my "progress," I record my starting weight, fat percentage, waist/hip/thigh measurements, flexibility, strength, blood pressure, cholesterol level, plus resting and exercising heart rates. I plan to weigh myself weekly and redo all these measurements after one month. And to make sure I stay committed, I've waited until the season of excess—that ham-gobbling, nog-swigging, kiffle-crunching time between Thanksgiving and New Year's. I wonder if the local fire company has found anyone yet to play Santa?

But I digress. It's almost noon. It's time for Potts.

It's exactly as I remember it—three steps up to a little shop on West Fairview Avenue, where three middle-age women work in synchronized precision. One puts the hot dogs on the grill, rolling them periodically until they're browned. Another prepares the rolls, painting them with mustard, ketchup, or onions. And the third calls out the orders, wraps the finished product, and collects the amount owed. The real art, though, lies with the griller as she creates the signature chili-cheese dog. She first slices it length-wise, then squirts in a generous line of Easy Cheese (straight from the can). After letting it melt for no more than 10 seconds, she nestles it cheese-side down into the bun and ladles on the sauce. I'm salivating as I watch this, and wondering whether I'm getting misty from the aroma of diced onions or from fond remembrance.

I take the three I ordered back to my car and notice that this lunch passes the Homer Simpson test: It has already stained the package. The first bite is heaven. Bits of onion crunching in my teeth, the bite of the yellow mustard, the gritty taste of the chili (which, incidentally, is made from old hot dogs withered on the grill), the pillow-soft feel of the bun, and the drip of the Easy Cheese down my arm. It's luscious. I wolf the first one, thinking I could eat five of these, no problem. But then the unexpected happens. I become satiated. Content. I eat the second one, but it's not as enjoyable. And the third, well, I could have done without it. I feel strangely unfulfilled, as if I were lying in bed next to a naked, exhausted Lola, but (damn!) it just wasn't that good. The anticipation, the first kiss, was better than the climax.

Midway through the afternoon, I visit the company cafeteria in search of some milk to settle my stomach. But old habits die hard. I buy skim without even realizing it.

Kevin Miller hands his admission ticket to the cheery woman at Paramount's Kings Island amusement park near Cincinnati. He has successfully herded his class of nearly a hundred middle-school band kids through the turnstiles and now he's next. "Have a great day!" the woman says. He smiles nervously, takes a deep breath, and begins to push through. There's a click and then, nothing. He sucks his gut in some more, but to no avail. He can't budge. He's stuck.

"C'mon, Mr. Miller!" his students scream. "We want to ride the roller coaster."

"Move it, hippo hips!" yells someone at the back of the line.

"Oh my!" says the flustered ticket taker. "I'd better get the manager."

And they scurry around him like Lilliputians, poking and tugging, but most of all gawking at this trapped giant who has suddenly become the park's main attraction. For a half-hour he stands there sweating in the mid-morning sun, wishing he could melt away, until a mechanic arrives to disassemble the turnstile and set him free—if only temporarily. Because this afternoon, tomorrow, and each day thereafter will continue to be filled with embarrassment, frustration, and impending disaster.

Chairs that must be inspected before sitting, narrow bathroom stalls that prevent him from peeing, closely parked cars that postpone his leaving, stores with skinny aisles in which he'll never browse, theater seats with armrests, restaurants with booths, seat belts, bathtubs, commuter jets, and everywhere stairs and more stares.

For 39 years, Miller has been what 45 percent of Americans fear becoming: fat. He's so big he no longer even knows how much he weighs. (The only scale that can hold him is used for laundry at the local hospital.) He estimates he's approaching 600 pounds. Most of this fat is carried between navel and knees, giving his 6-foot frame a tottering, Humpty Dumpty shape. His waist is a staggering 74 inches, making him bigger around than most people are tall.

In his hometown of Clendenin, West Virginia, he is the freak you don't have to pay to see. He appears Monday through Friday at Elkview Middle School as the music teacher, band director, and computer specialist. On Saturdays you might find him shopping at Kroger's or having a nonfat frozen yogurt with his wife and son at Dairy Queen. And on Sunday mornings he's at the Advent Christian Church playing piano and singing, perhaps too hopefully, the hymn: "Jesus Has Lifted Me."

Could that ever be me?

My car smells like chili dogs for days. I apologize to whoever rides with me. (No, that's not lipstick on my collar, dear; it's ketchup.) Word of my endeavor spreads fast, especially around the office, and everyone is eager to assist. One morning there's a box of doughnuts near the mailboxes and this sign: IT'S OFFER-JOE-A-DONUT DAY! FOUR BY FOUR O'CLOCK, 20 POUNDS BY NEW YEAR'S. GO! GO! GO! Women have a particularly pressing urge to feed me. They bring in candy, homemade cookies, leftovers from luncheons. It must be the mothering instinct. Maybe they've long thought me scrawny and are now jumping on the opportunity. Or maybe there's a more selfish motive at work. Perhaps they want me fat and out of shape so I'm less of a reminder to them. In other words, they're trying to break the mirror of comparison. After catching me eating a tuna-fish sandwich ("It has full-fat mayo, I swear!"), one coworker threatens to draft

169

a schedule where everyone rotates the responsibility of taking me to lunch. "We want you at McDonald's, Burger King, Taco Bell . . . every day! No excuses! It's obvious you can't be trusted."

My plump mother is delighted by my new lifestyle, if only because she can cook for me again. I stopped eating at her house years ago for a number of reasons. First, she considers Crisco the foundation of the food pyramid. Second, she's so eager to feed me that the various courses are served machine-gun style. (Dinner takes approximately 15 minutes.) Third, whenever she cooks meat she insists on "boiling the scum off it," which makes even the finest cuts of poultry and beef taste like indoor-outdoor carpet. Finally, she's big on simmering things. I'll call at 10:00 A.M. to confirm a dinner at 5:00 that evening, and she'll already be warming the chicken potpie.

But she's been vindicated now. Her wayward boy has come home, desiring some of Mom's comfort food. And in celebration, she lays out an impressive spread. There's lasagna, crab cakes, stuffed chicken breasts and, for dessert, a mail-order cheesecake so heavy it belongs on a dumbbell rack. "You should have seen the shipping-and-handling charge for that," she says proudly, dropping it onto the table. The impact makes the silverware rattle.

By 5:15, I'm comatose on her sofa—my stomach so overwhelmed by the influx of food that it has summoned all the blood from my head and limbs to help digest it. "You looked good when you were fat," my mother says, as if talking to me through a fog. "I'll put some meat on those bones. When are you coming over next?"

I have no recollection of how I got home.

Indeed, it seems the entire world suddenly wants to feed me, to stuff me like a turkey. Billboards, television commercials, grocery stores, restaurants, drive-thru windows, super-sizing options, buy-one-get-one-free coupons . . . there's just *so much food*. I want to open my mouth and scream, but I'm afraid someone will push in something filled with cream.

 The reaction strangers typically have to Miller is amazement followed by some degree of disgust. His gift, if you can call it that, is making everyone he meets feel closer to perfect. They look at him—a slow-moving, heavy-breathing, bespectacled fat man—and smugly congratulate themselves for not being that lazy and lacking in self-respect. Most people give no thought to the everyday enormity of what Miller must face beyond his very self.

Life becomes so challenging when you're obese that most of the spontaneity is squeezed out of it. Every action, no matter how minor, requires careful consideration and planning. Miller's brain is a crane operator's, delicately maneuvering a heavy, awkward load from one place to another. "All the things ordinary people do without thinking, I *have* to think about," he says. "It's the only way to avoid constant humiliation." For example . . .

Going to the bathroom: The regular-size toilets in Miller's home have no lids. He removed them to gain a few extra inches of sitting room. In public, he'll use the handicapped stall or just not go. "I try to case the place beforehand," he says. "If the bathroom is the size of a closet, I won't drink for eight hours ahead of time."

Bathing: Miller can't squeeze into a normal-size bathtub. In fact, when making hotel reservations, he has to request bigger facilities. At home he uses a "garden tub," which is a third larger than average and has a detachable showerhead. "Because fat people have a reputation for being sweaty, I'm paranoid about being clean."

Putting on pants: Since he can't balance on one leg, he has to sit on the edge of the bathtub, put both legs into his trousers, stand, and then pull up.

Bending over: "The problem isn't my belly, it's my knees," he explains. "Stooping to pick something up is like doing a 600-pound deadlift. I usually have to ask my wife to tie my shoes."

Walking: On pleasant West Virginia evenings, Miller doesn't reach for his wife's hand and suggest a stroll. It's challenging to walk 50 yards without stopping, difficult to complete a shopping trip to Wal-Mart without sitting, and impossible to mow his half-acre lawn in one afternoon.

Sitting: "The first thing I do when I walk into someone's home is look around for something that can hold me," he says. "I'm simply trying to protect their furniture and my dignity."

Sleeping: Miller has a waterbed because it supports him better than a conventional mattress. But he can sleep only on his side or back. "I can't get comfortable on my stomach."

Making love: Forethought is more important than foreplay. He must be careful never to rest too much weight on his partner, and he has to make sure he's on a stable surface. Other than that, it's both possible and enjoyable.

Driving: Miller prefers a van because it has big windows with lots of visibility, and a sliding door that can serve as an emergency entrance if other cars park too near. His biggest fear about driving, though, is the airbag. "I'm so close that if it goes off, it'll probably kill me," he says. "I'm sure they didn't have crash-test dummies my size."

Shopping for clothes: Miller buys most of his wardrobe from big-and-tall mail-order catalogs. Because of the extra material involved, underwear costs $20, pants $75, and an ordinary black suit $450. "You find yourself wearing things much longer than you should because the cost of replacement is so high," he says.

Eating out: He rarely goes to restaurants because of the stir that occurs. When he enters the Ponderosa Steakhouse and requests a table (never a booth), silverware stops clattering, forks pause in midair, and a look of apprehension settles on the lone girl behind the buffet bar. "Just once," he says, "I'd like to eat in public without being watched."

Flying: He can't afford two seats, so he reserves an aisle seat and hopes the plane isn't full. Before he can fasten his seat belt, he has to ask for a special extender, and when that "tiny meal" is served, he must eat it off his stomach rather than the unusable fold-down tray. If the person in front reclines his seat, Miller suffers in silence. "When you're fat, you don't want to call attention to it," he says. "You don't argue about details."

My appetite has inexplicably vanished. Despite all the tantalizing possibilities, I've lost my drive to eat. It's weird, as is the fact that even though I've been subsisting on junk food and not exercising for a week, I've only gained two measly pounds. It's as if my body is resisting this change on some rudimentary physiological level.

There's a scientific theory that may explain it. Supposedly, the body becomes accustomed to operating at a certain weight. This "set point," as it's called, is partly genetic but mostly learned. You can change your set point by modifying your eating and exercise habits, but it's very difficult. The body stubbornly clings to its usual way of doing business. This may be why it's so hard for chronically fat people to lose weight. When the body detects a drop in calories, it automatically lowers its metabolism (the rate at which food is combusted) in order to maintain that set point. So even though they're on a strict diet, they're unwittingly burning fewer calories. Such is the frustration of weight loss, at least for a while. Make the diet a lifestyle, and the set point will gradually reset itself.

If this theory is correct, then the opposite should also hold true: If a chronically lean person attempts to gain weight, his body should try to maintain its set point by *raising* metabolism. Therefore, even though my pockets are stuffed with Butterfinger wrappers, I may be burning more calories without even trying. In fact, researchers at the Mayo Clinic found that thin people who ingested an extra 1,000 calories per day burned as much as 600 of them through increased fidgeting. It was an adaptation they weren't aware of. Evidently, the body has many ingenious ways of protecting itself.

I'm also not enjoying these forbidden foods as much as I thought I would. Whoppers, Big Macs, Burrito Supremes . . . they all taste *different*. Instead of being this symphony of wonderful flavors, they're a disappointing drone. My initial reaction is to take them back, to argue that somebody forgot the special sauce. But no, it's right here, globs of it—on the bun, the car seat, my slacks. It's the chili dog phenomenon all over again. Apparently over the years, my taste buds have adapted to the relative lack of fat and sodium in my diet.

Here's another thing I didn't anticipate: How can I be eating so

173

much crap but not have any urge to take one? I'm so constipatded I can no longer spell it. Where is all this food going? My wife, who's a nurse, reminds me that junk food is finely processed, meaning most of the nutrients and fiber have been removed. Thus, a couple of SnoBalls has a much greater chance of being compacted than, say, a half-tray of whole-wheat fig bars, which will scour the pipes like Liquid Plumr. She recommends I relax with some Ex-Lax, but I don't want to sacrifice the weight I've gained, even if it is semitransient.

While I miss regularity (you wouldn't believe how far behind I am in my reading), I miss exercising even more. In fact, so far that's been the hardest part. It's not so much the exhilarating movement but the camaraderie of the guys I move with. There's a group of us that runs or plays basketball at lunch. We've been doing this for years. It's the conversation, the shared bitching, the good-natured ribbing that fuels us. Sitting at my desk, poking a slab of warmed-over meatloaf, watching them jog by my window, makes me feel like I've been forbidden to play with the neighborhood boys. Maybe the reason I exercise has nothing to do with staying fit or maintaining my weight. Maybe it's one of the few ways a guy my age experiences friendship.

You're probably wondering why I'm so despondent. How I can *not* be enjoying this. Why am I not holed up with my arm elbow-deep in a bucket of fried chicken, chocolate sauce on my wife-beater, take-out numbers scribbled on my thigh, and a stack of John Candy films atop the VCR? Why am I resisting living the dream?

Because it's not a dream to me.

Miller contends he is blameless for being so big. Although he admits to the occasional binge (like once swallowing 35 Reuben sandwiches in three days at a Manhattan deli), his refrigerator is filled with veggie burgers, low-fat dressing, and diet soda. "I've been fat my entire life, and I've been dieting for just about that long," he claims. "When I eat the same food everyone else does, I'm the one who gains weight."

It's tough to tell if Miller is stretching the truth. It's possible that his perception of what he ingests has been skewed by years of excess, or that he's just a gifted actor around journalists. James O. Hill, Ph.D., director of the Center for Human Nutrition at the University of Colorado Health Sciences Center, doesn't believe Miller is entirely innocent. "We've searched for about 40 years for someone who eats an extremely low number of calories a day and still gains weight," he says. "We haven't been able to find that person."

Indeed, Miller's long diet history, which includes Weight Watchers, TOPS, Richard Simmons, fen-phen, Pritikin, Slim-Fast, self-imposed hospitalization, and even a few weeks of nothing but bananas and ice, proves that when he musters the willpower to eat less, he can lose weight. The problem is keeping it off. In fact, whenever he has dropped a significant number of pounds, he has gained back almost twice as many. So consistent is the experience that he's fearful of what might happen if he diets again.

Aside from weighing more than three men, Miller has no serious health problems. He doesn't smoke or drink, and he claims that his blood pressure and cholesterol "check out." Still he worries, because there doesn't appear to be a limit to how big he could become. (Purportedly, one of the world's heaviest humans is a 1,100-pound Brooklyn man.) The reason Miller keeps rebounding ever higher is not clear. It could be the set-point theory at work, or it could just be that he has a genetic susceptibility to gaining weight that's being amplified by our food-rich culture.

Whatever the reason, Hill agrees that if Miller doesn't sustain a low-fat diet and exercise more, he could challenge that Brooklyn man for the title of world's biggest human. His alternative, Hill says, is to have his stomach surgically downsized, or stapled, a procedure Miller has resisted so far because it's "Frankenstein stuff."

Two weeks, four pounds, 169 on the scale. Okay, it's not an explosion of Brando-esque proportions, but it's progress. That equates to eight additional pounds in a month and 32 by swimsuit season.

175

My cannonball could still be devastating. All I have to do is keep eating like many Americans do. And with each passing day, I grow less tentative about that. Although the urge to do so and the enjoyment I derive from it remains stubbornly low, I'm lathering full-fat cream cheese on my bagel, asking waitresses to butter my baked potato, and continually pilfering my wife's stash of Christmas cookies. ("Who the hell ate all my fudge Jesuses?")

One thing I haven't lost my taste for is sweets. Chocolate is just as dreamy and Ben & Jerry's exactly as creamy as I remember it. This must be because I never swore off them like I did fast food. Rewarding myself with occasional nibbles must have kept those taste buds intact. When an unsuspecting Girl Scout comes to my door, I momentarily lose control and write a check for $75. Then I run after her, asking whether my Caramel deLites and Peanut Butter Patties can be FedExed.

I'm also getting a ton of work done. Because I'm no longer exercising, I can run errands at lunch and devote extra time on weekends to stalled projects. When you consider I'd been working out 10 to 12 hours per week, I've reclaimed almost half a day. I'm also noticeably less fatigued. Whereas I used to be nodding off by 9:00 P.M., now I'm still up reading at 10:00. Somehow I have *more* energy and am less achy in the mornings. I'm starting to wonder which lifestyle is really more productive.

It's surprisingly easy to live like this. It takes no effort or awareness. I no longer have to figure out when I can squeeze in a run, or which entrée on the menu will do less harm, or how I can lower my LDL cholesterol, or where I can buy fresh organic vegetables. I hadn't realized how much I'd been bucking the system. Maybe that's why I was so exhausted at the end of the day. It's so much simpler to let yourself be swept away.

And so much cheaper, too. At the local McDonald's, I can get all the cheeseburgers I want on Sundays for 39 cents apiece. How can that be? At the supermarket, white bread is cheaper than wheat, soda is significantly less expensive than juice, and ground chuck is far more economical than salmon or halibut. Who has decreed that we should pay a premium for healthful food? If anything, the crummy stuff should be taxed. The result of overindulging in it is no different than smoking or drinking too much alcohol. It should be discouraged.

But I'm talking like a skinny man again. I have to learn to keep an open mind, along with an open mouth.

Miller isn't one of those cranky, militant fat people who enjoy throwing their weight around. He refuses to become a card-carrying member of the National Association to Advance Fat Acceptance, and he didn't participate in its Million Pound March. He's a tolerant, easy-going man. But sometimes even *his* skin isn't thick enough.

Like when he interviewed for a teaching position at a local high school, and the principal ignored his eight years of experience and his five grand-champion bands and focused instead on his appearance. "He told me I didn't fit the image of the school," recalls Miller. "He didn't see my credentials. He didn't see the kids I had educated. He just saw a fat man."

Then there was the time his overweight son was being teased on the kindergarten bus, and he called the principal to intervene. But instead of asking for names, the principal asked Miller if there was a medical reason why his son was obese. "What he was saying is that it was *my* fault my boy was being abused," he explains. "Just like it's *my* fault people make fun of me. I'm supposed to be able to change. Well, I've spent my whole damn life trying to change. This is not a person who's unconcerned about his health. This is a person who's desperately trying to lose weight and be accepted. But nobody realizes that."

Miller isn't looking for pity, though. He's looking for meaning. And fortunately, he's found some in his music. The ounce of self-worth it gives him is enough to offset the pounds of sadness he carries. There was one evening in particular that he'll never forget, one night when he experienced for the first time what it's like to have people see *you* instead of the body you inhabit.

"It was the final band concert of my senior year," he recalls. "I had an alto sax solo, and I hit a note at the end that I'd never quite been able to get before. I held it, and when I cut it off, there was silence in the auditorium. There was this intake of breath, and then everyone cheered. I stood up, took a bow, and all the keys fell off my sax. But I didn't care. I knew what I wanted to do with my life—that there *was* some meaning to it."

Three weeks, five pounds, 170 on the scale. Damn! I never thought this was going to be so difficult! I've become the laughingstock of the office. People are accusing me of not trying. My wife says if I write honestly about what's not happening every woman in America is going to hate me. But I swear my pants feel tight around my thighs. Every time I sit down, they supply a snug reminder that I'll soon be shopping for Spandex.

To silence the critics, I visit a steakhouse and eat so much I almost get sick. A gristly T-bone, instant mashed potatoes, a half-loaf of garlic bread, all-u-can-eat salad, two pints of Guinness, plus a brownie sundae for dessert. All the plump, pasty people at the coat check are patting their stomachs and sucking on toothpicks—eyes half-closed, stifling burps. And I'm no different, except that I'm not fat—at least not yet.

I know why the menu boards inside fast-food restaurants are so huge. It's to give you something hypnotic to stare at, like the illuminated numbers above elevator doors, so you won't notice who else you're in there with. I'm waiting in line one afternoon at McDonald's, staring up at the board like it's ET's returning spaceship. Eyes wide, mouth agape—everyone else is doing the same. Including an old lady with a wispy moustache and goatee, a teenager with a bad blossom of acne, a workman with a twitch, and a fat guy in sweatpants showing some ass crack. Everyone seems broken, off center, lumpy, dull. They're nothing like the fit, happy customers who break into song on the TV commercials. Has the food done this to them? Maybe our definition of junkie should be expanded.

Yesterday I had a cheese-steak sandwich, three slices of pizza, and 24 ounces of birch beer for lunch. Then I got lost driving home. Somehow I turned onto an unfamiliar road, even though I grew up in the area. Somehow I made a big 20-minute loop. Somehow I ended up back at the restaurant.

Am I becoming one of them?

Researchers have found that if you feed one rat a diet that's 10 percent fat and another a diet that's 40 percent fat, the second rat will do significantly worse on a variety of mental tests. Scientists speculate that beyond impeding blood flow to the brain by narrowing arteries, fat also hampers the ability of cells to metabolize glucose, which is the brain's chief fuel. "It's remarkable how impaired these animals were," said the chief researcher.

Even worse than the disgust and sluggishness I feel from living like this is the iron ball of stress that's lodged in the middle of my chest. It's rounding my shoulders and folding me up, like I'm a wounded fighter trying to protect myself on the ropes. This morning I even had a nosebleed. I tried to convince myself it was just the result of dry winter air, but my worry is that it's a warning sign of heightening blood pressure. Last night, I even dreamed I was exercising. It felt *so good*, I woke up with an erection.

Evidently, I need exercise for reasons far beyond what the experts advocate. I need it for appetite and then satiation, for pain and then peace, for challenge and then pride. Without it, there are no peaks and valleys in my life. The days are just a steady smear. Life tastes the same. I'm asleep, just like those rats at McDonald's.

Something has to change. From here on, I'm adopting a new strategy. I'm reverting to the food I enjoy (pastas, soups, egg-white omelets, sushi, whole-wheat bread . . .). I'll just eat more of it. To get fat I have to enjoy eating, not want to puke whenever I'm finished or forget where I put the Yodels.

In the middle of the night, when my family is sleeping, I tiptoe downstairs, open the refrigerator, and gorge on nonfat frozen yogurt.

The conductor's baton looks like a toothpick in Miller's hand, but when he swings it down, the Pride of Elkview—94 strong—responds. The musicians launch into a rousing rendition of their fight song. Cheeks balloon around horns. Hands blur above drums.

And Miller, without a drop of sweat on him, conducts like he's in Carnegie Hall, not the half-full auditorium of a West Virginia middle school.

For a generally private man who winces at attention, Miller chose an occupation that puts him center stage each day with potentially the most insensitive species known to man—middle-school children. Yet he handles it with great skill and good humor. And he's eventually able to teach those kids to see the music beyond the notes—a skill that's instrumental in life as well as band.

For an hour, the final concert of the year goes on, and when finally his baton is still and the last note fades, the 94 faces turn in unison toward the audience and soak up the applause. Some show surprise at the perfection achieved; all display smiles like piano keys.

When you ask Miller if there are any advantages to being fat, he pauses as if you had just asked for the meaning of life, which in a way you have. "Ninety-nine percent of the time there's absolutely nothing positive about it," he concludes. "Most days I fluctuate between total depression and total incredulity at the kinds of things I deal with. Society treats fat people as subhuman.

"But I still have many joys in life—my job, my wife, my son, my music. Although others see me as pitiful, I am not. My problems are with people's perception of me, not with who or what I am.

"This has given me a certain drive and a different worldview," he adds. "I think I'm more aware of people's feelings than most. Every day I see kids who think they are the most worthless human beings on earth. I try so hard to connect with these kids because I know exactly how they feel."

After the concert, Miller takes the next hour to introduce each kid by name, giving individual awards and shaking tiny hands. He's bestowing much more than certificates and trophies, though. He's giving each one a taste of public praise. His unspoken goal is to make the experience so sweet, so memorable, that it will stand out in sour times as an example of what the child is capable of. Some kids are so overwhelmed that they hug him, not realizing—or caring—that no one's arms are that long.

Four and a half weeks. Thirty-one days. I'm holding steady at 170. Son of a bitch! How can this be? Everyone says I'm failing miserably, except one coworker who insists he can see some facial pudginess and the hint of a second chin. Bless him. I'm giving this my all, I swear. Just last night, I ate an entire box of Bugles. There are changes, I can tell. And to prove it, to silence them all, I redo my original measurements.

A body analysis determines that those five extra pounds are 100 percent Grade-A fat and, as suspected, they've been deposited around my waist and hips. Each has grown by three-quarters of an inch. "I don't think you have anything to be ashamed of," says Mike Siemens, an exercise physiologist in Tucson. "Let's do the math: Every pound of fat is 3,500 calories. Since you gained five pounds in a month that means you ate 17,500 more calories than you burned, or about 600 extra calories per day. Over a year's time that's 60 pounds of fat, which is pretty astronomical. I'd say you're well on your way."

As far as my strength, there's been little change. I can still lift as much weight as I ever could in the bench press and leg press. However, I'm able to do *more* pushups and situps within one-minute time limits. "That's probably because you're more rested," explains Siemens. "Even though you may not have realized it, you were probably overtraining before. The break did your muscles good."

This is also the case with flexibility. I can actually stretch three-quarters of an inch farther in the sit-and-reach. Once again, because I haven't been exercising (and in particular, running), my chronically tight hamstrings had a chance to relax. Hey, maybe this isn't so bad after all. I do nothing; I get stronger and more flexible. How's that for a revolutionary program?

My enthusiasm nosedives, though, when I look at my heart. My resting pulse has risen from 49 to 56 beats per minute, still good but an indication that my ticker is a bit weaker. It's not expelling as much blood with every beat as it used to. Likewise, when I finish a three-minute step test, my pulse is 16 beats higher than it was before. My heart is struggling a little more. And my blood pressure is up, as well. Not yet cause for concern, but perhaps a beginning.

I really get scared when I receive the results of my blood test. My cholesterol has always been borderline high, but through diet and exercise I've been able to control it. But in just a single month of nonvigilance, my total cholesterol has risen from 201 to 263, my LDL (the particularly bad stuff) from 131 to 164, and my triglycerides (another marker for heart disease) from 77 to 115. I am suddenly at risk of having a coronary, and my doctor soberly recommends that I start seeing him regularly.

I hold the report in my hand, stunned. This isn't a joke anymore. This is my heart. These are my arteries. This is my life spinning away from me.

It isn't the fear of getting fat that makes me call it quits. No matter how hard I try, I could never be Miller-size. I don't have that body type or those genes. At least now I know I can survive the occasional chili dog or Krispy Kreme.

It isn't the fear of getting fat that prompts me to lace on my Nikes and run away. I realize now that I exercise for reasons far beyond weight control. Although it sounds contradictory, movement is my balance.

No, it's not the fear of getting fat that compels me to return to my previous lifestyle. It's the fear of death. It's not my ego that I'm afraid will crumble, it's *me*. I want to live forever, and a healthful lifestyle is one way of fooling myself that it's possible. I need to believe this in order to truly live. Some people use religion to achieve the same thing. They convince themselves that those who lead moral lives will never die. But me? I guess my faith lies in diet and exercise.

No, it's not getting fat that I fear. That's not it at all. It's dying. It's the period at the end of our sentence. It's what I have to embrace to stop being so scared.

10

Dea⊤h

BEING A HUMAN TARGET

Bob Klingleman smiles

    at me

        from across a polished desk.

He's wearing a dark, lint-free suit and is perfectly groomed. He looks so sincere I wouldn't be surprised if he shed a tear. No reason, just because he cares. I remind myself, however, that this is his business, that he's wearing his game face, and that instead of a box of Kleenex on his desk, there's only a calculator.

I've come to the Klingleman Funeral Home to make my "prearrange-ments." That's the preferred term for deciding what to do with yourself after, as my father used to put it, "you get hit by the big beer truck." The funeral business has lots of preferred terms like this. For instance, it's a *casket*, not a *coffin*; a *disposition* rather than a *burial*; a *body pouch* instead of a *body bag*; and, above all, a *funeral director*, not an *undertaker*. These guys can be more careful with their diction than third-grade grammar teachers. You can almost hear the "Tsk, tsk, tsk" in their patient corrections.

Klingleman's is the marquee funeral home in my area, run by "a family dedicated to caring since 1928." Bob is third generation and proudly notes that his sons are already interested in the business, even though they're only in first grade.

I've always been fascinated by guys like Bob who draw their living from death—the original men in black. On average, he arranges 275 funerals per year. "Our busy season is all the time," he admits with palms turned outward. "We're fortunate."

But how can anyone cope with that? How do you not let some of the pain, the grief, and the loss creep into your soul? How do you continue to smile, to be optimistic, to be hopeful when you're reminded every day that it always ends this way? How do you maintain your respect for death, continue to hold it sacred, and not let it become just another paycheck? And most important, how do you come to regard your own—with resignation, indifference, or fearlessness?

"I'm not afraid of dying," says Bob, with a shake of his head, "because I have faith in the resurrection of the dead. You wouldn't be able to do a job like this without it."

So that's the secret. Instead of saying goodbye, he's whispering, " 'Til next time."

So far I've been unable to do that. My faith isn't strong enough to convince me that there's anything to look forward to. The only dead person I ever saw outside a funeral home was my father, who got hit by the big beer truck in his sleep more than a decade ago. Whether it was a heart attack or a stroke, I'll never know. When the alarm clock went off, he didn't get up. I remember kneeling beside his bed, trying to reach him one last time, but there was just . . . nothing. Such vacancy shocked me more than anything.

I fear death because I sense it is the end of much more than life. It is the end of dreams—the sobering realization of what I will never be. It is the end of control—the handoff of crucial responsibilities to those who'll never do them quite as well. It is the end of knowing—the sudden perception that a lifetime of learning has still left me help-

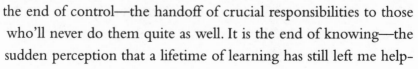

184

less. It is the end of numbness—the laid-open guts of my denied emotions as I descend into pain and penitence. It is the end of good fortune—the last laugh from whatever has me cornered. And, most worrisome, it is the end of myself—the too-soon departure of a stranger I would have liked to know better, someone who should have mattered.

For all these reasons and more, I believe the fear of death is the one that drives all others. After a year of digging up roots, I am finally tugging at the bulb. Without the fear of death, there is no fear of bogeymen, flying, heights, storms, or accidents. Without the fear of death, there is no fear of humiliation, rejection, or weakness. Rid yourself of it, and all worries and phobias vanish. Accept it and, ironically, you finally start to live.

There's a Latin phrase, *Memento mori*, that means "Remember you are dying." Trappist monks use it as a greeting. Their philosophy is that the meaning of life lies in the recognition of death. The more conscious we are of its inevitability, the more appreciative we become of living. The time to think about death is not when we're sad or sick or old, but rather when we're young, in love, on vacation, or laughing out loud. Instead of quelling the mood, it heightens it.

The deepest love I ever felt for my wife occurred after 13 years of marriage. We were at a couples' retreat, and the therapist/instructor told us to write each other's epitaph. Everyone in the group gasped. No one wanted to think about that. But she gave us 60 minutes to leave the room, walk separately about the grounds, and scribble something down. When I returned, it was with something profound. Envisioning my life without Maria made me treasure my life with her. Faults and differences disappeared; only appreciation remained.

It's a lesson that is still with me. When Maria kisses me on the cheek as she leaves for work, I imagine her never making it. Sounds morbid, I know, but it brings me totally into the moment and helps me cherish it.

Now it's time to write my own epitaph. And that's why I've come to Klingleman's. That's why I've asked Bob to make the introductions. Instead of pretending no one is home, as I've done for

42 years, I'm going to finally open the front door and let death stride in. I'm going to take its cloak, offer it my favorite chair, and try to get to know it as intimately as possible. I'm going to plan my funeral in detail and then, when all the prearrangements have been made, I'm going to face death in some realistic way. Hopefully, I'll walk away and, in the process, be done with all this bullshit. Be free of fear and, finally, be able to live.

"Shall we begin?" Bob asks, shooting his cuffs and deftly sliding a Pre-arrangement Planning Worksheet between us.

When I was a pimply, depressed, hormonally challenged teenager, I used to lie in bed at night and imagine my funeral, and how everyone would mourn and chastise themselves for not having been nicer to me. Parents, relatives, teachers, ex-girlfriends—they'd all inherit the eternal torment of regret they so richly deserved. I'd lie on my back in my casket of bedsheets, smile, and drift off into a sound, smug sleep.

But the process of planning your funeral is hardly so satisfying or dramatic. In fact, it's a bit like filing income tax. A life accountant behind a desk completes the necessary paperwork: social security number, date of birth, occupation, children's names, place of residence . . . an extensive five-page questionnaire. Along the way, there's even the temptation to cheat. When Bob asks if I belong to any organizations or clubs, whether I served in the military, or if the community has ever honored me in some way, I consider making something up. I mean, it's embarrassing to leave the whole damn section blank. And who's going to step forward at my wake and say, "Excuse me, but this guy never fought in the Persian Gulf, and I don't believe he was ever president of the Kiwanis, although I saw him at all the pancake breakfasts."

But no, I can't do that. I don't want to risk getting audited by St. Peter. So I joke that I better get busy, or I'll have the shortest obituary in history.

"Don't worry," reassures Bob, with a furrowed brow and a pat to my hand. "This can always be updated. Nothing here is etched in stone. This is only a guide for your loved ones in case, God forbid, something happens."

That's one of Bob's favorite phrases: *In case, God forbid, something happens.* Whenever he says it, I want to furrow my brow, pat his hand, and ask him (sincerely, of course) to cut the crap. This is all about being straightforward, isn't it? Something *will* happen, goddamn it, and my problem is that I can't accept that. Death has become this black secret I can barely talk about. I can't even say its real name. Instead, it's "passing away."

When the funeral people came for my father, they carried him out in a black vinyl body bag. It wasn't a nice little pouch, it was a fucking bag. I remember two men in dark topcoats struggling down the stairs with him, while my mother wailed in what used to be the family room. It took only 10 minutes for them to get rid of the sheets, the clothes, my dad—all bundled away and hauled out the door like a sack of early-morning trash. I remember standing in his bedroom afterward, unable to grasp what had happened. I closed the window they had opened, because I didn't want him out of my life so fast. Even the smell of his death was reassurance.

I saw him only once after that—lying in a coffin at the funeral home. Then, right on schedule, they closed the lid, lowered him into the ground, filled the hole with dirt, and tamped everything down. Just like that, he was gone. No wonder that after 11 years it still doesn't feel like I've said goodbye to him.

There is a woman in Sebastopol, California, named Jerri Lyons, who heads a movement called Final Passages. In her view, much of our anguish over death and the fear that surrounds it stems from not saying goodbye in a more personal way. Just as we instinctively know how to care for a baby, she says, we also know how to care for our dead—only the funeral industry deprives us of that. She encourages families to act as their own undertakers—to cleanse and dress the body themselves, to hold the viewing at home, to even build the loved one a coffin and decorate it.

I know what you're thinking. This sounds too much like the Addams Family. Who wants Uncle Fester festering upstairs? But

Lyons contends that a corpse is neither frightening nor revolting. When laid on bags of dry ice, it can last for days without smell or decomposition. In fact, some people say an unembalmed body eventually adopts a look of peace, with facial features softening and a smile appearing.

The point, she says, is to not totally lose your loved one in the death process, to not let all the final arrangements sweep by without ever saying a proper goodbye. There is no rush. There is no schedule. You have the right to hold his (or her) hand and weep and talk and smile and reminisce for as long as needed—so when you part, you'll already have grieved. That's how, Lyons says, it was meant to be.

Ideas like this make Bob nervous. They challenge his graciousness. Although he agrees that funerals are for the living and not the deceased, he can't help being dismissive. After all, this is his livelihood. This is how things have been at Klingleman's Funeral Home for 74 years. Death is enough of a change, he says. In times of shock, it's tradition that steadies us. The last thing you want is to risk making anyone more uncomfortable.

"Now," he says, putting both hands on the desk and rising up. "Would you like to see our showroom?"

I hesitate because I don't immediately know what he means. He mentioned earlier he had "two remains in the house," and I wonder if we're about to tour the embalming room. I swallow and nod. Then, with a ta-da flourish, he slides back a large, louvered partition. Behind it are almost two dozen gleaming caskets. (Fortunately, none are filled.)

"It's a nice bell curve of choices and prices," says Bob, with a proud smile. "Let me show you around."

The selection *is* impressive. From bronze to pecan exteriors, velvet to crepe interiors, plain to laser-engraved finishes, it's like being on the lot at Big Marty's World of Cars. I walk down the aisles as Bob explains the different features, encouraging me to look under hoods and even to get down on my knees to inspect the magnesium bar on the underbody that draws out moisture and prevents rust. These babies even have warranties (75 years against manufacturer defects), and a few are available for rent (the liner slides out for cremation). Sorry, though, no trade-ins.

I'm drawn to the Batesville Majestic Blue stainless steel model with royal-velvet interior for $3,200. The Batesville Nut Brown oak with spit-fire red crepe is also attractive, and it's a thousand less. I wonder if these prices are firm, or if the dealer invoice might be available from *Consumer Reports*. (Klingleman's does boast it won't be undersold.)

I picture myself lying in one, all pasty faced and stiff. Bob is apparently doing the same, but envisioning something far different. He's noting my eye color, my hair, my build, and asking if I have a favorite suit or tie I'd like to be buried in.

"It's your final picture I'm creating," he says, with building excitement. "It's the way everyone will remember you. If you prefer, I can give you color swatches to take home. Sometimes it helps to live with them."

In addition to the caskets, there are urns and lockets for housing ashes, plus registry books, prayer-card catalogs, cemetery directories, crucifix brochures, and lists of headstone manufacturers. In all, Bob says there are 80 different decisions involved in arranging a traditional funeral. I'm welcome to make each one separately (fresh undergarments with slippers are $24), or I can opt for a package deal (starting at $3,035, not including casket). To avoid the hassle, I'm tempted to do the latter. It would certainly be the easiest exit—what everyone would expect. Pay the respects, console the widow, then put this latest tragedy out of your head.

But traditional also means forgettable. It means we're used to this, we've seen it a million times, it's nondescript. I've spent my whole life wading through bullshit in search of the truth, trying to come up with fresh ideas, hoping to wake up just a few people (including myself). I can't let death dissuade me from that. In fact, it assures me the rapt attention of my biggest audience. To do the usual in the face of that would mean dying not just in body but also in spirit.

So I tell Bob I'm going to need some time. I'm going to have to think about this, discuss it with my wife, and get back to him with the particulars.

"Perfectly fine," he says, with fingers entwined. "I appreciate your coming by. Good night, and do be careful crossing the street."

I feel his eyes on the back of my head as I walk to the parking lot—just in case, God forbid, something happens.

In the ensuing weeks, death becomes less intimidating as I consider all the possible ways of exiting. Being proactive is giving me some control over it, thereby reducing its omnipotence. While part of me recognizes this is an illusion, action of any type feels better than avoidance. I go through different funeral moods—some dark, some humorous, some considerate, some vengeful, some earnest, some cynical. I change in and out of them like outfits, trying to decide which one looks best. I could do:

Something *outlandish*, like the ex-hippie who was buried in a tie-dye suit with marijuana seeds in the pockets. His wish was to have his friends smoke him. (Perhaps doing the same with zucchini seeds would allow me to delight my wife one last time from the grave.)

Something *creative*, like being cremated and having my ashes blended into the ink used to print this book. Not just my thoughts on these pages but my very body and soul. (Please excuse the typos.)

Something *riotous*, like throwing a death-day party at my home with unlimited booze, catered food, and a live band. (Get everyone embalmed, so the next morning I'd be the envied one.)

Something *cruel*, like purchasing a $175 pneumatic corpse lifter from the Special Effect Supply Company in North Salt Lake. (Your cue, son, is when the preacher says, "Rise everyone.")

Something *practical*, like building my own Boothill coffin from plans I bought for $19.50 on the Internet. (Prior to burial, it can be used as a coffee table, bookshelf, or entertainment center.)

Something *temporary*, like being cryogenically preserved or mummified so I can return to life some day. (Or else be discovered in some archaeological dig and be labeled Kita Man, circa 2002. Note the tiny cortex and bald head.)

Something *pretentious*, like hiring Klingleman's horse-drawn casket coach for $575, flying in a jazz band from the Big Easy, and buying a marble mausoleum. (If you fail at being impressive in life, there's always death.)

Something *environmentally sound*, like being cremated instead of laying eternal, selfish claim to an eight-by-four-by-six-foot piece of real estate that could be a parking space. (Correct me if I'm wrong, but wouldn't it be *more* ecological to insist on acres of rolling green fields?)

Something *thoughtful*, like purchasing a really nice bench instead of a headstone so visitors can relax and sit a while. (Rest your bones, soak up the sun, feel my life continuing on. . . .)

Or maybe something *philanthropic*, like donating my entire body to science. Transfer my organs to somebody else and put my tissue under the microscope. Perhaps the cure for cancer is in there somewhere. (Or perhaps, upon closer inspection, there's nothing worth saving.)

It's an exciting and difficult decision. Unfortunately, my family isn't much help. My mother doesn't want to consider her own funeral, let alone mine. My son, who just got his driver's permit, says he's mastered steering around cemeteries at 15 mph and can we please practice elsewhere. My teenage daughter doesn't understand; she thinks death is a pimple before the dance. My dog, though, seems partial to burial.

"Dear, you can make all the plans you want," says Maria, "but remember that how we get rid of you is ultimately up to me." And she smiles wickedly.

Damn, she's going to look good in black.

Honey, have I mentioned my idea about the zucchini seeds?

Che Che White Cloud is a Seneca/Onondaga Indian—claims he can trace his bloodline all the way back to Hiawatha. He has shoulder-length white hair and a stony stare. At 64, he's a piece of gristle that's been chewed up and spit out by the world. He refuses to be digested, to be assimilated. He stands separate. He'll look you in the eye and say he trusts no man, which is ironic because when you're looking at him trust is your consuming emotion.

Che Che is a knife thrower—the greatest, the fastest, the most spectacular . . . pick your adjective. His father, Chief White Cloud, taught him
the skill when he was seven years old so he could become part of a family
act that performed at Wild West shows across America. In addition to
throwing knives at human targets, he learned to toss tomahawks, hatchets,
and axes, plus shoot rifles, arrows, and blowguns. He is the classic carnival
showman—able to quick-draw a cigarette out of an assistant's mouth before you can say Pall Mall.

Che Che's skills brought him much success. He had his own carnival
for a while, complete with 48 elephants. He's been around the world seven
times. He's played Vegas and any town you can name in the Midwest. He's
appeared on the *Tonight Show with Johnny Carson*, *What's My Line?*, *Saturday
Night Live*, and even as a TV weatherman with a unique way of pointing
out low- and high-pressure systems.

But Che Che doesn't do much of that anymore. He's content to
hunker down and smoke cigarettes at his tiny house on the Indian reser-
vation in Salamanca, New York. It's not easy to get in touch with him. He
doesn't advertise. He has no agent. He rarely even answers his phone. After
a lifetime of traveling and entertaining, he's content to stay home. I track
him down through the American Knife Throwers Alliance. Its president
calls Che Che "a true professional, not a wannabe like a lot of guys out
there. Plus he's fully insured."

Now there's the type of knife thrower I'm looking for—someone with
good hands *and* AllState.

"His real name is Kenneth Pierce. I'll give you his number."

Wait a minute. His name is *Pierce*?

"Yeah, Pierce. . . . Ha! I never thought of that."

Che Che's wife, Nancy, answers the phone. She's his moat—a sweet retired home-economics teacher who listens patiently to my pitch, deems it
worthwhile, then tells me to hang on while she gets Kenny. I picture
him in the backyard practicing, always practicing.

"Ya-a-alow," he says in a nasal voice that momentarily disarms me. For some reason, I expected something deep and formal, like Sitting Bull in council.

I explain that I'm in the process of facing my biggest fears, and that I'd like to hire him to help me confront the greatest one of all, the fear of death.

He laughs. "I have no fears," he says. "I've been shot out of cannons, been in knife fights. . . . Fear isn't in my blood. I'm Indian. All these silly people with their phobias. . . . Sure, I'll do it for you. For $1,500."

Although that sounds expensive, I don't try to negotiate. The last thing I want is Che Che cutting corners, so to speak. He promises to drive down on the fourth. I mark my calendar as if I were engraving a tombstone:

JOE KITA

BORN: 8/26/59

DIED: 1/4/02

I get a chill. This is no longer just an idea. Suddenly, this is real, and I get the urge to gather as much reassuring information about Che Che as possible.

"Have you ever hit anyone?" I ask.

"Twice," he drawls. "The worst was my sister. I hit her right between the eyes from 40 feet. But instead of splitting her skull, the knife rode up across her scalp, and she took 290 stitches. There was a lot of blood. Then I hit her again a few years later. It was raining, I slipped, and a knife went through her thigh. That was a long time ago, though."

Of course. He's had years of practice since. Why, he must be throwing daily.

"I never touch a knife in between shows. Believe me, if I don't know how to throw these knives by now, I ain't gonna learn."

Makes sense. But when was his last show?

"Nancy, when was that? 'Bout eight months ago?"

I can't tell if he's putting me on, or if I've stumbled across some ornery old Indian with a vendetta against the white man.

I ask Nancy if she's ever been a target for her husband.

"Occasionally," Che Che jumps in. "But we were married five years before she'd let me even try this with her."

I figure I better stop asking questions. This may be the only instance where fear isn't lessened by knowledge.

Goodbye, I say.

"Good luck!" he shoots back.

At least he didn't ask for the money up front.

I update my last will-and-testament. I put it in the bottom drawer of my filing cabinet in a clearly marked folder. I'm satisfied that it takes care of all the legalities and distributes my valuables fairly. But I'm worried that it makes no mention of the invaluables—the stuff that neither lawyers nor government has any use for, but what I consider priceless. I guess it's up to me to distribute that stuff now, in case I don't make it.

But first I want to do a little demonstration. (Indulge me, please, I'm potentially a dying man.) I want you to hold your hand in front of your face, study it, and ask: "Is this hand me?" Then I'd like you to look at your arm with similar objectivity and ask: "Is this arm me?" Do this with as many parts of yourself as necessary until you become convinced, like I am, that we are not our bodies and that we exist beyond them. Only then will the gifts I'm about to dole out make any sense.

I believe in eternal life, but not in some heaven of angels in the sky. Rather I believe we live on in the people we influence. I'm convinced of this because I feel lots of dead people inside me. My father, friends, relatives, authors, actors, songwriters, even historical figures—anyone who has ever taught me or touched me in some way, for better or worse, is born again in that lesson and persists for however long I live it.

Life is energy. It is not matter. I do not sit or stand or lie down; *I* float like light from a bulb. I do not wrinkle or decay or get fat; *I* am what I always was, impermeable to age or physical effect. I do not think or feel or believe; *I* know like a tree or a rock or a mountain knows that reason is unnecessary for insight or worth or even existence. Life is an essence.

And although some people's sphere of influence may be great, it does not matter if yours is the circumference of a hug. That is enough. Life has no weight or other measure. It is just life, and the energy of yours persists whether you touch one or millions.

When viewed this way, death loses some of its scariness because it stops being so final. It replaces the period at the end of our lives with three dots . . . we are to be continued.

And so, for Maria, my wife, I am confidence. You are a smart, forever-beautiful woman whose good heart and common sense can steady any world. I am that strength, that faith. I am what you never saw in yourself, what you doubt, what you hold inside and think you can't let out. I am your potential, your bud.

For Paul, my son, I am curiosity. You are a worthy, talented young sponge with perception and vision and, most special, the humility to keep them in perspective. I am your questions, your wonder, but never the answers. Those you must find yourself. I am your undying interest.

For Claire, my daughter, I am the freedom you feel on a trampoline—six feet up in the air, wild hair, not a care. You are a responsible free spirit, of which few exist. Be proud of that. You can fly high with open eyes and not be scared. I am delight wherever you find it.

For Connie, my mother, I am whatever it is you wanted. I never could figure that out, and I've stopped trying, struggling, fighting. I am finally the perfect son, the one who always phones, the boy who helps his mom. I apologize for everything. You were right; I was wrong. I am your victory and the empty echo of "I told you so."

For my dog, I am a drawer full of old socks and shoes. They're all yours. Chew me with eyes half-closed, then run to the door convinced it's my key in the lock. I am your refusal to accept death. I am your insistence that "He's here!" And you're right. But as usual, nobody listens to you.

And that's all.

If you're disappointed about being left out, I'd caution you about jumping to conclusions. There's something for everyone. But it's your responsibility to find it. We all give each other lots of gifts; most go unnoticed.

Wednesday the second. I call Che Che to confirm our appointment and provide directions.

"Yaalow."

Are we still on for the fourth?

"When is that? Tomorrow?"

Oh my God. He's confused. He's forgotten. (Apparently, Nancy is out on some errand.)

"Oh yeah, right. *Friday.* Don't worry. We'll be there. Bringing the motor home. Taking the turnpike. What exit is it anyway?"

I give him the various route numbers. I hear him scribbling. I repeat things. His pen runs out of ink.

"Can you believe that? Hang on a minute."

Scrambling.

"Okay, where were we now?"

I spend 10 minutes on the phone with him. As insurance, I give him three numbers where he can reach me in case of emergency.

"Good luck," I say.

"Goodbye," he shoots back.

Why does any parting of his make me nervous?

Here are my final wishes. Here's how I'd like to be disposed of if, God forbid, Che Che slips.

If it's all right with Maria and the kids, I'd like to hang out at home for a few days afterward. If there is any semblance of spirit that lingers, I'd rather be around those I love and let them feel it. Bob can lend a hand with the details—paperwork, burial arrangements, a home viewing, plugging the knife wounds. I'd prefer my own bed if possible, but if that's going to ruin the mattress, one of his caskets will do. I'd like the least-expensive wooden model with the simplest interior. Dry ice is fine, but no embalming, makeup, or Sunday suit, please. Just let me be me. I want everyone to see what death really looks like—to realize that you can sit with it, touch it, chat with it, and it's not going to roar up and kill

196

you. I want to be a dead body, not a mannequin. I don't want anyone saying, "They did a nice job on him."

I'd like a long viewing. I'm talking a couple of days. I want the doors wide open. But don't fill the house with lilies of the valley and soft funeral-parlor music. I want people celebrating my life instead of mourning my death. There should be somebody fixing martinis. The pinball machines should be on, as well as the stereo. Dancing is encouraged, as well as pizza.

Instead of a formal registry book, I want a giant sheet of paper thumbtacked to the wall in the foyer. This is for wishes, memories, anger, photographs, drawings, anything people want to put there. And if a good chunk of it is blank, that's okay, too. Sometimes feeling nothing is the best feeling of all.

If anyone insists on spending money, I'd prefer it not be wasted on elaborate bouquets or big-time charities. Instead, donations should be made to the Joe Kita Let-Me-Help-You-with-That Fund—Claire Kita, executrix. She'll invest the money and, most important, distribute it. One rule: no dispersal greater than $50. Look for pain and suffering in the world that can be cured by just a little expression of understanding. It's not the money; it's the gesture.

And after everyone has said goodbye, after everybody has grieved, after I've started turning a little green, Bob can take me away. A simple ceremony at Neffs Church would be great. If it's a nice day, maybe it could even be held outside. I'd like Father John, my brother-in-law, to conduct the service. But no formal mass or communion, please. Just a straightforward memorial, interspersed by eulogies from these four people, and anyone else who feels so moved:

▶ Hugh O'Neill, because he's the wisest man I know. (Just don't let him go on too long.)

▶ Robert Sell, because he's the most generous. (And I have to be sure someone will pay me a compliment.)

▶ Mark Kovaleski, because he's so bizarre. (Consider him the entertainment.)

▶ And Paul Kita, because every son should do this for his dad. (It's the talk we never had.)

I'd like to be buried in the cemetery behind the church, if there's any space left. I didn't have time to check. Back by the trees would be perfect. Instead of a tombstone, I'd like that bench I mentioned earlier—high back, armrests, and a small plaque inscribed with my name, followed by three dots and the words *Memento mori* ("Remember you are dying"). Hopefully, people will sit down and think about that for a while, then stand up and live.

Before I'm put in the ground and covered up, Bob should secure a DNA sample—however that's best done. One day soon, this will allow my descendents to check if I passed along any genetic defects. A detailed analysis will help them live longer, healthier lives and be less surprised.

And finally, I'd like my family and whatever friends they can muster to go to The Downs Off-Track Betting Parlor in Allentown after it's all over. (There's a check for $900 in the folder with my will.) This should be apportioned over nine races—$100 to win on each horse whose name most reminds everyone of me. I'll see what I can do from the other side. I was lucky in life. I have a hunch I'll remain so in death. Have fun. Cheer me on.

Oh, and Bob. I'd like you to do one more thing. In that same folder is a check for $3,000. On my wife's birthday (July 12) and on my daughter's (October 15), I'd like you to send each of them flowers. Do it for as long as the money holds out, which I hope will be decades. Just a simple arrangement. Sign the card: "I miss you."

Yaalow! Joe? It's Che Che. I'm at the . . . Nancy, where are we? The Golden Corral Restaurant in Emmaus."

It's 7:00 P.M. on the third. I just got home from work.

"I blew a tire about 20 miles outside of Bradford, so we're running late. Now where is this place?"

I give him directions to a lot where he can park his motor home for the night. Fortunately, it's not too far away. He sounds road weary. I need him well-rested.

"I'll see you tomorrow at nine," I remind him.

There's only a click.

Dawn on the fourth. I couldn't sleep. Lots of popcorning thoughts. So I'm up, at my office in Emmaus, rereading my last wishes and funeral arrangements. Now they seem a bit over the top, too self-centered, melodramatic, a huge hassle. Perhaps such decisions *should* be left to loved ones. It's impossible for me to be objective.

Am I ready to die? No way. I have too much of my life yet to live. It would be stupid and tragic to go out like this. Lots of people worry that their work is killing them. Ha! Mine actually did. In fact, this could probably be ruled a suicide. I mean, I arranged it.

Che Che's motor home is parked in the lot across the street. I can see it from my desk. There aren't any lights on inside yet. Imagine that. The guy with the power to kill me, sleeping peacefully. My accidental assassin.

Am I scared? Yes and no. If I've learned anything to date, it's to tap into my instinct at times like this and listen for its whisper. And so far, I'm not hearing anything. It's calm at my center. There seems to be an assurance I will see tomorrow. But outside of this core is a swirl of apprehension. I try not to let my mind go there because I know it won't return. A knife in my heart is something I have to deal with only when it's there. I can do nothing about it now. Worry compounds fear. Plus, this all seems so vaudeville. An Indian in full costume driving down from rural New York to do a sideshow with me in it. It doesn't seem real. But maybe that'll change after I meet him, run my thumb across the blades, and better understand what he'll be doing. Right now, I only have a conception based on photos. I'm about to become his not-so-lovely assistant, the unsuspecting volunteer drawn from the studio audience.

What must a knife feel like when it slices into you? I bet you don't feel anything. I bet you look down and just see it sticking there. I bet there's a suspended moment of incredulity, when you can't believe that he (and you) fucked up, followed by a sharp instant of regret, of this is it, then blood and pain and finally blackness. What a bizarre way to go.

I'm both surprised and disappointed that my wife and children weren't more emotional last night. It could very well have been my *last* night. But they seemed unconcerned. I thought the kids might want to come, but they never asked. And Maria couldn't make it because she had to work. She said she'd look for me in the emergency room at her hospital and, as a joke, gave me an adult diaper to wear.

I'm going back and forth, emotions flip-flopping as the day gets brighter. There are lots of things I didn't have time to do. I didn't go to confession. I didn't get last rites. I didn't increase my life insurance. I didn't tell my family how much I love them. I didn't tell Bob about my final decisions. I didn't say goodbye to everyone I should have. I didn't pay all the bills. . . .

But amidst the anxiety, there is also the inkling of a thrill. I'm about to do something few people ever will. Does this mean I'm finally brave? Will people admire me if I walk away? I feel naturally caffeinated. And even if I don't survive, I'll still get to find out what everyone wonders about, whether the sequel is just as good. As a naturally curious person, a journalist, I'm tickled about getting the scoop on this. Fear is excitement, after all. It's just a matter of how you interpret it.

This whole scheme has too much momentum to stop it now. I must go through with it. There are too many players. I can't send anyone home. Che Che must be stirring in his Winnebago by now. At least I hope he is. I want him fully awake.

I wonder: How can I milk these final moments? Am I entitled to any last wishes? The cliché cigarette? A big charge on my Visa? Open-mouth kisses from all the hot women in the office? What was my last meal anyway? Damn, it was takeout from Sam's Pizza. How did I miss out on surf and turf?

I'm almost too busy to be scared. There's so much to think about. On my desk calendar, in between today's meetings, I've actually penciled in "knife throwing." Well, let's see here. I suppose I can squeeze death in, as long as it promises to be punctual and not stay longer than an hour. I'm probably the only person in the world who has made a specific appointment with death today. A lot of other people may have one, but they're unaware. Anybody could be struck dead at any intersection. But I know the exact location of my crossroad, and I'm voluntarily stepping into it at rush hour.

I still haven't arranged for an EMT to be present. Even though it's the smart thing to do, I don't want to admit it's necessary. Without one, I can continue believing this is an act, that the risk of death is an illusion. But I must, if only to create even more realism.

It's strange, but I'm not dreading this as much as some of the other fears I've faced. I was more worried about doing the comedy routine, in a way. Maybe that's because I don't have any responsibilities here. All I have to do is sit quietly and adopt a blank stare. If I die, it's Che Che's ass, not mine.

Despite how scary this stunt looks, it might not even be such a ballsy thing to do. After all, the alternative—never confronting your fears—kills you, too. There are all kinds of scientific evidence showing how anxiety and stress depress the immune system and produce biochemicals that create disease. It's almost better to go out in one mad grab for glory than to waste away like that.

There's still no sign of life in Che Che's motor home. I hope he's not hungover. I hope his wife is keeping him in line, getting him prepared.

Trust. That's what this is all about. I'm trusting Che Che to do his job. We have to trust millions of people every day in order to survive. It's probably the most pervasive emotion we have, yet we're rarely aware of it. I trust every other driver on the road not to veer into my path. I trust every person I meet not to punch me in the face or pull a gun. I trust the food I eat, the water I drink, the air I breathe, the medicine I take, the chairs on which I sit, the newspaper, the government. . . . With so much trust in the world, how can there be so much fear? It must be because people don't recognize all the trust they have, or else they don't trust themselves. In a way, that's what my entire quest has been about. The antidote to fear isn't building courage or confidence, it's learning to trust yourself. If you can do that, you'll never be scared because, deep down, *you know what to do.* You're programmed to survive. Your life instinct is so intense you won't go out without a worthy fight. Fear is self-doubt. Fear is mistrust. Fear is second-guessing yourself.

From "I *can't* handle this" to "I *can* handle this."

The challenge is that simple and that complex.

Che Che's motor home has KNIFE 1 plates. Large, threatening knives are scattered like road maps on the floor by the driver's seat, lending new meaning to "cutting somebody off in traffic." Che Che is no more than 125 pounds, but he is far from frail. His arms have sinewy muscles, and he moves confidently. He has the build of a soldier ant, a scrambler, a 20-to-1 underdog. His white hair falls from under a black felt hat, and his jeans are secured by a belt buckle that's the size of my fist. On it is (what else?) a knife.

"My whole life has been weapons," he says, sweeping his hand around the motor home's interior as if to indicate many more kept hidden.

Wife Nancy sits nearby knitting. I wonder how deadly she is with those needles.

"Sit down, and I'll show you some videotapes," he says. "It'll give you an idea of what to expect."

As I settle in, Che Che lights a cigarette. Just in case I was thinking about grousing, he points to a sign that warns: COMPLAINING ABOUT MY SMOKING MAY BE HAZARDOUS TO YOUR HEALTH.

"Been smoking since I was nine," he says proudly, as if he has even cancer intimidated. "But I don't drink. Never did. Never will. Can't handle the stuff."

I'm relieved. Let him puff all he wants. I can tolerate smoke, if it keeps him calm.

The videotapes are fuzzy, making me wonder just how long it's been since Che Che has worked. But it's obvious he's proud of them. And pride is a good sign. It puts an edge on talent. I watch as he throws knife after knife at people in all sorts of positions. The audiences are big and appreciative. There are clips from various events and news shows. All proof that he can do what he boasts.

But in the same way I'm feeling him out, I can sense him judging me. His biggest challenge in throwing at a live target is gauging how much he or she will flinch. Everyone moves; it's instinct. The question is how much. If it's someone from the audience, he'll give them a wide cushion, maybe inches. But with one of his professional assistants—women he's worked with for years and has conditioned to be like statues—he'll throw so close as to clip off their skirts, belts, and tassels. And while he no longer throws from 40 feet, even a dozen is plenty impressive.

"I've had to give in a little to age," says Che Che, flexing his hands. "Got some arthritis, and a few years back I had cataract surgery."

He grins. I can feel him testing me. I try not to flinch.

Che Che's target board is blood red. I check to make sure it's painted. He used the highest-grade pine to build it—the kind without any knots that might blunt his knives. It weighs 150 pounds. Ironically, it's shaped like an arched doorway or a tombstone.

Che Che single-handedly slides it out from under his motor home. He handles it carefully, like he's removing a car seat with a sleeping baby in it. I notice there are deep gouges all over it. The thing has been hit thousands of times. But there's no pattern. There are just as many marks in the heart of it as there are along the perimeter.

"Hey, nobody's perfect," he says with a shrug.

Nancy dusts off his costume. It's midnight blue with lots of long white fringe to accentuate his sweeping movements. It's patterned off of traditional Indian dress, and there are bands of intricate beadwork. Various fake jewels, big and small, are embedded to catch the spotlights and lend additional sparkle. It takes Che Che some time to dress. He methodically dons pants, mukluks, jacket, belt and, finally, his headdress. It's not the full war bonnet I expected, but rather a downsized skullcap of feathers and beads that—I'm pleased to hear him say—is less distracting. The total effect is a cross between Tonto and Liberace.

Che Che spends an inordinate amount of time wrapping a Velcro strap around the outside of each shoe. He puts them on and takes them off, cinching them tighter and tighter over the laces, until they're perfect. "Knife throwing is down here," he says, slapping his legs. "It's just like a baseball pitcher; your power doesn't come from your arm. These straps remind me of that."

I mention that I'm not so much concerned with power as I am with accuracy.

He grins and pulls out a squirt bottle filled with bleach, in addition to a pair of thick winter gloves. "That's where these come in."

The bleach is to dry his hands. It's the liquid equivalent of sandpaper for a safecracker's fingertips. The gloves keep his hands warm and the arthritis at bay, so he can move his fingers deftly. From this point on, he won't shake anyone's hands or touch anything but his instruments. He's like a surgeon, prepped and awaiting the operation.

And then come the knives. The reverence he showed for his board and costume is nothing compared to how he treats these. They were handmade by his great-grandfather from leather and steel. Each is 12 inches long and resembles a flattened bowling pin. The handles are white with thin red bands, and the blades are diamond shaped. He unrolls them from a chamois to let them warm. A knife is a living thing with a personality and a heritage and, if you're not careful, a mind of its own. There are nine of them, which Che Che holds in a fan. After all these years, they are like his fingers. He twirls and spins and maneuvers them. They're less sharp than I imagined. They wouldn't be able to slice a whisker and, in fact, Che Che can spin them point down on his palm with hardly an indentation. But it's their weight that makes them lethal—each a half-pound of tumbling momentum that'll burrow an inch and a half into that pine board from just 12 feet away. Human flesh would be far less challenging. It would slice like pork loin.

I want to touch the knives. I want to feel their heartlessness. I want to try to read their karma. Which of these nine is mine? But Che Che won't allow it. That would be like a priest permitting pagan fingers on the Eucharist. These are sacred. These are his.

"A guy offered me $300,000 for them once," he says. "But I'll never sell 'em. Everywhere I go, they go. They're a part of me."

Despite their beauty, I don't want them to be a part of me.

You ready, curly?"

It's one of the few times in my life I'm glad I don't have hair. Che Che will be able to see exactly where my scalp is, where my ears begin and end. I tell him I'd like to keep them.

In front of the board is a wood chair, dead center. I'll sit on this, hopefully motionless. I'm surprised that Che Che doesn't have any specific, last-minute instructions for me. I guess that's because this isn't an act. He's throwing sharp knives in my direction. That's a fact. There's nothing I have to do except sit here and not move.

"Did you happen to see that show on TV a while back," he asks, "the one where the masked magician gave the secrets to all his tricks? I think it was on Fox."

I nod that I had, my mouth suddenly feeling like it's been squirted with bleach.

"Well, he showed how knife throwers don't really throw knives, how they pop out from behind the board when the assistant presses a button. What bullshit! And people believe that! You're about to find out how real it is."

I try to settle him down by suggesting he have a smoke. Hell, at this point I'd even like one myself. But he refuses. He wants to get on with it.

"There was another guy who called himself the Master of the Blade. Master my ass! When I saw his advertisement, I threw my wardrobe in the motor home and drove 40 straight hours to the Hacienda in Las Vegas and challenged him. Turned out he was the biggest bullshitter in the world. No knife act today goes past 27 knives. Mine used to start with 90 to 100 throws and go up to 265. That's in 20 minutes. Believe me, that's a lot of chewed-up wood."

I'm worried Che Che is getting too cranked up. I try to settle him down with reassurance and compliments.

"No doubt about it, Che Che. You're the best. Everyone says so."

"You're damn right. But you reach a point in life where you just don't give a shit," he says.

"And what age is that?" I ask.

"Fifty-five."

I calculate, with a gulp, that he's nine years past that.

I sit down, strangely calm. It has become inevitable now. I am no longer anticipating or worrying. My brain has pulled back from what *might* happen to what *is* happening. It is focused on the known. It has taken control of what it can, telling me to stare straight ahead, grip the underside of the chair, rest the back of my skull against the board, and breathe slowly—all in order to remain rock steady. And after I have done all this, my mind turns off. There are no prayers, no thoughts of family, no life scenes tumbling past, not even a thread of panic or courage—just focus. I am precisely aware, but only of me, Che Che, the silver knives in his hands, and the blood-red board in my peripheral vision.

I am barely breathing. No trembling, sweating, fidgeting. Everything has stopped. This is fear in the starting blocks. This is what happens to all that accumulating adrenaline and angst at the sound of the words *Ready! Set!* It's something totally unexpected. The fear ends. Things settle. My heartbeat slows. Instead of feeling scared or brave, I just feel *ready*. For what, my mind is no longer concerned with. It is ready for *now*, and that is enough reassurance.

Che Che told me before that it's the same with him. As he assumes the throwing position, as he lets the tug of the Velcro around his feet center him, as he caresses the cold steel and feels its weight, it becomes just him and me and the board—a tunnel down which he'll throw, down which he'll flow. His mind has turned off as well. He is an animal ready to strike, and I am one, too: poised to react. We are both suspended in an age-old trance.

The plan is for Che Che to throw seven knives in quick succession, starting at my right elbow, then continuing in a semicircle to my right shoulder, right ear, the top of my head, left ear, left shoulder, and finally left elbow. They will thrum into the wood just millimeters away from me, the whole process taking five seconds. But as I sit here, distance and time lose their significance. There are only opposites: him/me, wood/flesh, hit/not hit. That's because I can react instinctively to black and white; it's those confusing grays that make me hesitate. So my mind has eliminated them. I feel like it's possible to float here forever.

The first three knives thunk into the board before I realize they've been thrown. Right elbow, right shoulder, right ear. They are suddenly all here, as if they just appeared. If one had been off target, I would never have felt it. I would have looked down in surprise at it lodged in me and watched it quivering. But just that quickly my mind adjusts. It focuses down to a pinpoint. And I actually hear that last knife vibrating next to my ear like the plucked string on a guitar. Then I see another one coming directly at my head. Even though it's traveling too fast to see, I see it perfectly. In fact, it becomes suspended three feet from my forehead, its tip pointing between my eyes, its diamond blade looking wide and bright, its polished handle pure and white. I see all this detail when, in fact, there should be no detail to see—just a blur, if anything.

But still there is no panic, no fear, no courage, just a cold assessment that this knife is going to be much closer. This knife may hit me.

Maybe that's all the moment of death is: just a flat, emotionless realization that it's over, that this is it. Fear is a survival instinct, after all. When there's no longer a chance of survival, there should no longer be a reason for fear to exist.

The knife rotates once, end over end, and splinters the wood above my head. The handle gives my skull a hard knock, like a marble has just been dropped on me. It hurts, but it's a dull pain, not the sharp slice of steel through bone. There is no trickle of warm blood down my cold temple.

This is all registering. My mind is assessing, assimilating, deciding. It's as if the knock was a wake-up call. Startled, I leave the now and jump to the possible consequences of the three remaining knives. There is a chance to survive, to do something. I feel the fear returning, myself flinching, my body leaning to the right as the next three knives thunk in beside me.

And just that fast, but just that slowly, it's over. I look up at the knife above my head. If I had had a cowlick, the knife would have clipped it. The curved blade actually follows the contour of my skull, the handle nudging the crown, and the knife tip dug into the wood about an inch farther down. It was a perfect throw. In fact, it borders on unbelievable.

Remarkably, my pants are dry, and when I stand, my knees don't buckle. I laugh nervously, because I don't know what else to do or say. When Che Che asks if I want to do it again, if I'd like to try a couple of different positions, I decline. My mind is already busy calculating the odds of him doing that repeatedly. It has jumped ahead again to all that could happen. And the fear has returned.

Later that night and all the next day, I feel electrified. I buzz with life. Part of it is a jolt of courage and confidence. I did it! I faced the fear of death. But another part is a gentle current of newfound appreciation. I see that knife blade suspended three feet away, coming at me.

Memento mori.

BEING Alone

11

LOCKED IN SOLITARY CONFINEMENT

So it looks like
death is it—
the fear that drives all others.

Not physical death but figurative death—that's the mother. It's not flesh I've been clinging to; it's spirit. It's not dying that's scared me so; it's losing my life. There's a difference. All these fears of mine weren't as much efforts to keep my body whole as they were attempts to protect my passion, my humor, my enthusiasm, my soul. No, I don't fear death. When my time comes, I'll face it with cold logic and resignation, if only because there isn't any other choice. I may sidestep it once, I may cheat it again, but I'll never escape it in the end. Ultimately, we all know that. There's acceptance in every last breath. No, I don't fear dying. I fear not living. And the older I get, the more conscious I become of how little time and energy I have left to do exactly that.

So maybe there's one more step. Maybe I haven't quite reached the end. Maybe what I truly fear is the opposite of everything I've been chasing here. It's not something; it's nothing. In all the confrontations I've manufactured, I never found my bogeyman. Not under the bed, up in the clouds, on some stage, out in the Great Plains, or even in a haunted house. He was never there. All my phobias turned out to be just elaborate disguises that he wears. And now that I've ripped off every last one, I'm seeing only the horror of emptiness—the blank life that awaits us when we surrender to fear. It's a safe, comfortable existence, to be sure, but it's also more lonely, vacant, and worthless than we'll ever admit. It's a single glass beside an empty bottle of scotch at 5:30 A.M. It's a king-size bed with no one else in it. It's an ashtray full of dreams, stubbed out. It's the day-after-day world of the living dead around us.

Maybe what really terrifies me is the suspicion of where my fears are leading me—to a life of isolation and sameness. Maybe I'm afraid of being sentenced, of finding myself in a prison of my own creation. And maybe that's where I have to finally go to face this, to find this thing I so intimately don't know. Perhaps I just need to be alone.

At first, confronting this fear—if it even is one—seems like an easy thing to do. No dogfights, marathon hikes, or tornado chases. Nothing palpable to point at and recoil from. Nothing even that I have to do, except survive with myself for as long as possible in a tiny room. No distractions, no interruptions, no news from the world. Most people would argue that's not frightening; that's potentially *enlightening*.

But before you jump to conclusions, think back on those times in your life when you were alone. And I'm not talking about that week in Aruba without the kids. I mean when it was just you for an extended period. No pets, no spouse, no telephone, no TV, no radio, no music, no reading material, no alcohol, no sleeping pills—no escape from yourself or the world around you. Don't be surprised if it's difficult to recall more than a few times that meet this criteria and if, in retrospect, the experience was not that pleasant.

Think about it.

Even though we yearn for a place of our own when we're young, we don't often spend much time there after moving in. Even though we swear we'll never remarry after a divorce, it doesn't take long before we meet someone new and begin considering it. And even though we look forward to a quiet night at home or a weekend in the woods, anything longer makes us bored and uneasy.

What is it about being alone that disconcerts us so, forcing us to double-latch the doors and hide a pistol in the drawer? Why do we punish criminals by putting them in cells? Why do we fill our lives with so much detail? What are we avoiding, almost without even knowing? What's so harrowing inside ourselves?

I suspect that the dread of being alone is one of the most pervasive fears in America. Only it never shows up on lists of common phobias because it isn't tangible. Instead, people think they're afraid of confined spaces, darkness, or death—when in fact it's the loneliness that exists at the core of each of these.

"A sheltered life can be a daring life," said the writer Eudora Welty, who lived all 92 years of her life in Jackson, Mississippi, "for all serious daring starts from within."

I'll face the fear of being alone at Eastern State Penitentiary in Philadelphia. It's where the concept of solitary confinement was pioneered. Built on an 11-acre site near what is now Fairmont Park, it was the most revolutionary prison in the world when it opened in 1829. Two things made it so. One was the architecture. Its castlelike exterior was grim and foreboding, designed to impress all who viewed it with the strength of the law and the misery of violating it. The interior layout resembled a giant wagon wheel, with the cell blocks radiating like spokes from a central hub or guardhouse.

The second thing that made Eastern State unique was the philosophy of rehabilitation behind it. In the late 18th century, most jails consisted of a single room in which large numbers of men, women, and even children were collectively detained. Conditions were poor, and most prisoners were corrupted further by the experience. A religious group in Philadelphia, called the Quakers, set out to change this. The Quakers believe that every person has a piece of God inside him. They reasoned that if a man reflected upon his crime in solitude for a suitable time, he would realize the error of his ways and discover this inherent goodness. The theory enjoyed much popular support (Ben Franklin was an advocate) and, as a result, Eastern State became the first prison in the world devoted to solitary confinement. Many foreign dignitaries, including the famous social commentator Charles Dickens, visited. In fact, the design inspired 300 similar prisons in Europe, Asia, and the Americas.

At the peak of the experiment, Eastern State housed 450 inmates. Each cell was about 8 feet wide by 12 feet long, with a high arched ceiling. At the top was a small skylight, not much bigger than a softball, fittingly called the "Eye of God." One oak door opened into the cell block, and another one opposite it led to a small private yard where the prisoner was allowed to exercise or garden for 30 minutes twice daily. Other than that, he had no contact with the outside world for his entire sentence. Talking, singing, whistling, correspondence, and family visits were all prohibited. His meals were delivered through a sliding hatch, guards wore thick socks over their boots to muffle footsteps, and the walls were so thick that communication with other inmates was impossible. All he had in his world was an iron bedstead, straw mattress, blanket, clothes rack, stool, toilet, tin cup, food pan, utensils, water basin, comb, cleaning brush, and towel. Good behavior might garner him a Bible, a loom for weaving or a bench for shoe repair, or a brief weekly visit from a "moral instructor." But for most of the time, he lived with nothing but his own thoughts. If he had to leave his cell for any reason, he was made to wear a hood.

Although this system captured the punitive imagination, it proved to be a miserable failure. For one reason, the prison was very expensive to operate. Since the inmates were prohibited from doing anything, an entire workforce was lost. By comparison, a competing prison system of the time flourished because it used its inmates to manufacture merchandise for commercial sale.

But beyond pure economics, the real reason solitary confine-

ment faltered is because it proved to be an inhumane and ineffective punishment. Many inmates lost their already-weak grip on reality, either going
insane or attempting suicide.

"Even extroverted prisoners who would stand up to anybody in any
dangerous situation absolutely caved in after a few days in an isolation cell,"
says Norman Johnson, Ph.D., a prison sociologist and professor emeritus
at Arcadia University. "Some of these tough guys would beg to be let out.
It clearly spooked them."

So instead of becoming peaceable penitents as the Quakers had hoped,
men often emerged less stable and manageable at the end of their sen-
tences. Because police records were poor, it's impossible to know the rate
of recidivism but, in retrospect, solitary confinement seems an illogical way
to reprogram a man for reentering society. How could isolation ever teach
someone to be social?

Eastern State abandoned solitary confinement by 1913, and the prison
closed entirely in 1971. Today it is a historical site, open for summer tours
and a Halloween Fright Night, ironically dubbed (in my case at least)
"Terror behind the Walls."

But Eastern State remains a grim and intimidating place. At least that's
what Sean Kelley, the prison's program director, tells me when I call. He
listens patiently to my eager request to be locked in a cell for a week, then
says: "Perhaps you better come down for a tour first. It may not be what
you expect."

By chance, a few days before my scheduled visit, I come across a kids'
TV show called *Scary Stories*. A group of young ghost hunters is combing
through Eastern State at night, searching for evidence of paranormal activity.
Deep in Cell Block 12, their flashlights, cell phones, and video cameras suddenly go dead. Something has sucked the energy out of their batteries. It
spooks one kid so badly that he runs off. Later, when they're safely outside
the prison walls, they play back the audio. Just before the equipment died,
a barely discernible voice can be heard hoarsely whispering: "Get out.
Get out."

Is it real? Sitting on my living-room couch, remote in sweaty palm, I can't immediately tell. I try to stop it from burrowing into my sub-conscious, but like a slippery red worm it's already in deep. Suddenly, there's another layer of fear I'll have to deal with—the manufactured demons of dark, solitary places.

The eventual sight of the prison, even on a pleasant morning, doesn't erase such thoughts. It looks like something Morticia and Gomez would have bought, rising unexpected and creepy from a neighborhood of restaurants, brownstones, and small businesses. Its turret-crowned walls are 30 feet high, and the thick stone blocks that compose them are cold to the touch. It takes me 10 minutes to walk around the perimeter. It looks as secure as ever, the only porthole being a padlocked set of double red doors that open onto Fairmount Avenue. Kelley is waiting for me there as I stroll around the corner. He's tall, thin, and dressed in a dark suit, with a funereal tone reminiscent of Lurch.

He unlocks the red doors, cranks up an iron gate, unchains a second gate, then thumbs the combination on a padlock. Evidently, security is still tight. But considering how grand this prison must once have been, it is now in hurtful condition. When we enter a cell block, it looks as if there's been a riot. Beds are overturned, doors hang from their hinges, rocks are strewn across the floor, and everywhere there's a thick layer of dust, rust, and must. The plumbing and heating systems no longer work, rat traps hide in the corners, and the paint peeling off the walls leaves spots that resemble scabs. It's hard to believe men actually lived here. When I poke my head into one of the tiny cells, my skin crawls. Although it's incredibly quiet, it's a disconcerting *dead* silence.

As he gives me the tour, Kelley explains that some of the country's most notorious criminals were incarcerated here, including Willie Sutton and Al Capone. Most, however, were run-of-the-mill murderers, rapists, and thieves—a bad lot whose legacy makes fine fertilizer for the imagination. I ask him about ghosts, and he laughs it off. He says he spent the night here once and didn't meet any, although he admits "it's a very spooky place after dark."

Although it doesn't look it now, he points out that the accommodations at Eastern State were quite luxurious when it opened. In fact, the prison cost $780,000 to build, which at the time was a fortune. The facility had flush toilets and central heating two years before the White House did, and prisoners were fed three ample meals a day to keep them fat and content. "If you could learn to cope with the loneliness," says Kelley, "it might not have been half-bad."

But there's no way I could spend an entire week in here. It's too primitive. In fact, I'm already whittling down the time I initially suggested. One hundred hours sounds just as impressive. Doesn't it? That's slightly more than four days. That'll be sufficient.

Kelley mentions that one of the cells is being refurbished. In a few months, it'll have a new wood floor and whitewashed walls, and be outfitted as neatly as it was nearly 200 years ago. With the addition of a fan for ventilation, he says, it will be quite livable. All I'd have to bring would be a camp toilet (since there still won't be any plumbing) and some basic necessities. He encourages me, explaining that no journalist he knows of has ever done what I'm entertaining: spend a length of time under solitary conditions, just as it was then.

"It would be extremely interesting," he says, deadpan, "to see what would happen to you."

In a few minutes, I'm going to sign off. My replacement will be the person I became once my prison sentence began. What you're about to read comes from the journal I kept. It captures my moods, loneliness, and even madness better than I can in retrospect. It'll help you better understand what occurred in my cell, what happens to the mind when it turns in on itself. In fact, I appreciate your coming along, because I never want to relive this on my own.

My confinement began on a Friday at 7:00 A.M. Like the original inmates, I brought nothing to occupy myself except a Bible and a writing tablet. I had no wristwatch. Although I was not locked in my cell, I was locked inside the prison. The staff delivered meals three times daily, but was told not to talk to me. The food was patterned after the original prison fare, heavy on meat and starch with no vegetables. Eastern State remained open to the public during my incarceration, but my cell block was closed to tours. I had no interaction with the outside world. After 6:00 P.M. each night, I was the only one on the entire 11-acre site. There were no security guards, no staff, no video cameras. I had only a lantern, an electric fan and, in case of emergency, a cell phone.

I was scared for reasons I could not grasp. How long, I wondered, would I last?

Friday morning. Very stressed, very nervous—that was how I felt last night, and I'm still not sure why. What is there to be frightened of? Spending time alone with myself? Who else could I possibly be more comfortable with? This is a strange sort of fear. It's completely illogical. What's inside of me that could hurt me?

How ironic that I had a new entertainment system installed in my home yesterday—big-screen TV, nine SurroundSound speakers, even a transducer to shake the floorboards. So much *stimuli*.

Now there's nothing.

My wife failed to cook me an elaborate last meal. I had to settle for leftover pasta. (She did, however, hint at a conjugal visit.)

All through my daughter's softball game, I worried. I was crabby. Part of me wanted to look forward to this as a vacation—some much-needed, restorative time away. But I couldn't do that. Why this dread?

I packed all my stuff (except for the camp toilet) in a large duffel bag. Bedsheets, pillow, lantern, flashlight, Bible, writing pad and pens, cell phone, drinking cup, wash basin, change of clothes, and (just in case) a hunting knife. I was embarrassed at how much of it there was, given how little I'd actually have to do.

After a fitful night's sleep, I left at 4:40 A.M. for the drive to Philadelphia. I kissed Maria, my son, my daughter, even my dog goodbye. Amazingly, these are the only ones who would really hurt if I were actually being put away. (And I'm not absolutely sure about the dog.) Forty-two years of life, and these are the only creatures I've let in. Maybe I'm already more alone than I realize.

I've been thinking a lot lately that I've missed an opportunity to be a better father. I've had such a short time with my kids. They're already 16 and 13, and I can't help feeling that I blew it. I could have taught them so much, taken them so many places, but instead I was always in a hurry to do something trivial by comparison. Maybe that's my crime, and I need to reflect upon it before they're lost entirely.

Kelley never showed at 6:00 A.M. We were supposed to meet outside the big red doors. I eventually had to call and get him out of bed. When he finally arrived at 6:40, he was flustered and apologetic. His girlfriend turned off the alarm without him realizing it. I told him not to worry, that for once I was under no deadline. "Just don't be late letting me out," I said—joking, but not really.

I pulled my car through the narrow entrance gate and parked in the prison yard. Kelley gave me the combinations to all the locks "in case something happens and you have to get out." Then we made the long, silent walk down the remains of my cell block. I was already sweating heavily in the humid air, lugging my duffel and toilet. We finally stopped in front of my cell—the number 66 nailed above it. When he slid back the door, it was more pleasant inside than I expected. As promised, the cell had been refurbished. The walls were plastered and freshly whitewashed, and the floor was planked with new boards. An old iron bed frame with an air mattress was against one wall. Elsewhere was a wood bench and table, a five-gallon container of water, and a large electric fan. But despite the hour, it was surprisingly dark. The Eye of God, far overhead, must angle toward the west.

Kelley handed me an ice pop as a final treat—a bright green, lime-flavored stick deliciously cold and sweet. He asked if I was nervous, and I replied, "Of course." He nodded and said he expected as much. We shook hands, said "See you soon" almost simultaneously, then he closed the door and gave a final knock for good luck. His footsteps echoed down the cell block.

And I am alone.

It has begun.

I am sweating so profusely that I take off my shirt and tie a bandana around my head. Opposite the door is a small iron gate, so ancient and rusted that it appears barnacle encrusted. This should have been the entrance to the exercise yard, but that section has yet to be restored. Now it houses a window fan. I plug it in and watch the blade start to spin. Unfortunately, it doesn't throw much cool air, but I like the whir. It fills the emptiness.

October 23, 1829. That's when the first prisoner was admitted to Eastern State. Kelley showed me the manifest: ". . . Charles Williams, Prisoner Number One. Burglar. Light black skin. Five feet seven inches tall. Scar on nose. Scar on thigh. Broad mouth. Black eyes. Farmer by trade. Can read. Theft included one 20-dollar watch, one three-dollar gold seal, one gold key. Sentenced to two years' confinement. Received by Samuel R. Wood, first warden. . . ."

I wonder if the spirit of Charles Williams is still here—somewhere.

I unpack my stuff. I put the sheets and pillow on the bed. I arrange the Bible, tablet, cup, and basin on the table. The camp toilet I tuck into a corner. And I put the empty duffel over a hole in the floor to discourage anything that might try to crawl in (or out?). Real inmates weren't allowed to have any personal possessions, nothing to make their cell feel even a little familiar. They wore prison-issued clothes and were given all their necessities. The only thing that made them unique was the number above their door.

I am fortunate.

There are faint, brown handprints on the walls. I hope they're from the workmen. There is also a lot of damp sawdust. They probably just finished the restoration and didn't have time to sweep up. I turn off the fan and listen. I hear traffic in the distance, an occasional plane overhead, the clutter of pigeons and, once, a songbird. But these are mere whispers. The walls are thick. I am surrounded as much by them as by the silence. I lie back on the bed and let the stillness blanket me. It's surprisingly soft and comforting. I feel the nervousness abating, like a fever breaking. I stop sweating and doze, for how long I don't know. There must be some way to gauge time by the way the light filters across the walls. Maybe I'll try to figure it out, scrape a sundial in the floor dust. Or maybe I'll just doze like a Mississippi bloodhound in August.

In a situation like this, is it better to use the mind or make it dormant?

The sound of a latch far down the hall. The scream of arthritic hinges. The clatter of what sounds like silverware on a dinner plate. It must be breakfast. A young man's face appears in the doorway. This morning, instead of giving tours, he's playing guard. As instructed, he doesn't say a word. He just hands over a cardboard box containing a bowl of oatmeal, a loaf of brown bread, a bottle of green tea, and some utensils. After he leaves, I position it all on the table. Even though I'm not hungry and the oatmeal is lukewarm and pasty, I eat greedily because it's something to do. Halfway through, I tell myself to slow down. I have the luxury to study each grain, chew my food well, and make the meal last as long as possible. I can make it nourishment for the mind, as well as the body.

I've been joking with my wife lately that I'm sick of personal hygiene—the whole daily routine of shaving, showering, and dressing presentably. Well, in here I don't have to worry about any of that. I can become a total pig. I can ignore the napkin and toothbrush—get crusty eyes, a dirty nose, bad breath, naked. The only mirror is the one in my head.

My spirits lift with the food. Things don't seem as intimidating. I'm more relaxed. Dare I say I might enjoy this? Nothing to do, nowhere to go, just delicious rest and solitude. I'll have time to reflect, get my priorities set, maybe even write some heartfelt letters to the people in my life who matter most.

The latch again. The hinges. More footsteps coming down the hall. Who could this be? I tense, put my eye against the peephole, but it's only the guard returning to pick up my dirty dishes. I didn't expect this. Either he only has one set, or he's worried about the breakfast remains attracting roaches and rats. I hand him the box, and he hustles off. After every visit, the quiet seems more absolute, more profound. I feel it settling down, dripping over me like warm syrup. It's pleasant. Maybe a way to bring this prison back to life is to rent cells to stressed-out business people for $200 per night. Bill it as the latest, greatest way to find peace. Much cheaper than a shrink! The overhead would be nonexistent. Oatmeal is cheap, a maid could clean one of these cells in minutes, and since no one is going anywhere you could dispense with the concierge. The media would love the concept. I'll have to remember to suggest it to Kelley.

Create. Plan. Scheme. That's what I do best. It's reassuring to know that even isolation can't deprive me of this.

I also thrive on getting things done. No day dawns in my world without a to-do list, and I judge its worth by how many items I've crossed off by sunset. I waste no time. I am one of the most productive people you'll ever meet. It's a discipline that I've sharpened. But while I'm proud of all I accomplish, I also worry about my ever-accelerating drive to stay so busy. Have I lost the ability to throw my mind into neutral and coast through at least a portion of life, like a kid on a bike with his feet in the air and a grin on his face?

I close my eyes and open to a random verse in the Bible. Looking for an answer. Although I've listened to many readings in church over the years, it's not a book that gives me much private solace. It has never spoken to me in the way some people claim. I brought it merely because it was the only book prisoners were allowed to read. Maybe enlightenment first requires despair.

My finger stops on the opening line of Joshua, chapter 8: "The Lord then said, 'Do not be afraid or dismayed. . . .'"

Hmmm, nothing cryptic there. I guess the Almighty is pretty busy Himself these days and needs to be direct. I'm tempted to shut my eyes and try again, to take another spin at religious roulette. But I decide not to push it.

Imagine all the people outside in the world doing so many different things right now. All the possibilities. All the choices. An entire aisle of nuts and bolts at Home Depot. One long avenue of cereal at the supermarket. The menu board that looms over you at the Taco Bell drive-thru. What should I choose? Every day is one continuous decision-making process. But suddenly, I am faced with none of that. Imagine being sentenced to solitary confinement for real—to be without options for 10, 20, or 30 years. Would it become a wasted life? Society assumes yes, but I suspect you could make it full—with introspection, with imagination.

I have a lot of things I need to get done in here. First up: Instead of dwelling on how great it will be to get out, I need to work on appreciating how great it is just to be. So I close my eyes and drift, until a ray of sunlight lasers down from the Eye of God, startling me into awareness. It's like someone turned on a movie projector. The star is an oval of bright light that slides across the wall and gradually elongates. Dust dances within it. I study it. Touch it. Try to catch it. Is it a sign from some convict spirit? An amendment to that quote from Joshua? How has it been encrypted?

But I'm just being egotistical. There isn't any meaning here; I just need there to be.

The scrape of the latch. Footsteps. Softer than the others. Is it lunchtime already? A tentative young lady appears at the door, eyes downcast, nervous. She hands me the same cardboard box, only this time filled with a plate of roast beef and mashed potatoes, a bowl of chicken soup, and another bottle of green tea. It's the biggest meal of the day. I'm still not hungry, but I nod my thanks, arrange it as before, and make myself eat every last scrap. I may need my strength later. This time I shovel the food with my hands. You can get a surprising amount of mashed potatoes on your index and middle fingers. It wouldn't take much of a nudge to become an animal in here. The more time you spend in this hole, the less respect you probably have for the rules. When they've taken your dignity and self-worth, what else is left? How crazy to think this could be a form of rehabilitation, that this was devised by a religious organization. What else do we live with now that will one day be deemed equally foolish?

Time feels like it's creeping now. I wonder if it goes slowly for guys in prison, or if they too look back at the end of a day or a decade and wonder where it all went.

From lunch I saved two packets of salt. I figure if I really get bored, I can compare the number of crystals. For a while, I consider digging a tunnel with my spoon, just to get a sense of how long it might take. Prisoners did escape from Eastern State. Despite the tight security, some managed to sneak out disguised as civilian workmen, while others crawled through sewers, hid in empty molasses barrels, or climbed the walls with homemade ropes and ladders. Evidently, the toughest thing to break is a desperate man's ingenuity. Something tells me, though, that getting out was only a peripheral goal. Keeping occupied, staying busy—that was the real escape.

The light changes so swiftly in this place. Moments before it was stark; now it's becoming warm and golden. It reminds me of a chapel. The arched ceiling, the Gothic doors, the seamless walls—it really is an impressive piece of architecture. So much effort, so much thought, devoted to something we all forgot.

The girl comes back to collect my dishes. I take notice of her this time. Brown curls, buttermilk skin, fresh lips, peach fingertips. . . . Masturbation was a troublesome problem at Eastern State. It was called the solitary vice, and frequent indulgence was said to cause everything from insanity to death. In fact, it was listed on many convict death certificates. The only time I'd ever been in a prison before this was as a newspaper reporter covering a concert. The guards had distributed 8-by-12, black-and-white glossies of the young girl who was performing. But instead of waiting to ask for her autograph, many inmates ripped a hole where her mouth was and fucked it later.

Where is love in a place like this? When no compassion is being shown, how can you cultivate it on your own? I love my wife and kids, but it seems like such a distant emotion in here. I can barely feel its pulse.

A car horn blows. How ludicrous that someone is so impatient.

A plane passes overhead. Imagine all those passengers clutching their itineraries. They're so conscious of the clock, so hateful of delays.

I keep trying to think of this cell as a little bungalow. If this were Puerto Vallarta, and I had tipped the doorman and hung out the Do Not Disturb sign, I would be relishing the seclusion. It's all a matter of perspective.

The shadow I've been watching has stopped moving across the floor. It can't be my timekeeper. Like me, it has stalled. The light is weakening, becoming almost fragile. It's going to be very dark in here later. What will I do if the power gets sucked out of my Duracells?

But I can't let myself think like that. I can't permit my mind to run amok with possibilities. I have to remain in the present, where it's safe and comfortable. What might be is always scarier than what is. The mind manufactures most of its fear.

Whenever I start to get uneasy, I pick up my tablet and write. I feel less lonely when I'm talking to myself. Most of the early prisoners didn't have that option. They were illiterate. At least I have paper, and the skill to fill it. No matter how dire the situation, there are always blessings.

The wall is cool against my bare back.

An artful spider web overhead.

Doing time. The phrase suggests you're in control. But I don't think that's true. Time does us all.

Friday, early evening? I wake to someone whistling. How dare they be so carefree. It's a new guard delivering dinner—a girl with close-cropped hair, thick glasses, and a navy-blue polo shirt. Unlike the others, she talks. She hands over oatmeal and says she'll be back in a little while. Whistles some more as she leaves. I despise her for her freedom. In less than an hour, she'll be driving home, listening to the radio, deciding what to do this Friday night. And I'll be here, trying to tune out the static in my head, deciding nothing more vital than what to dread next.

I'm angry. I'm sick of doing nothing. My personality demands that I wring every last drop of life out of life. Only then am I satisfied. So it's decided. I'm leaving. The hell with this. It was a stupid idea to begin with. I'll tell the girl when she comes back. I'll go home, hug my family, and get lots of things done this weekend. I refuse to lie on my back and stare at the ceiling any longer.

But when the whistler returns, I don't say a word. I hand back the box and withdraw like a varmint into his burrow. "Don't try to escape now," she says with a laugh, closing the door.

I want to bust her.

Dinner made me gag. Even with some Grandma's molasses as a sweetener, the oatmeal was only slightly more palatable. In prison, they even take the enjoyment out of eating.

I notice a string on the desk. It's very old, about 18 inches long, and coated with a wax. Some prisoners were given menial, mechanical jobs like chair caning and shoe repair. Perhaps Kelley left this for me intentionally. I play with it. Winding it around my finger, pulling it taut, tying it up in knots until it resembles me. The mindlessness of it helps.

I should exercise—exhaust myself with situps and pushups until I'm sweaty and hard. Maybe emerge with biceps so big a tattoo artist would consider them billboards. But the floor is too dusty. I'd get filthy. Instead, I do some standing stretches to thwart the lethal lethargy that's building. And it gets things moving. I squat in the corner and take a shit. I turn my friend the fan back on.

I'm shocked that I'm feeling the urge to leave so soon. It comes and goes. For 10 minutes I'm content, then for 10 minutes I pace. Because I have the option, because there's no lock on the door, the temptation is powerful. It begins as a deep unease, then builds into a yearning, a burning, that's almost sexual. It would be so easy to do. A single finger would roll back that door. Thirty steps would put me at the end of the corridor. A hand would lift the latch. Two would push back the gate. And just that quickly, I'd be in the yard. It would be over. No guards to fight. No spotlight to elude. No wall to scale. It would be that simple.

But instead of the law, I'd eventually have to face myself. Although running feels good at first, you can't do it forever. Sooner or later, I'd stop and condemn myself for it.

Who is this situation tougher on: the intelligent man or the stupid one? Who has more fear: the one who understands little or the one who knows too much?

I love the sound of the fan. It fills the void with something close to human. It is dependable. Right now, I am not.

The prison is deserted. I can feel its emptiness. No visitors, no staff, no security system. There's nobody watching over me—or is there? Keep writing. Must keep writing. Need to have the company of my own thoughts.

What am I so afraid of? I can't figure it out. And that makes me more afraid. If I can point to it, I can stand up to it. I need to be rational. I'm in a room with a bed, and that's all. It's unfamiliar, it's quiet, but nothing more. Steady the mind. Make it sit still like the body. Where's that string?

Suddenly I miss the richness of life intensely—all the stimuli that normally wash over me and make me crazy. I can't believe I miss the stress. Could it be I'm addicted to it, and these are the first symptoms of withdrawal?

Maybe some fears grow as you confront them and get to know them. I never thought I was afraid of being alone, but it's slowly becoming my worst nightmare. I honestly don't know if I can survive this.

A piece of string is a wonderful thing. Tying little knots stops the thinking process. Maybe I'll make a rosary, or a bracelet . . . or a noose. Ha!

I turn off the fan, sit on the floor, and listen. No more traffic noise. No more planes. No more anything. Once in a while, I feel a cool lick of breeze. Where is it coming from? It's the only sign of life or movement beyond myself. The Eye of God is dim.

An alternative escape is sleep, but I can't go to bed yet. I don't want to wake in the middle of the night thoroughly rested. Or worse, have something wake me—a sound, a presence. . . .

This is crazy! Why am I thinking this way? Why is this so tough? What a ridiculous idea to rent cells to stressed-out business people. They'd go nuts.

Am I going nuts? Is this how it starts?

That cool breeze again. It's like a gas. I wonder what Timothy McVeigh felt like sitting in his cell the night before he was put to death. A little like this? I can understand why cell mates have sex. Any closeness—anything. I'm pathetic. POWs or guys who have been in jail will laugh at me. I've only been in here about 12 hours! The string is half its original size. The knots in it get me thinking about the knots in the floor planks, so I count them. There are 82 in all. What's next? The knots in my head for thinking I could do this? Outside there must be a beautiful sunset. Most days, I don't even notice. There is no help in the Bible. I read the entire book of Revelations but find nothing but wrath and punishment. God doesn't care. No one cares. What I'm doing here won't make one iota of difference in the world. The spider is in his web far overhead. He chooses to live here. I can walk out that door so easily. I remember sitting on the stoop with my best buddy Mark when I was a kid. We had nothing to do, but we had everything to do. I wish I'd brought a sleeping pill. The sound of pigeons coming home to roost. The fear of the unknown, whether it's out there or in me. I'm a coward. Paint the walls with molasses. My hunting knife! Maybe if I carry it, I'll feel braver. Some fears beat you; that's nothing to be ashamed of. My daughter's softball game. A perfect evening. Everything. What am I doing here when I could be out there?

Trying to develop appreciation for it, silly.

Would it help if I sang? There's a better echo in here than in my shower. Some Harry Chapin maybe. "Taxi" or "Cat's in the Cradle." I know all the words. Or perhaps "American Pie." Something mournful. When was the last time these walls heard song? It's always toughest right before nightfall—even dogs get unsettled then. They sense something coming. Suppose there's a secret way into the prison that Kelley doesn't know about? Suppose gang kids come in here on weekends to drink or hang out? Suppose they find me? I put the knife and a pack of matches in my pocket, just in case. I want to lie down, close my eyes, and sleep through the night. Wouldn't that be wonderful? But I'm not tired anymore.

Look at all these pages I've filled with my ramblings. My brain just keeps racing. Who really controls it? I go back to the Bible again and read the last few chapters of John—the part about the crucifixion and resurrection. It makes me feel strangely calm. I remember listening to these stories when I was a boy in Catholic school and being comforted by them. No one was more alone than Jesus before he died. Everyone deserted him. I'll keep that in mind.

I'm listening to everything. Trying to familiarize myself with every little sound. Lots of pigeons squabbling and kicking debris from the rafters. They aren't afraid to sleep here. Psalm 142 is called Prayer of a Prisoner in Dire Straits. I'm feeling humble. Ego fading away like the light. Exhausted but not sleepy. Fearful. Vulnerable. Greasy. I am just one speck on this planet, yet I feel like all the energy from everywhere is focused on me. Almost not enough light to see this page. It's getting cooler. Hope I have enough battery power to last the night. You bet I'll get down on my knees and pray before I go to sleep. Isn't the presence of a ghost supposed to feel cool? Hope not. Maybe it's passing through, checking me out. Is that you, Charles Williams?

Friday, 10:00? 10:30? 11:00? A loud boom. Not thunder. Not a truck backfiring. More like one of the heavy cell doors hitting the ground. It resounds. Then another. And another. Like thousand-pound dominoes toppling over. Holy shit! Someone is searching for the intruder, checking every cell, furious. *Get out! Get out!* I turn off my lantern, so it doesn't betray me, and squat in the dark—listening, waiting, shaking. What the hell is going on? I am trapped. I grab my cell phone and scroll to Kelley's number. He said to call him if there was trouble. But I can't make my finger push the call button. What will I tell him? That I heard a noise and now I'm scared? He's not going to come running and help me check under the bed. It must be my imagination. It can't be my imagination. I'm tired. I'm wired. I've been trying to kill time, but time is killing me. I'll never be able to get to sleep. Maybe Hell isn't fire and brimstone like Revelations predicts. Maybe it's nothingness like this. Suddenly,

11 acres seems no bigger than an elevator. The walls are closing in, and so is whatever's out there. Control. Get control. You're stronger than this.

BOOM!

That's it. I'm out of here. I have no idea what that is, but it's damn close. This is no longer spooky; it's dangerous. There's something out there, and it's pissed. I don't care if people call me a wimp. I'm cornered in here with no way to defend myself. This is stupid.

I turn on my lantern, pocket my tablet and pen, and unsheathe the knife. Slowly, I slide open the door and peer along the corridor. It looks like I'm inside the hull of an ancient ship. Everything is shadowy and gray, and as far as I can tell, deserted. But I hesitate. My next step will take me past the threshold, and it will be over. I will have failed. Fear will have beaten me—already. I take a deep shuddering breath. I try to steady my-self, to tap into some auxiliary tank of courage. But there's nothing left. My power has been sapped. I know, true and deep and sure, that I can't spend the night in here. No way. *Get out! Get out!* Is that my hoarse voice I hear, or someone else's? So I take that step with no regrets and start heading toward the gate. All I can hear is my heart pounding in my ears. The cells on either side are completely demolished. Beds overturned, desks shattered, walls crumbling. I don't remember them looking so bad this morning. I avoid peering inside any of them, afraid of what I might see. A skeleton in a convict suit, perhaps, laughing at me? Nothing seems far fetched now. In fact, I'm convinced that if I turned around and went back to my cell, it would be wrecked. Whatever is loose would have torn it apart. Where is that fucking gate? I thought it was closer. I look over my shoulder, back toward the rotunda. Are any of the old guards watching? Taking aim? Grinning? I start to run, knuckles white around my knife. Survive. The gate! The bolt slides without complaint, but as I push it back it screams like I want to. I'm out of the cell block, in the open air beneath the southwest tower, but I can't stop here. I need to get to my car. Only then will I be safe. Only then will I have escaped. The next gate is chained and locked. What did Kelley say was the combination? It had something to do with the history of the prison. A date. Yes, a year. Was it 1913? That's when the prison abandoned solitary confinement. How ironic. I fumble with the lock and lantern, still worrying that something is coming. I work the tumblers until they show 1-9-1-3, hit the lock with the palm of my hand, and it opens! My car is tucked against the wall, across the yard, and I run for it.

Once inside, with windows closed and doors locked, I am instantly relieved. Even though I've just exchanged one cell for another, the familiarity of this one makes all the difference. There's another iron gate and those big red doors between me and the outside world, but I'm content to sit here and catch my breath. Let my heart slow. Let the paranoia go. The yard is bathed in the soft glow of a vapor light, and there are stars and a fingernail moon overhead. Leafless vines snake around the entrances to the various cell blocks. I feel like the warden now, surveying each one to be sure nothing is creeping out. It's the perfect vantage point. My car is backed into a corner. No one can approach without my knowing. I crack the windows to get some fresh air and hear (what?) the twinkle-tune of a faraway ice-cream truck. I close my eyes and smile. It's the first time I've done that in a while.

BOOM!

I nearly jump through the sunroof. My hand reaches for the key in the ignition. My foot floors the accelerator. I'll bust through that gate, out those doors, and into the street! Adrenaline is coursing through my veins like gas through the fuel lines. And when I glance in the rearview mirror, I actually see the whites of my eyes they're so wide. Then. . . . Far overhead. . . . A pinwheel of sparkling color. . . . A giant blossom of brilliance. . . . Fireworks! I should have guessed. Some sort of celebration in Fairmount Park.

So it wasn't ghosts. It was my own uneasy spirit. I am simultaneously relieved and embarrassed. I fled from what my mind created.

But even though I know my fear is unfounded, I can't go back in there. Not in the dark, anyway. For some reason, I'm not ready. So

I sweat and squirm the rest of the night, too hot and cramped and humiliated with myself to get much sleep.

Saturday morning. My plan is to wait for the light to strengthen, then head back to my cell and pretend this never happened. No one will know. This place is full of lies, and I'll merely be following precedent. There's only one problem. When it's time to leave my car, the driver's seat gets stuck in the reclining position. And no matter how hard I try, I can't push it upright. So there's a clue. Someone may notice.

I put the lock and chain back on the outside gate and spin the tumbler. My cell block isn't as frightening now. In fact, I even do some poking around. How could I have been so scared? Man, I actually lost it! For a few minutes, I became an animal—teeth bared, desperate, ready to claw my way out of this corner. But my cell is just as I left it—untouched by rampaging evil spirits. As I slide the door shut behind me, it all seems like a dream. Did I really hear a truck selling ice cream?

Napoleon said, "I have very rarely met with two-o'clock-in-the-morning courage." The little Frenchman knew what he was talking about. Studies have shown that we're more susceptible to fear when we're alone. Even combat veterans perform poorly and are more likely to surrender under solitary conditions. In fact, one theory holds that courage is merely the result of vanity and pride. We act valiantly not out of selfless concern and responsibility but out of our own conceit and egoism. If not for an audience, there would be far fewer heroes.

What to do now? I'm coated with a veneer of sawdust and salt, and there's a stale taste in my mouth that's the bad breath of cowardice. I feel empty and numb. I've been beaten. But the more I ponder what happened, the less insane my behavior seems. Did fear twist my thinking, or did fear focus it? My brain assessed the situation and compelled me to flee from potential danger. That's the survival instinct. It was simply per-forming the job it had been programmed to do by hundreds of thousands of years of evolution. Fear is the drive to stay alive, whether in the face of a perceived or a real threat. That's why it's such a tough adversary. Ignore it, make a mistake, and you could be dead.

The world is coming to life again. The pigeons. The traffic sounds. The Eye. But none of it awakens me. I feel like day-old bread.

I sit stupidly in the corner, exhausted from everything. I tried to get away from it all and, in a strange twist of fate, found more than I bargained for. The more closed in you are, the more open you become to yourself. Who would have thought that confinement could make someone so susceptible?

Footsteps in the corridor. It's the guard—the same guy as yesterday morning. He asks how I slept, and I don't lie. I tell him poorly, that it's creepy in here at night, that the loneliness plays tricks on your mind. He tilts his head and smiles. He doesn't even look real. I want to talk, to make him understand, but he just says he is going to get breakfast and will return.

Feeding time at the zoo. I pace like a caged animal, anticipating . . . what? Being caught? That must be it, because I'm certainly not looking forward to more oatmeal. In fact, I'm not hungry at all. Originally, I thought of fasting during my sentence but decided that would make it doubly tough. But I could have done it. I guess my head has bigger things to worry about than filling my stomach. In stressful situations, it squelches the appetite, knowing that when the belly is full, the mind is dull.

I'm beginning to see the patterns, the logic in the irrational. On the surface, fear appears to be frenzy. But the more you analyze it, the more good sense it makes. It just has a bad rep. If more people examined their fears instead of shutting their eyes, maybe they wouldn't be so paralyzed. It's the avoidance and the shame that sharpens their insecurities.

It's the shame that's starting to gnaw at me. It's like a rat trying to get its tail out of one of those traps; I can feel part of myself being chewed away. I didn't have the courage to spend the night in here, but I can still be brave by confessing to my fear. In some ways, that takes more guts. Admitting weakness. Or at least that's what I tell myself.

Those handprints on the wall I noticed before—brown on white. No doubt left by workmen trying to steady themselves. I put my hands on them now. They are so much bigger than mine. Fear makes you small. I catch my balance.

What's the point of continuing? If I stay it will only be to save face, to make Kelley and his staff believe that I'm tough. Where's the victory in that? This ended when I picked up that lantern and walked out that door, when I gave in to the fear. This now is just deceit. And it feels even more dishonorable.

But to actually pack my bag and surrender, to utter the words of defeat, that's a tall order. Give it some time. Maybe I'll change my mind.

I don't want to think anymore. I want to turn my brain off, pull the plug. So why can't I? The harder I try, the faster the gears spin. Without distraction, it's burning itself out on introspection.

The guard returns. I can't meet his eye. I'm skittish and preoccupied. Does he notice the difference in me? Does he suspect how close I am to quitting? Oatmeal, Grandma's molasses, green tea, and another loaf of bread—rye this time. I chew, tasting nothing.

Voices. At the far end of the cell block. When I look through the peephole, I can just make out faces pressed between the bars of the gate. It's a tour group, mostly kids. Kelley mentioned that Saturday was the prison's busiest day, that visitors often came early. I press my ear to the door and hear the guide explaining that this is one of the original cell blocks but, unfortunately, it's closed today because a reporter is experiencing what it's like to be in solitary confinement. She says it with reverence, and it sparks many questions.

"How long is he in for?"

"Does he have a real long beard?"

And from one particularly small, clear voice, "Can I get his autograph?"

And that's when I realize I'm not worthy of admiration. To fool someone else is even more of a crime than to fool yourself. It's time to get out. Thirty hours is what I'll do—a measly sentence but a nice round number. I'll ask to be let out at one o'clock.

Surprisingly, the decision to quit doesn't make the remaining time pass more quickly or even become more precious. I hate this. I try to write, but there's little left to say. I try to sleep, but there's no accessing peace. So I sit and wait, rehearsing what I'll say to the guard so it won't sound crazy. Nonchalance is what I want.

I don't doubt my decision. The more time I spend in here, the more convinced I become that I have to leave. The nervousness is creeping back. Even though I know the cause of those sounds, I'd never be able to spend another night in here. The same thing would happen, I'm sure. Something else would spook me. I am a loner who can't stand being alone. Go figure.

What's taking so long? The beam from the Eye is about where it was yesterday at midday, but there's no sign of lunch. Tour groups continue to shuffle past in the distance. The staff must be very busy. I suddenly remember that there's a clock on my cell phone, and I check it for the first time. It's 12:15. Maybe they've forgotten about me. The bastards.

I pace. I stretch. I want to scream. You'd think I'd be used to this by now, but it's only getting more tedious.

And finally it comes. The bolt scraping across the faraway latch and the familiar whistling. Suddenly, I don't know whether I'll be able to go through with it, to admit. She knocks on the door. I don't instantly respond. She knocks again. I stammer, "Come in."

"I just need to collect your dishes," she says, "and I'll be right back with lunch."

"I'm not going to be able to go through with this," I blurt. "It's too tough. Can you find Kelley and tell him I want to get out, sometime around one?"

Disbelief and puzzlement behind those thick glasses. "Are you sure?"

"I'm sure." Wavering conviction.

"Okay. He's doing a tour right now, but I'll tell him when he's finished."

This time, she doesn't close the door behind her. I guess that means I'm no longer a prisoner. And she doesn't whistle as she walks away. Have I made her unhappy?

One o'clock comes and goes.

233

Then 1:15 and 1:30.

I keep checking my cell phone, just now realizing the irony of its name. Maybe Kelley is refusing to let me out. Maybe now I'm a real inmate. Even though I'm free to do so, I refuse to leave on my own. I need to bring this thing full circle.

1:35, 1:40.

Where the hell is he? Did he oversleep again?

1:45. Voices. Approaching.

Kelley has brought a gang. Many of the guards, some friends. He introduces me all around. I shake hands, act nonchalant, as planned. I tell them what happened. That for the first portion at least, it was luxurious, a wonderful retreat. But then as I found less and less to do, my mind went into overdrive and turned inward on itself. And come nightfall, it was just as spooky as he had said. There were loud noises. Unexplainable creepiness. I stop just short of telling them everything, of confessing. It's obvious they still admire me, and I don't want to disrupt that. Until the whistler asks, "Did you make it through the night in here?"

I hesitate. I stall. Then I hang my head and say no.

"I knew it," she says. "I just knew it."

While I'm walking back to my car, behind the rest, Kelley pats me on the shoulder. Now it's his turn to confess.

"Remember when I told you that I spent the night in here?" he says. "Well, I didn't make it either. I stayed until 10:00 or 11:00, went home, and came back the next morning."

In front of the big red doors, I shake his hand and thank him, as much for his hospitality as for his honesty.

Maybe there would be a little less fear in the world if we all had the courage to share our own. Maybe then we wouldn't feel so alone.

After

When I'm asked to pick the scariest thing I did
during this year of facing my fears,
I reply without hesitation that
it was being in isolation.

I would do everything else again, except get locked in that prison. Most people find this hard to believe—and, truthfully, so do I. When I began this search, I never suspected it would lead to this. As it turns out, what I'm most afraid of is myself—or more accurately, my *lack of self.*

Here I was thinking I'd made admirable progress during my 40-some years, that I knew myself pretty damn well, when in fact I had yet to scratch the surface. Once I'd cleared out the hubbub in my head, I didn't find peace and contentment like I had expected. I found emptiness.

For a long time after my abbreviated stint in jail, I hunted for an answer—or, more honestly, an excuse—for why I cracked. Norman Johnson, Ph.D., the expert I had consulted initially, told me that he routinely put volunteer students in solitary confinement when he was teaching criminology at Arcadia University.

"It was very interesting," he explained, "because at first they all thought it was fantastic. They didn't have to do any work. But after about 20 hours it got to every single one of them. One student even had a minor seizure. They succumbed to the madness that comes from listening to yourself live."

Charles Dickens, after touring Eastern State in 1842, said: "I hold this slow and daily tampering with the mysteries of the brain to be immeasurably worse than any torture of the body. Its effects are cruel and wrong. [The confined] is a man buried alive."

And that's exactly how it felt—like I was lying in some loamy hole, hoarse from screaming, exhausted from struggling, yet at the same time realizing I'd been the undertaker of my own soul. I'd confined myself to this cell of existence. I'd been dying all along.

I suspect most of us are more familiar with this horror than we care to admit, that the fear of ending up alone, of disappearing, of not mattering, is an undertow that tugs at all of us. It's so quiet and deep that we don't recognize its power until it pulls us under forever.

"The sole cause of man's unhappiness is that he does not know how to stay quietly in his room," wrote Pascal in the mid–1600s. "What people want is not the easy peaceful life that allows them to think of their unhappy condition . . . but the agitation that takes their minds off it. That is why we prefer the hunt to the capture. That is why men are so fond of hustle and bustle; that is why prison is such a fearful punishment; that is why the pleasures of solitude are so incomprehensible."

"The brain is mortality phobic," adds Paul Pearsall, Ph.D., a scientist and author. "Its greatest fear is its own end or any consciousness state [such as deep meditation] that approximates the selflessness it may experience at the end of its existence. . . . The brain is afraid of cognitive darkness. It constantly seeks input and feeds on new, different, intense stimulation."

So it turns out I am most terrified of having nothing, being nothing, amounting to nothing, living as nothing. Whether my mind has created this 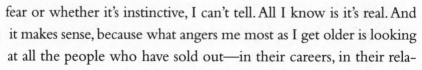 fear or whether it's instinctive, I can't tell. All I know is it's real. And it makes sense, because what angers me most as I get older is looking at all the people who have sold out—in their careers, in their relationships, in their religions—they're just showing up and going through the motions. They may claim they're happy and content, but I don't believe them. I think deep down they're disgusted with themselves, and they're relying on a habitual existence to avoid the truth. Chronic fear is a sign that we're living too comfortably, that it's time to shake things up. Fear drives us to false contentment at the same time that it points the way out.

A year ago, when I started this project, I viewed my fears and phobias as problems. I even apologized for them. But after facing each one, I see they were really opportunities. Instead of being embarrassed, I should have been grateful. They weren't my failings; they are my potential.

In life there are two diametrically opposed forces: self-preservation and self-development. They are at continual war—our fear of the new and uncomfortable versus our desire to learn and grow.

Robert Maurer, Ph.D., an associate clinical professor at UCLA School of Medicine, goes so far as to say that the more fears we have, the more interesting our life potentially is. It's a sign, at least initially, that we're bumping up against the perimeter of our comfort zone. It's evidence of a lust to explore, imagine, and live. But instead of going one step further when we hit it, most of us pull back. We get scared. And eventually our comfort zone contracts.

This is a far different view of fear than society holds. It would seem that in order to be as courageous as Chuck Yeager or any of America's most vaunted heroes, we must treat fear as an impediment that needs to be crushed, banished, and never tolerated. We must spit on it because it's worthless.

But fear has purpose. I've seen it. I've felt its protective, guiding hand. I've come to accept it as a wise friend. I'd never want to crush or banish it, because if I did I wouldn't have much longer to live, both physically *and* figuratively. Fear is a gift, a guardian angel, a valuable emotion worth cultivating.

But yes, it's volatile. Even man's best friend must be leashed. The key to managing fear, to making sure it empowers rather than impairs, is not to cop some holier-than-thou attitude but to simply

237

allow ourselves to be scared. I know that sounds counterintuitive. How can you learn to control an emotion by yielding to it? My only answer is: Try it. By taking that extra step when you're at the comfort edge, by pausing to let the anxiety build a minute longer, you'll begin to see the difference between fear that is genuine and fear that is imagined. And that marks the beginning of courage and enlightenment.

The moment you stop facing your fears, the second you squat down and cower, is the instant they double in power. They become problems instead of opportunities.

Fear compounds when you do nothing. Fear subsides when you do *something*. Fear is a stationary emotion that only strikes when you're not moving.

This is the minefield through which I've spent the past 12 months walking.

But now that I've reached the end, I'm realizing there is no other side to this. I can stop, but I can never emerge. I can't truthfully say I've made it. I need to keep walking, staring at the ground every second, looking for any little bump in the dirt, grabbing my legs to keep them from shaking, just like Schwarzkopf did. I have to do this for the rest of my life, or at least for as long as I want to keep living.

How ironic. I've faced my greatest fears. I've risked not only my life but also my ego. I've every right to feel like a hero. But I don't. I can't honestly say I'm fearless. All my original devils are still with me to some degree. I don't even feel significantly more brave. My courage, if you can call it that, is accidental—I sort of stumbled upon it.

But I've learned, and I've grown. My life has more balance. I've made the war between self-preservation and self-development a little less one sided. And I've gained perspective. I've gathered yardsticks. I know that every time I look up at a fear I stand a little taller, until one day I'll be eye to eye with it.

238

A year ago, courage and fearlessness were my goals. I dreamed of how wonderful a life without fear would be, how tremendous it would feel to be free. But now I know differently. Instead of being rich and full, such an existence would be flat and dull. My heart would never race. My eyes would never widen. I would never again feel the urge to run to someone. I would be imprisoned.

Fear *is* life. Fear *is* freedom. It is the protector as well as the director. Fear makes life uncomfortable, and thereby, it makes life interesting, challenging, and potentially exciting. This past year has been the most nerve racking one of my life. But it's also been the most exhilarating. I've never felt more alive. What I truly fear must be the lack of fear, the absence of the only emotion that matters. It is the experience of fear that takes us into the experience of life. We would be nothing without it.

"Fear not
that life shall come
to an end
but rather that
it shall never
have a beginning."
— JOHN HENRY CARDINAL NEWMAN